Return of the a priori

Return of the a priori

Edited by
Philip Hanson
and
Bruce Hunter

©1992 Canadian Journal of Philosophy

The University of Calgary Press
Calgary, Alberta, Canada

ISSN 0229-7051   ISBN 0-919491-18-9

© 1992 The Canadian Journal of Philosophy
ISBN 0-919491-18-9
ISSN 0229-7051
First published in 1993

University of Calgary Press
2500 University Drive NW
Calgary, Alberta
Canada T2N 1N4

Canadian Cataloguing in Publication Data

Main entry under title:
Return of the a priori

    Includes index.
    ISBN 0-919491-18-9

    1. A priori. 2. Knowledge, Theory of.
I. Hunter, Bruce A., 1949-   II. Hanson, Philip P., 1948-
BD81.3.R48 1993   121   C93-091303-5

Cover design by Art Design Printing Inc., Edmonton, Alberta, Canada

Printed on acid-free paper
Printed and bound in Canada

Table of Contents

List of Contributors   vii

Introduction — Return of the A Priori   1
Philip Hanson and *Bruce Hunter*

A Rationalist Manifesto   53
Laurence BonJour

Analyticity, Undeniability, and Truth   89
James Van Cleve

Analyticity and the A Priori.   113
Albert Casullo

The Doubtful A Priori.   151
John Bigelow

Some Remarks on Indiscernibility   167
Ali Kazmi

The Constitutive A Priori   179
Graciela De Pierris

Kant's A Priori Methods For Recognizing
Necessary Truths 215
J.A. Brook

EPR As A Priori Science 253
James Robert Brown

Gaps, Gluts, and Paradox 273
A.D. Irvine

An Essay on Material Necessity 301
Barry Smith

Index 323

CANADIAN JOUNRAL OF PHHILOSOPHY
Supplementary Volume 18

Contributors

John Bigelow is Professor of Philosophy at Monash University. He taught previously at Victoria University of Wellington and La Trobe University. He writes primarily on topics in metaphysics, philosophy of mathematics, and philosophy of logic. Among his publications are *The Reality of Numbers* (Oxford University Press, 1988) and, with Robert Pargetter, *Science and Necessity* (Cambridge University Press, 1990).

Laurence BonJour is Professor of Philosophy at the University of Washington and currently visiting Professor of Philosophy at Illinois Wesleyan University. He is the author of *The Structure of Empirical Knowledge* and of papers in the areas of epistemology, philosophy of mind, and metaphysics. The present paper is drawn from a forthcoming book on a priori knowledge.

J.A. (Andrew) Brook is Associate Professor of Philosophy and Director of the Institute of Interdisciplinary Studies at Carleton University in Ottawa. His research interests include Kant, cognitive science, and philosophy of psychology, foundations of psychoanalysis, and environmental ethics. His book *Kant and the Mind* is to appear in 1993 from Cambridge University Press.

James Robert Brown is in the Department of Philosophy, University of Toronto. His interests are mainly in topics in the philosophy of science, including foundations of physics, philosophy of mathematics, social relations of science, realism, and thought experiments. He is the author of *The Rational and the Social* (1989), *The Laboratory of the Mind: Thought Experiments in the Natural Sciences* (1991), and two forthcoming books: *Smoke and Mirrors: How Science Reflects Reality* (1993) and *Proofs and Pictures: Introductory Topics in the Philosophy of Mathematics* (1994).

Albert Casullo is Professor of Philosophy at the University of Nebraska-Lincoln. He has published articles on a number of topics in metaphysics and epistemology, including a priori knowledge, mathematical knowledge, the nature of perceptual experience, the identity indiscernibles, and the relationships between universals and particulars.

Graciela De Pierris received a degree in Philosophy from the Universidad Nacional de La Plata, Argentina; and an MA and a PhD from the University of California, Berkeley. Her research is in epistemology, Kant, Frege, and History of Modern Philosophy. She has taught at Indiana University, Bloomington, and has visited several Latin-American universities. She has articles and critical studies appearing in *Revista Latinoamericana de Filosofia, Pacific Philosophical Quarterly, Synthese, Canadian Journal of Philosophy, Noûs,* and *Dialogos.*

Philip P. Hanson, a graduate of the University of Calgary and of Princeton University, is currently Associate Professor of Philosophy at Simon Fraser University, having also taught at the University of Toronto. He has published principally in the areas of epistemology, philosophy of language, philosophy of mind, and environmental ethics, including two anthologies: *Information, Language and Cognition* (University of British Columbia Press, 1990, and now Oxford University Press); and *Environmental Ethics: Philosophical and Policy Perspectives* (Institute for the Humanities, Simon Fraser University, 1986).

Bruce Hunter teaches philosophy at the University of Alberta. He received a B.A. in Philosophy and English from the University of Toronto and a Ph.D. in Philosophy from Brown University. He has published articles in epistemology, political philosophy, and early modern philosophy.

Andrew Irvine received an Honours BA from the University of Saskatchewan in 1980 and an MA from the University of Western Ontario in 1981. In 1986 he received his PhD from the University of Sydney for work on mathematical truth and scientific realism. Since then he has written on various topics in the philosophy of mathematics, the history and philosophy of logic, and political theory.

Edited books include *Physicalism in Mathematics* (Kluwer, 1990) and *Russell & Analytic Philosophy* (with G.A. Wedeking, forthcoming with the University of Toronto Press, 1993). Together with John Thompson he is also the author of *Reforming the Red Chamber* (forthcoming with McGill-Queen's University Press, 1993).

Currently an Assistant Professor in the Department of Philosophy at the University of British Columbia, he has also been a Visiting Fellow at the University of Pittsburgh and has taught at the University of Toronto.

Ali Akhtar Kazmi is Associate Professor of Philosophy at the University of Calgary. He has written in the areas of Philosophy of Language and Philosophy of Logic.

Barry Smith teaches at the International Academy of Philosophy (Lichtenstein) and at SUNY Buffalo. He has held visiting positions in Erlangen, Graz, Innsbruck, Paris, Irvine (CA) and Turku. He is the author of *Austrian Philosophy* (Amsterdam/Atlanta 1993) and of some 100 papers on metaphysics, phenomenology, and the history of philosophy. He is editor of *Parts and Moments. Studies in Logic and Formal Ontology* (Munich 1982) and *Foundations of Gestalt Theory* (Munich 1988), and co-editor of the *Handbook of Metaphysics and Ontology* (Munich 1991). He is currently director of a project sponsored by the Swiss National Foundation on the role of formal ontology and naive physics in artificial intelligence research.

James Van Cleve teaches philosophy at Brown University. He received his BA from the University of Iowa and his MA and PhD from the University of Rochester. His principal interests are epistemology, metaphysics, and the history of modern philosophy, especially Kant. He is currently writing a book on problems raised in Kant's *Critique of Pure Reason*.

CANADIAN JOURNAL OF PHILOSOPHY
Supplementary Volume 18

Return of the A Priori

PHILIP HANSON
BRUCE HUNTER

I Introduction

A priori knowledge has been a central topic in modern philosophy. Philosophers before the seventeenth century were concerned with the prospects for knowledge in mathematics, logic, and the natural sciences, and with the roles to be played by reason and experience in achieving it. In the early modern period they became preoccupied with these concerns and with concomitant fears for the prospects for knowledge in theology, ethics, metaphysics, and philosophy itself.

For us, the a posteriori/a priori distinction is fundamentally an epistemic distinction between kinds of knowledge, evidence, or warrant — empirical on the one hand, non-empirical on the other. The original seventeenth century distinction was between reasoning from what was prior and reasoning from what was posterior. Origins, causes, principles were prior, effects or consequences posterior, essence prior, existence posterior. Reasoning from causes to effects was a priori, reasoning from effects to causes a posteriori. A priori reasons for thinking that something was so were reasons why it was so, and the knowledge based on such reasons a priori. Hence, what we know about something by reasoning from its sensory effects would be known a posteriori, and the reasons for belief provided by such sensory effects a posteriori reasons.[1] Even so, the distinction doesn't match ours. First, we might have a priori knowledge in at best a relative sense — if the *causes* from which we know why things are so are *themselves* always ultimately known from (their) other effects and empirical consequences. Second, some things might be known other than on the basis of reasons. That even leaves open the possibility that some effects (e.g. our existence) are non-empirical givens, known non-empirically and non-inferentially, but serve as a posteriori reasons for inferring causes (e.g. God's existence), or that some a priori reasons (e.g. God's existence) are empirical givens.

There are many well known controversies concerning what might be warranted empirically. What, if anything, may become evident to us in various sorts of sense perception — that we see a chair or just that we seem to see a chair? What, if anything of this, may continue to be warranted in memory or recollection, and what, if anything, about our feelings, experiences, and thoughts themselves, may be warranted in introspection? What conclusions might any evidence from experience warrant concerning what we don't observe, remember or introspect? Most philosophers have nonetheless insisted that things can be evident or warranted a priori without being empirically warranted, chiefly for three reasons.

(A) There are propositions which we think of as universally and necessarily true but on the basis of experience we can have reason for thinking only that they hold in experienced cases or in cases similar to experienced cases, or only that they always happen to hold, but not that they must always hold.[2] If something must always be so, it will

---

1   Cf. discussion by Ferdinand Alquié, ed., Descartes, *Oeuvres Philosophiques*, Tôme II, (Paris: Éditions Garnier Frères 1967), 582, n. 1; Graciela De Pierris, (this volume), n. 2, G. Leibniz, in Remnant and Bennett, eds., *New Essays Concerning Human Understanding* (Cambridge: Cambridge University Press 1981), 293-4, and 475.

2   Cf. Leibniz, *New Essays*, Preface, 49-50, and I. Kant, *Critique of Pure Reason*, Kemp Smith, ed. (London: Macmillan 1968), B3. What's needed to warrant them is non-empirical insight into their universal necessity, perhaps from 'a priori'

always be so in cases similar to experienced cases, but not necessarily vice versa. Thus, whatever reasons might be contained in experience for thinking something universally necessary must include something additional to the reasons experience might contain for thinking something will hold in cases similar to experienced cases. But what could that be? There is nothing extra, no extra experience, for experience to provide.

(B) Even if experience can provide reasons for thinking a proposition universally and necessarily true, e.g., because the hypothesis of universal necessity provides the best explanation of why experience conforms to the hypothesis, or simply because heretofore reliable authorities testify to it, there often is no obvious connection between the degree to which their universal necessity is warranted and the degree of warrant any such confirmation in experience would provide. In grasping a proof of a proposition, the conclusion may have, Leibniz suggested, an 'evidence' or 'luminous certainty,'[3] that exceeds the sort of practical certainty experience can provide. A young prodigy may quickly grasp a basic principle like the transitivity of identity after considering and thinking about only a few varied examples presented by her teacher. But the principle, it appears, isn't any less evident to her then than it is to a child of dull mind but long memory who catches on only after being presented with far more varied examples. Nor is it equally evident to the dull child who accepts it only on his teacher's authority. Her degree of warrant transcends what empirical confirmation might provide in the circumstances, and thus is independent of her empirical warrant. To some, this claim is a confused relic of Platonic metaphors of cognition as enlightenment, and ignores the pervasive, mundane, confirming instances in the lives

---

reasons which explain why they are universally and necessarily so. An equally traditional, 'Platonic,' variation is that mathematics concerns 'abstract' objects that need not, perhaps indeed cannot, be exemplified in the world we experience, and thus cannot be known on the basis of that experience.

3 *New Essays*, 445. Cf. also, 'The senses can hint at, justify, and confirm these truths, but can never demonstrate their infallible and perpetual certainty' (80).

of ourselves, our fellows, and our ancestors, however little we may be able to recall them. To others, appealing to such pervasive instances in human experience to explain an individual's current warrant depends on a doctrine of original evidence as murky and confused as the doctrine of original sin.

As well as distinguishing two kinds of knowledge, Leibniz also distinguished two kinds of truths: truths of reason or a priori truths, and truths of fact or a posteriori truths. The former were necessary and their opposite impossible, truths of fact contingent and their opposite possible.[4] Not surprisingly then, much debate surrounding the a priori concerns the metaphysical distinction between the necessary and the contingent, and the metaphysical status of truths in mathematics, physics, and other disciplines. However, as we have just seen, there might be a definable a priori/a posteriori distinction between types of truths, without an exclusive distinction between types of truths that can be warranted only a priori and those that can be warranted only a posteriori.[5] Defining a useful notion of a priori

---

4 Leibniz, *New Essays*, 434, and *Monadology*, sec. 33 from *Selections*, Wiener, ed. (New York: Scribners 1951); W.A. Tait, 'The Concept of A Priori Truth' in *Proof and Knowledge in Mathematics*, Michael Detlefson, ed. (London: Routledge 1992) argues that Leibniz's notion of a priori truth as truth whose reason is discoverable by analysis shows it is a non-epistemic notion of truths derivable from primitive identical truths and definitions. Albert Casullo (this volume) points out that many recent philosophers, e.g. Ayer, do work with some such non-epistemic notion of 'a priori' truth. But Leibniz is more problematic, since he also claims that 'a reason is a known truth whose connection with a less well known truth leads us to give our assent to the latter' and that a reason isn't an a priori reason (a known truth which is 'a cause not only of our judgment but of the truth itself') unless it and its connection with its consequence are known, or at least knowable, non-empirically (*New Essays*, 475).

5 For example, if only certain types of truth can be certain a priori, or follow from a priori certain truths in a priori certain ways, perhaps they can be called 'a priori truths,' even if they are susceptible to some degree of a posteriori warrant. If certain types of truth can be known only a posteriori, whereas others can be warranted either a priori or a posteriori, then perhaps the latter can be called 'a priori' truths.

truth seems secondary to understanding a priori knowledge and warrant, their possibility, and their scope.

(C) Empirically warranted conclusions require principles the validity of which is a priori warranted.[6] We can't be empirically warranted in drawing conclusions from past and present sense experience concerning further phenomena, e.g., that the sun will rise tomorrow or that the sun always rises, unless our sense experiences (or the premises they provide) are relevant to our conclusions and we are warranted in thinking the premises relevant to our conclusions or, at least, unless warrant for thinking the premises relevant is available to us by reflecting on our premises and their relevance. Otherwise it is pertinently an accident that our conclusion is true or likely to be true, and it isn't epistemically warranted for us. However, the relevance of our premises about experience to our conclusions can't ultimately, on pain of circularity, be itself empirically warranted.[7] There is an equally traditional variation. Empirical reasoning and thought proceeds in accordance with metaphysical distinctions, e.g. cause/effect, substance/accident/alteration, that cannot be derived solely from marks in experience. The validity of whatever principles licence the application of these categories can't ultimately then be empirically warranted.

An account of the a priori thus faces three tasks. First, to determine what is distinctive, if anything, about the subject matter or metaphysical status of the possible objects of a priori knowledge. Second, to indicate precisely what distinguishes a priori knowing or warrant

---

6 Cf. Leibniz: 'the truth of sensible things is established by the links amongst them; these depend upon intellectual truths, grounded in reason, and upon observations of regularities among sensible things themselves' (*New Essays*, 444).

7 Laurence BonJour (this volume) endorses an argument of this sort, acknowledging its 'internalist' presuppositions, and the opposition of 'externalist' critics for whom warranted conclusions may require warranted and relevant premises, and thus valid principles of relevance, but doesn't require warrant for the validity of the principles themselves, or even the availability of such warrant by reflection alone. See James van Cleve, 'Reliability, Justification, and Induction,' *Midwest Studies in Philosophy* 9 (1984).

from a posteriori knowing or warrant. If a proposition is made evident by certain sorts of considerations — other evident propositions that constitute evidence for its truth or just distinctive features of the way we contemplate or accept the proposition — what constitutes a priori considerations? If what warrants a belief is the sort of process that produces it, what distinguishes those processes whose products are a priori warranted from those that are a posteriori warranted? Third, to determine whether, and above all how, anything may be a priori warranted. Dissatisfaction with the history of answers to these questions has produced much skepticism concerning a priori knowledge in recent years. Many authors in this volume resist such skepticism. Let us begin, however, with a review of this history, focusing on the second and third questions and some issues they raise.

II Intuitive Induction and Demonstration

Among necessary truths putatively known a priori, it is common to distinguish axioms — propositions that are evident without proof — and theorems known because a sound proof from axioms is evident. Our knowledge of the theorems is often called demonstrative, our knowledge of the axioms intuitive. Thus an account of the nature of proof is crucial to an account of the a priori.[8] However, the key epistemological issues concern a priori knowledge of the axioms and proof procedures themselves. Leibniz wrote, 'You will find a hundred passages in which scholastic philosophers have said that such propositions are evident ex terminis — from the terms — as soon as they are understood.'[9] In contrast, the proposition that the Prime Minister is in Ottawa isn't evident as soon as it understood, but only by having

---

8 That's so even though our knowledge of theorems often depends on recalling steps in proofs, and thus isn't entirely a priori.

9 Leibniz, *New Essays*, 406. Leibniz isn't endorsing the 'scholastic' claim wholeheartedly since he thinks it doesn't properly appreciate the possibility and epistemic significance of demonstrating what are *commonly taken* as axioms.

relevant experiences that give us a reason for thinking it true, e.g., seeing him there on television, and the Pythagorean theorem isn't evident as soon as we understand it but only by proving it, or being told it by a reliable authority, etc.

The legacy from the Aristotelian and scholastic tradition concerning the a priori is more ambiguous than Leibniz suggests. Within a demonstrative science concerning what is necessarily and inherently so, we understand and know many things to be so by demonstrating them from first principles. The first principles are not themselves known by demonstration. Nor are they known by sense perception since 'it is impossible to perceive what is universal and holds in every case.'[10] Instead they are known by induction from perceived instances. We perceive many *A*s to be *F*, remember them to be so, recall that every *A* in our experience has been *F*, and by induction grasp that being *A* includes being *F* or that *A*s are necessarily *F*.[11] Traditionally

---

10 Aristotle, *Posterior Analytics*, trans. J. Barnes (Oxford: Clarendon Press 1975), Book I, ch. 31

11 The characterization of 'induction' follows Barnes's notes, *op. cit.*, 259-60. As Barnes notes, this process mirrors, or perhaps is identical with, the process by which we acquire the concept of *A* (so as to understand and know what is included in its definition) by induction or abstraction from the several images of *A*s we retain in memory from our various perceptions of *A*s.

   The universal is 'grasped from seeing' and so is grasped 'from the posterior.' But whereas 'seeing occurs separately for each' (particular instance), 'comprehension grasps at one time that it is thus in every case.' The Aristotelian view contrasts with the Platonic, in which sense experience and conversation concerning *A* prompt, or serve to recall from a prior disembodied life, a pure intellectual perception or intuition of a perfect *A* (form) to which physically perceived and discussed *A*s may approximate, but which nonetheless transcends and is separate from these *A*s. It also contrasts with the Leibnizian, according to which the content of our fundamental mathematical and metaphysical ideas can't be explained as arising from features of experience or our interaction with the world. Ideas with such content must be innate, or our capacity to have them must be innate, with sense experience providing the 'occasion' for its activation and for reflection on our ideas. Although knowledge of mathematical and metaphysical truths requires only examining these ideas, the ideas aren't innately distinct or adequate, and our knowledge isn't innate.

Aristotelian induction is construed as a process of intuitively grasping the fundamental nature and interconnections of universals by reflecting on their instances in experience, not as a process of arriving at empirically warranted conclusions from particular experiences. Some contemporary scholars challenge this view.[12] The issue depends on details the Aristotelian tradition doesn't straightforwardly provide. As Wilfrid Sellars noted,

> to say that the reasonableness of asserting "All *A* is *B*" does not rest on knowledge of the form "It is probable on e [empirical evidence] that all X is Y" is but a pedantic way of saying that the reasonableness of asserting "All *A* is *B*" does not rest on, or is independent of, experience.[13]

Consider then the following suppositions. (a) We can be warranted in accepting a first principle by considering imagined or supposed in-

---

Barnes thinks the innatist claim is either the dubious one that we have innately occurring ideas or knowledge, or the trivial one that we have an innate capacity to know things or have ideas upon external sensory stimulation, apparently overlooking the issue of the content of ideas (250-1).

12 Cf. Barnes, *op. cit.*, 256-60. For Barnes, knowing that *A*s are necessarily *F* by understanding *A* and *F*, and their connection, isn't a matter of grounding knowledge in some distinctive act of understanding terms or a distinctive intuitive grasp of necessary connections. It's just a matter of understanding or comprehending that *A* necessarily includes *B* — by accepting this generalization by induction from perceived and remembered particulars. For a more traditional interpretation, see R. Chisholm, *Theory of Knowledge*, 2nd ed., (Englewood Cliffs: Prentice-Hall 1977), reprinted in Paul Moser, ed., *A Priori Knowledge* (Oxford: Oxford University Press 1987). There is also some dispute about the extent to which Aristotle's own most mature views concerning our knowledge of first principles differ from the historically influential views presented in *Posteriori Analytics*. See Terence Irwin, *Aristotle's First Principles* (Oxford: Oxford University Press 1988).

13 Sellars, Wilfrid, 'Is There A Synthetic "A Priori"?' *Philosophy of Science* (1953), reprinted in *Science, Perception, and Reality* (London: Routledge and Kegan Paul 1963), 300 (bracketed insertion ours). He adds 'But if the reasonableness of asserting "All *A* is *B*" does not rest on experience, on what does it rest? ... The reasonableness, we are told, rests on a correct understanding of the meanings of the terms involved. In short, a priori truth is truth *ex vi terminorum*.'

stances, e.g. a teacher says 'Now class, picture...,' as well as perceived or remembered ones. (b) If the warrant we have for accepting putative first principles can be undermined by counter-examples to the principles or to logically equivalent principles, it can be undermined by counter-examples which we imagine or conceive in thought experiments — perhaps with prompting from others — as well as by ones we actually perceive or remember. (c) It isn't undermined simply by discovering that the putatively perceived instances upon which we based our acceptance of the principle were really hallucinated. (d) Above all, and this is really the crucial point, warrant for the principle isn't a function of the number and variety of perceived instances we recall.[14] (Recall [B] above.)

It's not clear that the Aristotelian and Scholastic tradition rejects any of these suppositions.[15] But if it doesn't, the inductive process whereby

---

14 This isn't to say that degree of empirical warrant can't be affected by other factors as well, e.g. coherence with other empirically warranted propositions, or that empirical warrant for a hypothesis must be a matter of confirmation by instances rather than a function of the number and variety of observed phenomena and kinds of phenomena it explains.

Nor does it mean hypothetical cases that are neither perceived nor remembered can't be relevant to the *empirical* confirmation and disconfirmation of generalizations as well. In thinking about an hypothesis, we might realize that it implies that if circumstances C were to occur, Y would occur. If we have independent empirical evidence for thinking that it is likely that Y would occur, or that it wouldn't occur, if C were to occur, we can respectively confirm or disconfirm the hypothesis without any empirical evidence that Y actually does or doesn't occur. Moreover, a single observation can greatly confirm a hypothesis when we are empirically warranted in thinking the observed event unlikely if the hypothesis is false. In both cases, the empirical confirmation or disconfirmation of the hypothesis is nonetheless ultimately a function of the number and variety of perceived and recalled events.

15 Indeed many philosophers sympathetic with this tradition endorse them. Chisholm, *Theory of Knowledge*, 2nd ed., (Englewood Cliffs: Prentice-Hall 1977), ch. 3, and the various philosophers he cites, e.g. Duns Scotus. Though Aristotle suggests the need for several experienced particulars in several places, (e.g. *Post. An.* A 31, *N. Ethics, VI*, 8), he doesn't suggest that the degree of warrant is in any way proportional to the number and variety of instances. Eleanore Stumpf, in

we grasp first principles is epistemically quite different from inductive methods for empirically confirming hypotheses concerning populations as a whole ('m/n As are F') by examining an actual sample of the population ('m/n examined As are F'). In the former, perceived instances function as *illustrations* that allow us to understand the general principle in question and thereby know it to be true. In the latter, they function as empirical *evidence* for the truth of the principles. Many Aristotelians may find (a)-(d) implausible in the case of our knowledge of the nature of natural species like man or horse, but less implausible with respect to mathematics, logic, perhaps even physics. That may just be reason for them to distinguish more sharply the role of experience in the knowledge of macroscopic observable natural species from the role of experience in knowledge of first principles of mathematics or fundamental principles of physics and natural science. In both cases we move from particulars to universals, but the way we gain knowledge is otherwise quite different.

If, as Aristotelian immanent realists suggest, universals and real necessary connections don't exist apart from actual particular instances, knowledge of real necessary connections may require some perceptual knowledge of instances, not just knowledge of imaginary instances or the results of thought experiments. But the necessity of a connection still won't be empirical knowledge warranted by the empirical evidence (or a posteriori reasons) for it. We can say either that it presupposes empirical knowledge, but isn't empirical knowledge, or that though some of its warrant derives from the empirical reasons for thinking the universals are instantiated, at least some of its warrant does not. We might then wish to acknowledge an equivocation in 'a priori knowledge,' but in so far as the most significant epistemological classification of knowledge concerns the nature of the evidence or warrant for the proposition known, knowledge of first

---

her valuable 'Aquinas on the Foundations of Knowledge' *Aristotle and his Medieval Interpreters*, Bosley and Tweedale, eds., *CJP* Supplementary Volume 17, presents a view of Aristotle and Aquinas similar to Barnes's but neither she nor Barnes really addresses the issues that Sellars and (a)-(d) bring to the fore.

principles or at least some of its warrant will be non-empirical, and thus a priori rather than a posteriori.

Yet, if an inductive grasp of first principles isn't an empirically warranted induction from experience, what distinguishes it from empirically unwarranted generalization? The difference can't just be that unwarranted prejudices and the conclusions we jump to on too little evidence are either false or aren't necessary truths. Nor can it just be that when we inductively grasp first principles on the basis of a few cases, we wouldn't accept the principles on the basis of those cases unless the principle were true. This condition is met by any necessary truth we happen to accept, no matter how hastily. Nor can we simply say that in grasping first principles we exercise induction concerning topics in ways that, as a matter of design, reliably yield true judgments of universal necessity independent of the number and variety of actual instances, without saying precisely what these blessed ways, topics, and judgments are. This is a tall order.

One suggestion is that some basic necessarily true propositions are evident to anyone who accepts them, no matter how many or what sort of examples led one to accept them. If so, when we accept a necessary truth that isn't inherently evident to anyone who accepts it (or understands it), or that doesn't follow from such propositions in inherently evident ways, it isn't a priori evident. When it also isn't empirically warranted, we are simply jumping to conclusions. But critics may protest that (just about) any proposition can be accepted for bad reasons as well as good reasons or no reasons, empirical reasons or a priori reasons. So how can any sort of necessarily true proposition be inherently evident and so a priori evident?[16] Yet empirical warrant for necessary truths isn't empirical certainty. In response, then, Chisholm, for example, can define an axiom as any necessary truth that necessarily is certain for anyone who accepts it. An axiom becomes axiomatic and thus certain for us when we actually accept it, and our a priori knowledge is defined as whatever (i) is

---

16 Kitcher, Philip, *The Nature of Mathematical Knowledge*, (New York: Oxford University Press 1982), 15. Hereafter '*NMK*.'

axiomatic for us or (ii) is accepted by us and follows axiomatically for us from other propositions which are axiomatic for us.[17] But what is it about the intrinsic character of some necessarily true propositions that would allow them, but not others, to be certain for anyone who accepted (or understood) them?[18] Furthermore, Leibniz noted, many propositions or maxims that classical mathematicians took to be evident without demonstration and employed in the demonstration of other truths, are themselves susceptible to demonstration from propositions which, to those who accept them and recognize the demonstration, are more basic and more certain. That produces a dilemma. Either these demonstrable propositions are a priori certain and known a priori without demonstration, in which case there is no epistemological gain to them in demonstrating them,[19] or they aren't

---

17 In the second edition of *Theory of Knowledge* (Englewood Cliffs, NJ: Prentice Hall 1977), Chisholm defends 'intuitive induction' as a method whereby propositions become axiomatic for one by understanding universals and grasping what they include and exclude, but drops his discussion from the third edition (Englewood Cliffs, NJ: Prentice Hall 1989). What remains from the second is the account of a priori knowledge above in terms of the inherent certainty of certain propositions for anyone who accepts them. The shift may reflect a recognition that the latter view makes reflection on instances epistemically irrelevant, however psychologically relevant it may remain to producing acceptance.

18 And why should we restrict a priori knowability to necessary truths, by definition rather than by philosophical argument. Philip Kitcher (see Mathematics, below) provides a definition which leaves out Chisholm's stipulation but implies that some self-knowledge, e.g., 'I exist' is a priori (*NMK*, 24, 27) Leibniz, on the other hand, thinks that 'I am' and other 'first experiences' are axioms in the sense that they are immediately known without proof and are certain to anyone who accepts them, no matter what her experience. But he classifies them as a posteriori, because in accepting them we don't see why they are true. That allegedly distinguishes them from those necessary truths known a priori without proof, the 'first illuminations' (*New Essays*, 434, 411). This either seems just as 'stipulative' as Chisholm or appeals to the 'original' sense of 'a priori' mentioned above.

19 Despite their demonstrability, despite their apparent acceptance by some persons simply because experience confirms them, indeed despite the apparent rejection of some propositions we once took to be certain without demonstration.

a priori certain, in which case neither they nor the propositions demonstrated from them are a priori known or warranted at all, and no matter how many thought experiments underlie our acceptance of them, they are warranted for us only to the extent that they are empirically probable. Neither horn fits the apparent epistemological facts.

Another suggestion is that the inductive grasp of first principles is distinguished from hasty generalization by the role of the former in demonstrating theorems so as to produce a body of scientific knowledge.[20] However, if the results are to be a priori knowledge, what matters can't be the role of axioms in systematizing our whole body of knowledge and explaining the empirical data, but simply their role in providing premises for demonstrating putative necessary truths. Since that depends solely on their logical relations with those propositions, critics may protest, that's surely a role that could be performed as readily by hasty generalizations as by axioms! It seems, as foundationalists have always insisted, that some a priori warranted propositions must derive at least some of their a priori warrant from something other than their logical (or probabilistic) relations with other propositions, and so provide a foundation for the a priori warrant of the rest.[21]

Leibniz seemed to have thought that they gained in epistemological status since whatever degree of evidence or illumination they had before being demonstrated from more primary truths was less than what they had after being demonstrated. Cf. *New Essays*, 414.

20 Our knowledge of the axioms would then (contra Aristotle, *Post. An.* Book A, 2) be as much based on our knowledge of the theorems as the latter is on the former, since what would then matter for the warrant of axioms is their interconnection with theorems.

21 Cf. Roderick Firth, 'Coherence, Certainty, and Epistemic Priority,' *Journal of Philosophy* (1964).

III Rational Intuition and Coherence

For many foundationalists, distinctive intuitive grasps of necessity and possibility constitute the marks of a priori evidence for judgments of necessity and possibility. We know first principles by accepting them on the basis of a grasp of the very necessity of the principles we accept. We may understand other propositions by grasping their essential necessary or inferential connections with further propositions, but we don't grasp the very necessary connections that are the objects of our judgments. Laurence BonJour (this volume) dubs this view 'classical rationalism,' and vigorously argues that some form of it is the only viable approach to a priori knowledge. It needn't be combined with Aristotelian induction, but it can be. If understanding and knowing first principles requires reflecting on actual or hypothetical instances, it will be the distinctive grasp or awareness of the very universals and their necessary connection that we accept in our judgment, and which are exemplified in whatever particular instances we reflect on, that constitutes our understanding of the principles and makes our acceptance a knowledge of first principles rather than unwarranted or even empirically warranted belief. In any case, rationalists need to describe the distinctive psychological and semantic features of intuitive grasping and explain its epistemic relevance.

Suppose intuitively grasping the necessity of the transitivity of identity differs from judging that identity is transitive, and warrants the judgment, in something like the way seeing a black bar as over a white bar differs from and warrants thinking a black bar is over a white bar. The perceptual experience (empirical intuition) of something is often understood as a sensory effect, at least in optimal conditions, of the very state of affairs it represents, and as representing a state of affairs, not by virtue of its inferential connections with other representations, but by having features that are typically caused by features of the state of affairs. So what distinctive psychological character in 'intellectual intuition' corresponds to the distinctive sensory characters of empirical intuition? What distinctive feature of intuitive mental acts can correspond to the necessity of a state of affairs, and how can intuitive mental acts be the effects of necessary connections or what holds in all possible worlds? We might instead understand intuitively grasping the necessity of a pattern (e.g. 6 dots containing 3) as having the necessary pattern itself instanced in the representation of the pattern, and noticing thereby that in representing (perceiving, conceiving) one aspect of the pattern we are representing another. Yet, as John Bigelow (this volume) notes, part-whole relationships between representations *needn't* reflect a corresponding part-whole relationship between the patterns represented. On either suggestion, then, we might think our faculty of a priori intuition may represent what isn't necessary as necessary, and so gives us ostensible grasps of necessity which confer warrant that is prima facie and defeasible by broader considerations. If we insist that a priori intuition, properly understood, can't represent what isn't necessary as necessary, we still seem to allow that our capacity for intuitively judging necessity is fallible and the warrant for its products is defeasible.[22] The pattern or state of affairs we judge necessary needn't be (the) one whose necessity we intuitively grasp. That, it seems, will also be so if grasping a necessity isn't to represent it, but, mysteriously, to have it consciously and directly before (or united with) the mind in one seamless mental act.

Rationalists may wish to avoid issues about the representational / non-representational character of mental acts, and simply identify intuiting the possibility or necessity of something with being consciously able or unable to think of something upon trying to do so. Conceivability and inconceivability, so construed, also seem fallible and revisable, and the warrant they confer on judgments of possibility and necessity defeasible. If in trying to conceive A without B, we are consciously unable to conceive A without conceiving B, we are prima facie warranted in thinking A necessitates B. If we are consciously able to do so, we are prima facie warranted in thinking A without B possible.[23]

---

22 These conclusions are resisted by Ernest Sosa in 'Knowledge and Intellectual Virtue,' *Monist* (1985).

23 When we can't conceive A without conceiving B, our warrant might be undermined when various other propositions we can or can't conceive false imply, in

BonJour, Brown, and Bigelow (this volume) embrace the fallibility of a priori intuition and the beliefs it warrants, and the defeasiblity of a priori warrant by broader considerations. This idea is not new. Concerning logic and mathematics, Russell thought,

> self-evidence is never more than a part of the reason for accepting an axiom, and is never indispensable. The reason for accepting an axiom, as for accepting any other proposition is always largely inductive, namely that many propositions which are nearly indubitable can be deduced from it, and that no equally plausible way is known by which these propositions could be true if the axiom were false, and nothing which is probably false can be deduced from it.
>
> The object is not to banish "intuition" but to test and systematize its employment.... In all this logistic is exactly on a level (say) with astronomy, except that in astronomy verification is effected not by intuition but by the senses.[24]

The suggestion seems to be that our logical and mathematical intuitions give some initial or prima facie degree of warrant to propo-

---

ways we can't conceive as not holding, that *A* may occur without *B*. Or because we are also unable to conceive of the impossibility of *A* without *B* without thinking that there must be some reason why, and yet be unable to conceive of any way to prove the impossibility. As Arthur Pap notes (*Semantics and Necessary Truth* [New Haven: Yale University Press 1958]), inconceivability can't be a criterion of impossibility if what is relevantly inconceivable is defined by what is logically impossible. However, much of the force of Pap's criticisms of conceivability and inconceivability as criteria is lost when the criteria are construed, not as definitions of possibility and impossibility, but as giving marks of defeasible or prima facie warrant for ascribing possibility and impossibility. When we try to conceive *p* and are consciously unable to do so, that doesn't entail that *p* is impossible.

24 A.N. Whitehead and B. Russell, *Principia Mathematica to *56* (Cambridge: Cambridge University Press 1973), 59; Russell, 'On "Insolubilia" and Their Solution by Symbolic Logic,' in *Essays in Analysis*, D. Lackey, ed. (New York: Brazilier 1973), 193. Cf. Albert Cioffa, *The Semantic Tradition from Kant to Carnap: To the Vienna Station* (Cambridge: Cambridge University Press 1991), ch. 7. In 1912, Russell also suggested that some logical principles at least (e.g. the law of non-contradiction) were absolutely self-evident or certain, e.g. *The Problems of Philosophy* (London: Oxford University Press 1912), ch. 7.

sitions stating the content of our intuition, but their warrant may be increased by systematic logical connections with other such propositions, and may cease when their absence would increase the overall coherence of the system of propositions. There is epistemic point in demonstrating propositions we have thus far taken as intuitively true without demonstration, and in demonstrating connections we have thus far taken as intuitively valid without demonstration. There is epistemic gain in accepting propositions as true (or connections as valid) without demonstration and without intuition, so long as many propositions that are intuitively warranted can be demonstrated with their help. For Russell, paradoxes or contradictions generated by a system of intuitively evident propositions were a chief motive for making adjustments, introducing new postulates or restrictions on inferences.

Finally, multiplying and varying thought experiments and explorations of logical connections in an unsuccessful search for counterexamples can shore up our intuitions and increase the warrant of intuitively evident propositions. But when, and to what degree, does this make a difference? Critics might argue it all depends on the degree to which multiplying intuitions and thought experiments increases the empirical data, often introspective, concerning our mental states and the results of our thinking, and increases the *empirical warrant* for accepting various necessities and possibilities on the grounds that they *best explain* our intuitions and thought experiments. However, people who acquire warranted beliefs in various necessities and possibilities on the basis of what they intuit or think aren't always prepared or able to explain their psychological states or thought processes as the products of these necessities and possibilities. Their warrant isn't, it seems, empirical. But if it's a priori, we still need an answer to our question.

Once we have allowed that intuitive a priori warrant for a proposition is a priori defeasible, surely we must recognize that such warrant can also be undermined empirically, e.g. by evidence that a usually reliable authority tells us that what we judge necessary isn't necessary at all, or that she doesn't share our intuition, or by evidence that we were on mind altering drugs during the thought experiments or reflections that produced our intuitions of possibility and necessity, etc.?[25] Further thought about the issue may undercut the relevance of such empirical evidence to our warrant, but that isn't to say that the empirical evidence can't defeat the warrant conferred by our original intuition. Doesn't this then show that the warrant for judgments of necessity and possibility isn't really a priori in the first place?[26]

However, if we take the notion of prima facie warrant seriously, we must distinguish how a proposition is warranted from how its warrant is defeasible, and thus whether a proposition is a priori warranted from whether its warrant is empirically defeasible. If a proposition can be warranted for us in the presence of favorable evidence so long as undermining evidence is absent, but cease to be warranted when undermining evidence *is* present, there seems no reason why recognizing that a proposition is empirically defeasible means that its warrant can't be (entirely) a priori.[27] When we have prima facie warrant for accepting something, we don't need *independent* evidence that considerations defeating or undermining our warrant won't obtain. At most, the empirical defeasibility of a proposition's warrant implies that the proposition can't a priori be entirely certain.[28]

Still, once fallibility for our capacity of intuitively judging necessity is conceded, or defeasibility for the warrant it confers is conceded, why should we think following a priori intuition has anything to do

---

25 Cf. John Pollock, *Knowledge and Justification* (Princeton: Princeton University Press 1974), 329. Pollock provides the most comprehensive account of the structure of defeasible a priori warrant.

26 *Contra* Philip Kitcher, 'The Naturalists Return' in *Philosophical Review* (1992), 72.

27 After all, the warrant we have for thinking there is a tree before us when we ostensibly see one may be undermined when a reliable authority tells us our vision is unreliable or when we also reach out and don't feel a tree. That doesn't make our knowledge really testimonial or tactile knowledge when, in the absence of undermining evidence, we ostensibly see and take there to be a tree before us.

28 Thus, though there may a priori knowledge, there might not be any a priori truths *in the sense of* propositions that can have a warrant that isn't empirically defeasible or to which empirical evidence can't even in principle be relevant.

with getting judgments which are warranted, albeit a priori, rather than simply with getting judgments for which there is no warrant and for the truth of which there is no evidence? Although some epistemologists might be content to think this a brute fact about our warrant, revealed by critical reflection on our warrant and its sources, Bigelow, Brown, and Smith (this volume) seem willing to take an increasingly popular naturalist stance toward the question.[29] What makes a priori intuition a mark of warrant can only be just the reliability with which our practice or process of basing judgments on it serves, in our world, the desirable cognitive goal of getting truth and avoiding error, regardless of whether it would necessarily do so in quite different environments or for creatures with quite different evolutionary or cultural histories. Understanding a priori knowledge of various subject matters then may be advanced by examining the processes that underlie our judgments concerning various subject matters. Though particular experiences may play a role in making such judgments, what makes their warrant a priori will be the independence from experience of our judgments and their reliability, perhaps in the various traditional ways described above. The processes that provide a priori warrant may even turn out not to involve distinctive intuitions of universal necessity at all, but might instead simply be ones in which, on the basis of various patterns and relations presented in particular situations we perceive, imagine, or conceive, we reliably judge universal necessity. The process might still be loosely described as one of intuitively grasping necessity, or, perhaps better, as intuitive induction. In any case, whether there are such processes, or a priori warranting processes at all, is neither necessary nor certain.

Reliabilism may be challenged from two quarters. First, whatever perceptual processes we have developed for reliably detecting relevant

---

29 Pollock, however, argues that logical intuitions of possibility and necessity and implication constitute prima facie warrant for assertions of possibility and necessity, because it's in terms of these intuitions that we learn to make and correct such assertions and their meaning is determined.

features of our environment presumably are the product of interactions between these sorts of features and our perceptual processes. But how can there have been interaction between universal necessities and our cognitive processes to produce mechanisms for reliably detecting the former?[30] And why would nature design processes for detecting necessity as well as for detecting predators and the coming of winter? Naturalism and a priori warrant may make an unnatural mix if the latter depends on detecting real mind and language independent necessities. Second, BonJour and other traditional internalists argue, not only must intuitive a priori warranted judgment be based on internal states of mind that are accessible on reflection and can guide us in checking and correcting our judgment, but the reliability with which such states indicate the truth of the judgment must also be accessible on reflection in ways that will be warranted, and not just reliable, independent of experience. For BonJour, a priori intuition must provide a reason or warrant for thinking a proposition at least likely true, without simply reliably indicating truth, and without any independent warrant for thinking it indicates truth. The relevance of a priori intuition, he argues, is an inescapable presupposition of any attempt to justify, criticize, or assess a belief or the rationality of an argument — even an argument against a priori knowledge.

Perhaps the demand for some further reason for thinking reliance on a priori intuition reliable can instead be met by internalists with a coherence theory of knowledge. Beliefs are warranted to the extent that they form part of the most coherent overall belief system available to us, one which allows us to give reasons for the truth of our beliefs in terms of other beliefs we have, and which allows us to give reasons for thinking the various sources of our beliefs — experience, a priori intuition, convention, etc. — are reliable. But what could warrant us in thinking our beliefs coherent? Traditional a priori intuitionists like BonJour or Russell will insist a thorough-going coherentist must answer this question, but can't coherently do so. If anything is to be

---

30 Cf. the challenges concerning the efficacy of laws of nature from B. van Fraasen, *Laws and Symmetry* (Oxford: Clarendon Press 1989).

warranted by coherence, some logical relations between beliefs must be intuitively evident without any independent reason for thinking a priori intuition reliable. But, naturalistic defenders of a priori knowledge may object, doesn't this leave traditional internalists without any real explanation of how a priori warrant is possible? So much the worse for internalism, and so much the worse for internalist criticisms of reliabilism, say they.

In any case, for the thorough-going coherentist, it may seem the a priori/a posteriori distinction isn't a fundamental epistemic distinction concerning sources of warrant, but is really a causal distinction between sources of belief that may, depending on what sources our system of beliefs recognizes as relevant, matter for their justification. Our system of belief may allow that the reliability with which certain sources of judgment indicate necessary truth is relatively independent of experience or favorable testimony. But what warrants all our beliefs is ultimately *the coherence of the whole* — the network of relations among experiential beliefs, beliefs about necessity, and beliefs about the reliability of their respective sources. However, perhaps the coherentist can insist that warrant for some beliefs is presupposed by any warranted belief whatsoever, experiential or non-experiential, and by whatever sources we are warranted in thinking yield true belief. Their warrant is thus in a quite distinctive way a priori. Hilary Putnam, for example, suggests that the warrant or rationality with which we accept most fundamental logical principles as true rather than false might, traditional defenders of the a priori to the contrary, depend on what else we happen to believe and can cite as reasons for these principles. But he grants that there is at least one that can't, viz., 'not every statement can be true and false.' He writes, 'to believe all statements are correct (which is what we are talking about) would be to have no notion of rationality.'[31]

Few modern philosophers share Putnam's doubts concerning the a priori status of traditional logical principles. But most would agree

---

31 Putnam, H., 'Analyticity and Apriority: Beyond Wittgenstein and Quine,' *Realism and Reason* (Cambridge: Cambridge University Press 1983)

that in some way the ground of a priori knowledge is in the very way we think or perceive things or in what that presupposes.

IV Analysis and Presupposition

Leibniz sets the stage by explaining a priori knowledge of primary truths in terms of the form of the propositions with which they are expressed or of the judgments with which we accept them — that of identical propositions whose opposite involves an express contradiction. In thinking *A* is *A* or everything which is *A* and *B* is *A*, 'nothing comes between the subject and the predicate,'[32] and we cannot think of any way our judgment might be false without thereby thinking that a contradiction holds. There is thus no further reason why it is true rather than false, and its reason is thus evident in the form of the thought with which we accept it. When a proposition we accept is necessarily true, either it is an identical proposition, or its reason for being true rather than false can be discovered by a process of analysis in which it is reduced to an identical proposition by resolving its component terms or ideas into simple ones that cannot be defined, so that its demonstrability via the law of non-contradiction from identical propositions and definitions is evident. Kant introduced the term 'analytic' for truths that are so reducible, 'synthetic' for truths that aren't.[33]

Successful analysis and demonstration requires an 'intuitive awareness of (the) content'[34] of our ideas — a knowledge in which we have before the mind or think at once all the constituent characters of a complex idea. It may also require an intuitive awareness of logical form.

---

32 Leibniz, *New Essays*, 434. Non-identical propositions like '*A* is *B*' are evident only by experiencing instances of *A* and *B* together, or by demonstration, e.g. via a middle term '*C*' linking *A* and *B*.

33 Falsehoods that are reducible to express contradictions by analysis are analytic falsehoods; those that are not are synthetic.

34 Leibniz, 'Reflections on Knowledge, Truth, and Ideas' in *Selections*, 286

But it doesn't require any induction from actual or hypothetical instances, much less empirical evidence of the existence of things corresponding to our ideas. Necessary truth for Leibniz doesn't depend on our accepting it, but the form and content of the thoughts with which we accept it contain the reason why they are necessarily true.[35] The analytic/synthetic, identity/express contradiction distinctions are semantic and/or structural distinctions. They do double duty in the Leibnizian tradition: first, to explain how propositions can be necessarily true/false (true/false in all possible worlds), and others contingently true/false; second, to explain how necessary truths can be known a priori. Challenges to the Leibnizian account are legion. The most common objection is that there are necessary truths that are not identical propositions and are not reducible to such, perhaps because their terms are unanalyzable. Both their necessity and our knowledge of them stand in need of explanation. Kant charges that arithmetic and geometry consist of necessary synthetic truths concerning quantity. Following Reinach, Barry Smith (this volume) argues for non-formal, material but qualitative necessary connections, e.g. between being red and being colored, being promised and being obligatory. Moreover, what explains the necessity of logical truths and the validity of the principles required to reduce their negations to express contradictions?[36] Finally, what explains the truth of state-

---

35 'Our certainty regarding universal and eternal truths is grounded in the ideas themselves, independently of the senses' (*New Essays*, 392). Leibniz's distinction between truths of reason and truths of fact is justly often cited alongside David Hume's distinction between relations of ideas and matters of fact. Relations of ideas don't depend on the existence of anything in nature corresponding to the ideas and thus can be discovered without empirical evidence for such things, and there is no contradiction in denying matters of fact. However, for Hume even God's existence isn't a relation of ideas. More importantly, ideas for Hume are always (ideas of) imaginable, recallable, or introspectible particulars. Relations of ideas are thus relations between ideas of particulars, rather than truths about what is universally and necessarily the case.

36 The classic full length treatment of this charge and similar ones remains Pap's *Semantics and Necessary Truth*.

ments of definitions themselves? That is left as a primitive fact about what our words mean or what is contained in our concepts.[37]

Nonetheless, most philosophers assume that if a truth is analytic, it's a priori knowability is unproblematic. BonJour and Casullo (this volume) attack this assumption. How, BonJour asks, do we know that any proposition that is expressly contradictory is always and necessarily false? We need a positive account of how it is known a priori, not simply a negative claim that our reasons aren't or needn't be empirical. The supposed analytic character of a truth in no way explains how it may be known non-empirically without presupposing an appeal to an a priori intuition of necessity. Casullo argues that deriving mathematical truths from logical truths with the help of definitions of mathematical concepts doesn't alter their prior epistemic status. Adequate definitions of customary mathematical concepts are ones whose substitution in mathematical propositions we accept as true (false) leaves them true (false). If analysis can't disconfirm such propositions, it can't genuinely confirm them either. Leibniz might respond that we may be mistaken about what our ideas contain and what is possible concerning their content and thereby falsely accept something as possible or necessary. By telling us why a proposition we accept is true, analysis can give us a (degree of) a priori warrant we didn't already have. Yet, BonJour may again ask, why should knowing what one's idea of X contains tell us anything about the nature of X and thus what is possible or necessary concerning X?

Leibniz may respond that 'essence is fundamentally nothing more than the possibility of the thing under question.'[38] A priori demon-

---

37 Kant, *Critique of Pure Reason*, Introduction, B 10-11

38 *New Essays*, 293. 'Something which is thought possible is expressed by a definition; but if this definition does not at the same time express this possibility then it is merely nominal, since in this case we can wonder whether the definition expresses anything real — that is, possible — until experience comes to our aid by acquainting us a posteriori with the reality (when the thing actually occurs in the world.) This will do when reason cannot acquaint us a priori with the reality of the thing defined by exhibiting its cause or the possibility of its being

strative knowledge concerning X requires a distinct idea of X, i.e. knowing what, according to our idea of X, is necessary and sufficient for satisfying our idea, and also an adequate idea of X, i.e. knowing that it is possible to satisfy the idea. Without adequate ideas we engage in problematic symbol manipulation, and in drawing conclusions about the nature or existence of things, we lack reason for thinking those conclusions true rather than their contraries or contradictories, and lack reason for thinking our premises and conclusions applicable to anything real. A priori knowledge of the nature of something requires 'that we have carried the analysis through to the end and no contradiction is visible'[39] We may lack adequate or even distinct ideas for ordinary things like gold or red. But that doesn't mean we can't have recognizably consistent, distinct definitions for mathematical, physical, or metaphysical ideas employing basic, unproblematic notions the content of which we are immediately aware, and thereby have a priori knowledge of the nature of everything that is so definable.

However, Leibniz acknowledges we may never obtain a perfect analysis of our ideas. And denying possibility and compossibility for ideas that are unanalyzable or just yet unanalyzed isn't expressly contradictory. Leibniz should simply concede to BonJour — or perhaps was himself supposing all along — that when an idea is completely analyzed and we are aware of its components, what is simple (i.e. simply possible) and what is compossible will be intuitively evident. Analysis for Leibniz, then, may facilitate an intuitive grasp of possibility and necessity, but doesn't replace it.

'Moderate' empiricists, who wish to preserve a priori knowledge, but think only experience informs us of mind and language independent relations of things, typically argue that Leibniz's problems are resolvable by clearly recognizing that necessary truth and defini-

---

generated. So it is not within our discretion to put our ideas together as we see fit, unless the combination is justified either by reason, showing its possibility, or by experience, showing its actuality and hence its possibility.'

39 Leibniz, 'Reflections on Knowledge, Truth, and Ideas,' *Selections*, 288

tion aren't matters of real necessity and possibility. They depend on our inabilities, resolutions, or conventions in thinking and speaking. What makes a sentence (e.g. 'all bachelors are unmarried') necessarily true, for example, are our resolutions, conventions, or dispositions never to deny it or assert its negation, or its logically following from such sentences. What makes certain principles of logic valid are our resolution or conventions not to make or permit certain types of inferences. The unanalyzability of 'X,' and its possible satisfaction, are just matters respectively of its being treated as primitive, and its ascription being consistent, within the system of rules and definitions governing our symbolic activity. Analytic truth is now truth solely by virtue of the meanings of our terms or the conventions governing their use. Casullo's concerns thus reappear.

However, some empiricists will argue, this also lets us think of definition, not atomistically as analyzing terms into unanalyzable terms, but holistically as specifying the interconnected meanings or uses of terms.[40] Necessary truths that aren't reducible to identities by substituting definitions for defined terms are nonetheless analytic — true by virtue of the meaning of terms or the conventions governing our use of terms. Yet the degree to which we are warranted in accepting the transitivity of identity bears no obvious connection with the degree to which introspective and behavioral evidence empirically warrants conjectures about our psychological, sociological, or linguistic proclivities. Empiricists might respond that nondemonstrative a priori warranted acceptance or assertion is acceptance or assertion that is unconditionally licensed by our *rules* for thinking or speaking, regardless of what particular experiences we might have or proofs we might provide. Such rule-governed warranted assertion may presuppose knowledge of the rules, along with readiness to cite empirically warranted facts about what we would and wouldn't say to support claims about the rules and to

---

40 R. Carnap, *Meaning and Necessity*, 2nd ed. (Chicago: University of Chicago Press 1967), Appendices; W. Sellars, 'Is There a Synthetic A Priori?' in *SPR*. See also A. Cioffa, ch. 7.

criticize violations.[41] But it isn't itself knowledge of the rules. The rationalist might respond that surely it's our knowledge of the transitivity of identity that makes it wrong to deny it, and grounds our knowledge that it's wrong to do so? Barry Smith argues that even the necessary connection between obligation and promising isn't constituted by our adopting social rules or conventions, but underlies and constrains rule-formation in the institutional sphere. A more common criticism[42] is that accounting for all and only necessary truths requires appealing to what can't be denied without *contradiction* or to what *logically* follows from our resolutions/conventions of speech, or to what is a *consistent* application of our resolutions/conventions of inference — precisely what needs explaining. Quine expands these concerns to argue that the appeal to dispositions or conventions of denying and asserting to fix truth solely by virtue of the meanings of our terms and necessary truth can't succeed. However, BonJour argues that Quine's further rejection of a priori warrant altogether leaves any set of non-observational beliefs or sentences as rationally warranted or acceptable as any other. BonJour's goal isn't to restore 'moderate empiricism,' but to show the incoherence of any non-skeptical theory of knowledge which doesn't allow for a priori knowledge grounded in a priori intuitions of mind and language independent necessity.

We are usually content, Leibniz notes, to establish the possibility of something a posteriori from actual instances in experience. That doesn't mean such definitions yield conclusions that are merely empirically warranted by the evidence in their favour. They can just be less evident that those whose reason is a priori evident because we recognize a priori the adequacy of our ideas and definitions. However,

---

41 Cf. Sellars, 'Is There a Synthetic A Priori?' Empirically warranted assertions, Sellars adds, may even give us reasons for adopting or modifying our rules, including those unconditionally licensing assertion, without these assertions thereby being warranted by empirical evidence for their truth.

42 Besides concerns arising from Gödel's theorem, an elementary statement of which can be found in Pollock *op. cit.*

their epistemic status is still puzzling on Leibniz's account. Experience alone leaves problematic exactly what possibility is being shown to be actual. The fundamental ontological categories of reality aren't given in experience, and 'the linking of phenomena which warrants truths of fact about sensible things outside of us is itself verified by means of truths of reason' (*New Essays*, 375) and must have a reason drawn from the a priori known or knowable ultimate nature of things.

Why not appeal to a priori knowledge of actual instances to establish the adequacy or inadequacy of our ideas? The problem, as Hume and Kant emphasized, is that objects don't come into existence on being conceived by us, and there seems no way finite beings such as ourselves are presented with objects except through their effect on the faculty of sensible intuition. Hume went on to deny the a priori knowable necessity of the causal principle that every event has a cause, and of Leibniz's more fundamental general principle of sufficient reason — that nothing can be 'real or existent, no statement true unless there be a sufficient reason why it is so and not otherwise.' There is nothing in their concepts to make their denials self-contradictory, and no a priori intuition of their necessity.

However, Kant firmly maintained that there were some synthetic universally necessary principles concerning notions like causality, as well as substance, that were a priori knowable. Although the causal principle isn't reducible to an identical proposition, it is necessary at least in so far as it is instanced by any possible empirical phenomenon or object of experience, i.e. in any situation in which concepts or their complements may be applied in judgment to the sensory matter of intuition. Thus the principle holds whatever judgment about experience we might make or have reservations about making, and its truth is presupposed, whatever happens to be true of the experience ('it's a dog' vs. 'it just looks like a dog'). In order to make any judgment that is true or false of objects of experience we must synthesize and order the manifold of sense experience in accordance with the principle. It and its constituent concepts, Graciela De Pierris argues (this volume), are thus constitutive of any possible experience. Warrant for it (and other such constitutive principles) is thus a presupposition of whatever empirical warrant or doubt we might have concerning what is true of empirical phenomena, and can't be undercut by empirically warranted discoveries.

We know synthetic necessary truths in mathematics by constructing our mathematical concepts and propositions, or their proofs, in an a priori intuition in which we represent the process in time of producing (e.g. by drawing) and reproducing instances of them in space and time — the form with which things appear to us in sensible intuition. Since we can supply our concepts with objects adequate to them through this activity of pure imagination, mathematical truths become evident to us without an intellectual intuition of their necessity but independent of any empirical intuition of instances we might have. Thus in mathematics we have a priori evident axioms and demonstrations. Since space and time exhaust what can be given to us a priori in intuition, philosophical principles like universal causality can't similarly be proven. So how do we know them to be true, even for all possible objects of experience?

BonJour (this volume) argues that Kant's position, on pain of infinite regress, can only reduce to a version of moderate empiricism — e.g. to claiming (1) 'Every event that is a possible object of experience has a cause' is analytically true and thus knowable by conceptual analysis. But Kant can't think (1) any more analytic than 'every event has a cause' since neither 'object of experience' nor 'cause' are analyzable concepts.[43] De Pierris emphasizes that Kant doesn't think of such philosophical principles as demonstrated truths — as they would be if they were knowable by conceptual analysis — or as axioms ('first principles' in the traditional sense) from which various conclusions may be demonstrated, much less as conclusions demonstrated from facts we experience. Rather, by showing that they are constitutive of any possible object of empirical judgment, their deduction is 'juridical.'[44] Our right to claim a priori knowledge of their necessity is

---

43 Kant, B 756

44 She doesn't elaborate but cites Dieter Henrich, 'Kant's Notion of a Deduction' in *Kant's Transcendental Deductions*, Forster, ed. (Stanford: Stanford University Press 1989).

established by showing its basis in the way objects may be presented to us and judged, the requirements for the salient operations of our cognitive and sensory capacities, showing other claimants appeal to grounds that presuppose the legitimacy of our claim, etc. Some claimants (e.g. Putnam) may still question Kant's claim. And long forgotten relatives do show up from Australia to claim estates. Why then should the conclusions of such arguments be anything other than defeasible? These challenges, however, still presuppose the relevance of the style of argument. BonJour might instead ask why the sort of argument provides us with any reason for thinking the principles are in fact constitutive of experience, and thus ones we are entitled to. Is it because they are ways of establishing that something is analytically true? We return to these issues below.

Andrew Brook (this volume), emphasizing Kant's claim that the method of proof in philosophy is ostensive, suggests that Kant at least should have said that to prove the causal principle in application to objects of experience we must perform thought experiments in which we imagine ourselves fixing an event in time and we explore through the imagination what we would have to know in order to do so. The criterion of a priori warrant thus seems to be unimaginability, albeit 'pure.' Brook himself expresses doubts that this could establish necessity, or give us certainty. BonJour would doubtless concur, but also wonder why we should think the criterion even relevant to the question. Is its (even defeasible) relevance guaranteed by the very nature of the concept 'what we would have to know in order to do something' or 'constitutive of experience'? Is it simply that satisfying the criterion is a reliable method for persons like us to answer the question, and moreover we can tell a coherent story about our cognitive place in the world which explains why, and which is itself arrived at in a reliable way that accords with the very story we tell? But that's an answer that can be given by any naturalist — those who think there is warrant independent of experience and those who don't. It nonetheless invites us to look more specifically at the processes at work in making mathematical and other allegedly a priori warranted judgments.

V Mathematics

In his important book, *The Nature of Mathematical Knowledge*, Philip Kitcher conceives of mathematics as

> ... an idealized description of [collecting and ordering] operations on objects in our environment.... If we say that a universal affordance is an affordance which any environment offers to any human, then we may state my theory as the claim that mathematics is an idealized science of particular universal affordances. In this form, the theory expresses clearly the widespread utility of mathematics and, given the ... claim that affordances are the objects of perception, it is also easy to see how mathematical knowledge is possible.[45]

In elaborating his theory, Kitcher attacks 'mathematical apriorism,' traditional appeals to the role of proof and intuition in mathematics in support of apriorism, and 'platonism' in mathematics, which he conceives of as giving mathematics a subject matter inaccessible to ordinary perception.

By contrast, John Bigelow (this volume) tries to initiate a 'back to Pythagoras' movement in the philosophy of mathematics. To do justice to the nature of mathematics, he says, '... a theory must allow mathematics three distinctive characteristics: mathematics contains a priori knowledge of *necessary* truths about *intangible* things' (000). According to the 'Pythagorean' theory envisaged, a priori knowledge of mathematics is possible via the intuitive grasp of proofs, or of results of experiments in the imagination, where what is proven or what results are truths about mereological — part-whole — relations among 'universals.'

---

45 Philip Kitcher, *NMK*. 'Affordances' is a technical term borrowed from the psychologist J.J. Gibson, referring to what the environment offers, provides, or furnishes animals, either for good or ill. For example, krill affords nourishment to baleen whales, a wetland affords a habitat to ducks, and the African savanna affords predatory cats to gazelles. According to Gibson and his followers, it is the affordance that is perceived. Cf. *NMK*, 12 and J.J. Gibson, *The Ecological Approach to Visual Perception* (Boston: Houghton Mifflin 1979).

On the face of it Bigelow's account of mathematics opposes Kitcher's at least with respect to the a priority and the abstractness of mathematics.[46] Yet Bigelow himself elsewhere pays homage to Kitcher's perceptually based and 'historicist' epistemology of mathematics, and poses his own deciderata for a theory of mathematics, more circumspectly, as the requirements that the *apparent* a priority, necessity, and abstractness of mathematics be adequately explained.[47] The term 'apparent' leaves open an important loophole. For instance, it allows Bigelow's explanation of the intangibility or abstractness of mathematics to be, not in terms of transcendental Platonic forms, but in terms of 'concrete universals,'[48] perceivable structures immanently present in the objects that have them. So if Platonism is the belief in universals, Bigelow is a Platonist; but clearly as he construes it Platonism is compatible with mathematical knowledge having a basis in the 'perception of affordances,' à la Kitcher. Thus the apparent disagreement about Platonism turns out to be more verbal than real, more about what is or should be meant by the claim that mathematics has an 'abstract' subject matter than about what the subject matter of mathematics is.

Do Bigelow and Kitcher also mean different things by 'a priori'? As it turns out, they do, and in ways that turn out to connect interestingly with issues raised in other contributions to this volume. But as we shall now elaborate, this disagreement is not *merely* verbal. Its deeper

---

46 It is less clear what Kitcher wants to say about the modal status of mathematical truths. He never outright denies their necessity. However, he has denied that our knowledge of them as necessary need involve an a priori warrant (or, conversely, that our knowing them a priori would imply their necessity). Cf. Philip Kitcher, 'Apriority and Necessity,' *Australasian Journal of Philosophy* **58** (1980) 89-101.

47 J. Bigelow, *The Reality of Numbers* (New York: Oxford University Press 1988); cf. 3-4, 110-17

48 Cf. the tradition of D.M. Armstrong, *Universals* (Boulder, CO: Westview Press 1989); and D. Lewis, 'New Work For a Theory of Universals,' *Australasian Journal of Philosophy* **61** (1983) 343-77.

sources are: first, an underlying methodological or strategic disagreement about the way the history of the issue is to be approached; and second, a substantive disagreement concerning the nature and role of representations — external and internal — and attendant reflections on them, in mathematics.

We begin with Kitcher's carefully articulated account of mathematical a priority. Kitcher takes as his '... starting point the obvious and uncontroversial thesis that most people know some mathematics and some people know a large amount of mathematics' (*NMK*, 3). Allying himself with the late twentieth century 'back to psychologism' movement, he argues for the following broad condition, in which X is a cognitive agent, p a proposition, and t a time.

(1) X knows at t that p if and only if p, and X believes at t that p, and X's belief at t that p was produced by a process which is a warrant for it.[49]

---

49   *NMK*, 17. We have added the temporal indices; Kitcher acknowledges often leaving these implicit (cf. *NMK*, 22). Kitcher also leaves the notion of 'warrant' officially unanalyzed, but it is significant that he cites Alvin Goldman's recent 'externalist' treatment of the notion (cf. *NMK*, 18, n. 6; and Alvin Goldman's 'What is Justified Belief?' in Pappas, G., ed., *Justification and Knowledge* (Dordrecht: Reidel 1979); and his *Epistemology and Cognition* (Cambridge, MA: Harvard University Press 1985). What externalists like Goldman deny is the more traditional 'internalist' claim that the warrant producing process need involve the internal possession — in principle available to conscious reflection — of a reason for thinking the belief true. Of course, from the internalist's standpoint, such externalism opens the door to skepticism, since it allows that we may have no reasons for our beliefs. Larry BonJour argues (this volume) that externalists avoid traditional skeptical problems only by changing the subject. For instance, on its externalist construal, Kitcher's initial assumption of mathematical knowledge would be worth little in the eyes of an internalist, since it does not imply that we have any (good) reasons for the putative items of mathematical knowledge, which is what was originally at issue. An externalist conception of warrant would seem to be a particular affront to the traditional conception of a priori knowledge as knowledge gained by conscious reasoning, thought, or reflection alone, although we note below that on a certain construal the issue of a priority can nevertheless be seen to arise even within the externalist's framework.

But thereafter he mainly defers to the eighteenth century, and in particular to Kant (cf. *NMK* 23-4), in elaborating his account of a priori knowledge. First, Kitcher defines *X*'s 'life' at *t* as *X*'s total sequence of experiences up to *t*; a life at *t* is said to be 'sufficient for *X* for *p*' if *X* could have had that life and gained sufficient understanding to believe at *t* that *p* (*NMK*, 22).

(2) *X* knows a priori at *t* that *p* if and only if *X* knows at *t* that *p* and *X*'s belief at *t* that *p* was produced by a process which is an a priori warrant for it.

(3) α is an a priori warrant for *X*'s belief at *t* that *p* if and only if α is a process such that given any life *e*, sufficient for *X* for *p*,

(a) some process of the same type as α could produce in *X* at *t* the belief that *p*;

(b) if a process of the same type as α were to produce in *X* at *t* the belief that *p*, then it would warrant *X* in believing at *t* that *p*;

(c) if a process of the same type as α were to produce in *X* a belief at *t* that *p*, then *p*. (*NMK*, 24)

A fourth condition concerns a priori mathematical knowledge in particular.

(4) There is a class of statements *A* and a class of rules of inference *R* such that

(a) each member of *A* is a basic a priori statement; [i.e. its a priori status is taken as already established by (1)-(3) above without any appeal to a 'proof' (see below)],

(b) each member of *R* is an a priority-preserving rule;

(c) each statement of standard mathematics occurs as the last member of a sequence [called a 'proof'] all of whose members either belong to *A* or come from previous members in accordance with some rule in R. [And each statement of standard mathematics can be known by following its proof.] (*NMK*, 39; scare quotes and insertions in brackets ours)

As Kitcher summarizes (3), the processes in question must be *available* independently of experience, produce *warranted* belief independently of experience, and produce *true* belief independently of experience. We shall not dispute that these three aspects are present in Kant's idea of independence from experience. Also Kantian is the specifically *epistemological* character of the 'independence' invoked; it is not, e.g., merely logical or causal. This allows warrant to be epistemologically independent of experience though still logically conditional on and causally dependent on the experiences that go into a life sufficient for *X* for *p*.

But embedded in (3) is a further implication of a more modern, Quinian cast. The status of the process as a warrant must be 'unrevisable' in the sense that no subsequent experience is relevant to, or able to effect it. This follows because a process of the same type is held to be warrant-producing for *any* life sufficient for X for p — i.e., no matter what experiences X has, will have, or would have.

Thus armed, Kitcher is able to argue that mathematical beliefs supported by the intuitive grasp of proofs (or the results of experiments in the imagination) do not thereby qualify as having a priori warrant, for the reason that the basic a priori statements on which these proofs rest fail to satisfy (3 b), because there are *some* conceivable lives sufficient for X for p that undermine the warranting power of X's grasp of those statements. They may do so either by containing sufficiently bizarre perceptual experiences that pose a *direct* challenge, or, more subtly, by involving an *indirect* 'theoretical' or 'social' challenge. A theoretical challenge might be a sequence of experiences which suggests that the denial of the claim would provide a simpler over-all scientific view of the world than its affirmation. A social challenge might be a sequence of experiences in which apparently reliable experts deny the statement and offer hypotheses about the errors we have made in coming to believe it.[50]

In a more recent paper, acknowledging the complaint of some that his sense of a priori is 'strained and idiosyncratic,' Kitcher responds thus:

> I claim, however, that the traditional notion of a priority rests on the idea that a priori knowledge is independent of experience, and that, when this is articulated, it is seen that claims that *p* is a priori imply that *p* can be known in such a way that the knowledge could not be undermined by any experience. Hence ... the usual sources of philosophical knowledge [e.g., logic, conceptual analysis] do not yield a priori knowledge. I sympathize with those who think that my analysis of a priority somehow stacks the deck, and invite them to articulate a notion of a priority that will both cleave to the venerable idea of

---

50 *NMK*, 55. Cf. also Pollock.

independence from experience and also avoid the negative conclusions that I reach....[51]

If the deck has been stacked in Kitcher's analysis, it is surely, in the first instance, with its implication of unrevisability. Can Bigelow's (largely implicit) account of a priori mathematical knowledge be regimented in response to this challenge? Let us try. Bigelow sees himself as a 'naturalist,' a 'physicalist,' and in broad sympathy with a 'causal-theoretic' approach to knowledge.[52] So we may assume that Bigelow accepts at least the spirit of Kitcher's conditions (1) and (2). We begin to glean how his conception of a priori warrant differs from Kitcher's in the following passages:

> Mathematics not only has a distinctive subject matter, it also has a distinctive methodology. The characteristic form of justification found in mathematics is one which has traditionally been called a priori. A mathematical opinion is supported, not by assembling sensory observations, but by proofs which do not make any appeal to any contingent observations that anyone happens to have made. Such proofs are said to be a priori because the order of justification begins without (prior to) any assumptions about any experiences of any agents. Experiences will be required to help someone understand a proof; but no assertions about those experiences feature as premises in the proof. Different people have different experiences which lead them to understand the proof; but it is the very same proof that they come to understand. ('The Doubtful A Priori,' this volume, 159)

> History has taught us to be wary of any pretensions to infallibility. Yet this should not mislead us into denying the existence of a priori justifications in mathematics.... Mathematical justifications often do have a distinctive status, even if they do not establish their conclusions beyond all reasonable doubt. We need a name for the distinctive kinds of justifications which we find in mathematics; and "a priori" is the name which best fits. However epistemically fallible mathematics may be, its justifications are nevertheless a priori.
>   What makes a mathematical justification a priori, I propose, is the way in which the part-whole relations which constitute the necessities in nature are

---

51 Philip Kitcher, 'The Naturalists Return,' 53-144; cf. esp. 77 n. 72. Insertion in brackets ours.

52 Other authors in this collection who share this perspective include Andrew Irvine, James Brown, and perhaps Barry Smith and Albert Casullo.

reflected in part-whole relations among the representations in the mind or in language. (Ibid., 161)

In perceiving or conceiving he more inclusive pattern, a person necessarily also perceives or conceives the constituent pattern that it contains. It is not possible to conceive the one pattern in that way without also conceiving the other. (Ibid., 155)

Judging from these passages, Bigelow would both weaken and strengthen Kitcher's conditions on a priori mathematical warrant. He would strengthen (4) with the addition of the following further constraints.

(4 d)B A does not include any statements about particular experiences of particular agents; and

(4 e)B proofs are, au fond, about necessary mereological relations in patterns, and our warrant for believing them comes from perceiving or conceiving of these relations as evidenced in their very representation in the proof.

He would weaken (3) by *somehow* disarming Kitcher's Kantian conditions (3 b) and (3 c) so as to allow an a priori warranted belief to be false, and a would-be a priori warrant of (even a true) belief to be undermined by experience. The challenge, of course, is to allow a priori warrants to be fallible while sufficiently preserving their independence from experience, and thereby their distinctness from a posteriori warrants.

It is tempting to try modifying the preamble of (3): instead of requiring that (a)-(c) hold for *all* lives sufficient for X for p,[53] requiring only that they uniformly hold for some special subset of the lives. But there are problems with this approach. First, the 'availability condition' (a) intuitively still holds for all those lives. Second, the 'truth' condition (c) should surely *not* hold even for a privileged subset of lives. P's truth value is not function of these lives, and if a priori warrants do not guarantee truth, then they do not guarantee it with respect to any of these lives. At the same time, though, we need a priori

---

53 And for α. The lives must be sufficient for X to, e.g., comprehendingly follow a proof of p, if that is what α involves.

warrants to make the truth of *p* very likely, to reflect the relatively high level and stability of the confidence which we place in propositions so warranted.[54] So far then, what seems to be required is a *differentiated* approach to availability, warrant, and truth, Kitcher's three aspects of independence from experience.

But third, and most difficult, is the problem of identifying the warrant producing subset of lives in a principled way. Clearly one would want the sorts of lives that Kitcher appeals to as counterexamples to be among those excluded, but *that* way of identifying them seems pretty *ad hoc!* This is a difficult issue which we cannot adequately treat here, except to suggest an approach once used in the broader epistemological context by Gilbert Harman. In his book *Thought*,[55] Harman suggested that the fact that we accept that we know some things shows that it is a simpler and more plausible hypothesis than the skeptical alternative (16). The way to deal with skepticism, then, is simply to 'turn it on its head' by using intuitive judgments about when people know and do not know things to discover when reasoning has occurred and what its principles are (112). A prominent example of a principle of reasoning to which we are then led is Harman's Principle Q: One may infer a conclusion only if one also infers that there is no undermining evidence that one does not as yet possess (151). In effect, Harman accepts that if *X* knows that *p* at *t*, then it is rational for *X* at *t* to disregard as 'misleading' any evidence that would appear to defeat *p* or call *p* into question. But, according to Harman, the temporal index is crucial here. If *X* is actually confronted at some later time *t'* with some would-be defeating evidence, *X* may no longer know that it is misleading, and so of course may no longer disregard it, thus defeating *X*'s claim at *t'* to know that *p*.

We propose, on Bigelow's behalf, turning skepticism about the a priori on its head in roughly the same fashion. A version of Principle Q

---

54 Internalists and externalists may disagree about whether the epistemically relevant sort of likelihood is subjective or objective.

55 Gilbert Harman, *Thought* (Princeton, NJ: Princeton University Press 1973)

then suggests itself, to the effect that if one infers on a priori grounds that *p* then one infers at the same time that there is no 'undermining evidence,' of either an empirical nature (e.g. authorities asserting the contrary) or of a conceptual/inferential nature, that is, no evidence such that if one possessed it one's claim to know a priori that *p* would be undermined. So for here and now, what we propose is the following.

(3)B α is an a priori warrant for *X*'s belief at *t* that *p* if and only if α is a process such that

(a)B given any life *e*, sufficient for *X* for *p*, some process of the same type as α could produce in *X* at *t* the belief that *p*;

(b)B among the lives sufficient for *X* for *p* there is a non-empty subset, *L*, containing no 'defeaters,' with respect to which if a process of the same type as α were to produce in *X* at *t* the belief that *p*, then it would warrant *X* in believing at *t* that *p*;[56]

(c)B with respect to the lives in *L*, if a process of the same type as α were to produce in *X* a belief at *t* that *p*, then, very likely, *p*.

A priori warrants retain their full independence from experience as regards 'availability.' But experiences in lives sufficient for *X* for *p* that are outside *L* may undermine warrant. Even so, recalling (4 e)B, those experiences cannot be experiences in which *X* manages to perceive or conceive of, e.g., an arithmetic pattern, without at the same time thereby perceiving or conceiving of the constituent parts of that pattern in the relations to the whole which in fact bear on the arithmetic truths at issue. Finally, although an a priori warranted belief can be false, this can only be because of the fallibility and limitation of our abilities, e.g., to grasp whether or not some would-be proof is a proof, not because a genuine proof might have a false conclusion.

Kitcher would be right to insist that Bigelow's notion of independence from experience is weaker than his own. Bigelow can counter that he is trying to preserve, not just a recognizable core of

---

56 *One* such life should be sufficient for an externalist. Internalists might insist that *L* represent a *substantive* proportion of such lives, so that warrant isn't undermined by mere reflection on the probabilities of defeaters occurring.

that notion, but at the same time the traditional *belief* that the grasp of proofs is an a priori warrant-producing process in mathematics and that by this process we can and do come to know mathematical truths a priori. There is a problem when this traditional belief is interpreted in terms of Kitcher's 'venerable' notion of independence of experience. It seems that the latter precludes the former; indeed it turns out that we scarcely know anything a priori. Bigelow therefore takes as *his starting point* not only that we know quite a bit of mathematics, but that we know quite a bit of it a priori. He in effect takes a priori warrants in mathematics to be *whatever* in the character of mathematical warrants turns out to be in some respect distinctively independent of, or in addition to, experience, and that distinguishes them from ordinary a posteriori warrants. It is one thing to insist that all warrants are fallible and can be undermined by sensory experiences. Bigelow concurs. But it is quite another to suggest in addition that our sensory experiences all by themselves, without the aid of any (principled) reasoning or thought, yield warrants for *anything*, much less mathematics.[57] Kitcher wants to be postmodern about knowledge but merely modern about the a priori. Bigelow, straight and single-minded Aussie that he is, wants to be thoroughly postmodern! If Kitcher is prepared to reject, say, Cartesian epistemology, and take as his starting point the antiskeptical stance that we know lots of mathematics, why not go further, take as one's starting point that we know lots of mathematics a priori, and set out to formulate an account of a priori warrant (sufficiently and recognizably related to traditional accounts), on which this can be true? Why burden a late twentieth century conception of knowledge with an eighteenth century (cum

---

57 BonJour (this volume) makes this point forcefully. We would surmise that, in thinking of warrants as the externalist does, one tends to undervalue the role of conscious reasoning, thus making it easier to lose sight of its contribution entirely. Although it is worth pointing out that to the extent an externalist takes unconscious but purely internal information processing to play a distinctive role in a certain class of warrants, she is in effect countenancing a priori warrants à la Bigelow.

mid twentieth century) conception of the a priori? This, then, is the nub of the underlying *strategic* disagreement between Kitcher and Bigelow. One striking thing about it is where it leads Bigelow: back to Pythagoras. The nub of the underlying *substantive* disagreement is as follows. Against Bigelow's acceptance of his version of (4), Kitcher notes, correctly, that to grasp a proof as a proof, one must not simply see that the conclusion follows from the premisses, but also see that the premisses are true. Barring an infinite regress of proofs, we must therefore eventually come to basic underived premisses somehow grasped a priori, and mightn't this essentially involve perceptual experience? To this Bigelow's reply (perhaps also echoing Leibniz — see section IV above) seems to be that while to grasp such basic premisses as true may indeed involve a perception of their representations, what is represented are certain structural properties — certain 'patterns' of things — such as part-whole relations that they exhibit. *And the way these patterns may be represented is simply by being instantiated by the representation itself;* Pythagorean 'square number' representations and 'gnomons' provide a graphic illustration. What is grasped (by Aristotelian induction? — see section II above) via a perception of the representation that is relevant to grasping the proof as a proof is the necessity of these merelogical relations which are instantiated by their own representations. No particular perceptual experiences are *essentially* involved: since any instantiation of the merelogical relations could, in principle, and ceteris paribus, serve as the representation, none is itself essential to the proof. What *is* essentially involved is the internal, non-sensory process of reflecting on the properties of these particular representations and drawing the appropriate general conclusions. Ironically, at this juncture Bigelow invokes Kitcher's own historicism to make plausible the idea that even today's very abstract and complex mathematics can nevertheless ultimately be linked conceptually with such humble ancient origins.

Note that while one can be a fallibilist about the a priori without being commited to representations in this role, the *converse* may not hold (see section III above).

Kitcher's implicit reply (at least in *NMK*) to such a line seems to be that the intuitive grasp of features of representation is a nebulous or at any rate fallible process and therefore cannot provide a priori warrant. Bigelow, of course, concedes the fallibility, stressing instead the *distinctiveness* of our access to necessary feature of patterns through representations which represent by instantiation.

VI Other Cases

If with Bigelow we allow a priori warrants to be fallible, then prospects thereby increase for extending their scope well beyond mathematics, perhaps along the lines of other papers in this volume. Critics will no doubt say that it opens the flood gates. What about Bigelow's other idea, that the a priority at least of basic arithmetical truths has to do with patterns in their representations instantiating the patterns they are semantically about? How generalizable is this within mathematics, and how generalizable beyond it? Take the principle of mathematical induction, i.e., Peano's fifth postulate. It says that for any property, if zero has it and if given that some natural number has it its successor does too, then all natural numbers have it. The postulate is admittedly impredicative, applying as it does to the property of natural number in terms of which it is formulated. But should we thereby say that it represents a truth about a pattern in denumerable series by instantiating that pattern? How so? Where is the denumerable series in the representation? Yet isn't the postulate relevantly basic? Or what about when we simply a priori grasp an analytic truth, such as 'All spinsters are female' as an analytic truth? This would seem to have little to do, in general, either with pattern recognition or with any sort of fancy syntactic/semantic interplay. While one could say that many analytic truths share with our example the pattern that the criteria expressed in their predicates are contained in their respective subjects, that fails to capture what matters most to us about the analyticity of a given truth, which is always specific to it.

Several papers in this volume feature examples from logic and semantics of natural language involving some form of self-reference, impredicative definition, semantic sensitivity to orthographic features, or direct reference. It is hard to know how to generalize from them. Still, the examples are intriguing, and may be representative of a significant and revealing class of a priori warrantable truths.

For instance, Ali Kazmi argues persuasively for at least the formal coherence of false 'indiscernability principles.' According to Leibniz's Law, identical individuals have just the same properties. One might have thought, then, that if individual variables α and α' pick out the same individual, then anything true of that individual that is expressed using α will remain true when the occurrences of α are uniformly replaced by occurrences of α', which is just what happens in an indiscernibility principle. Not so. There are clear counterexamples, e.g., VxVy(y=x → (OCicero=y → OCicero=x)). We can simply see from its syntactic structure together with the meaning of the sentential operator 'O' that this is false. 'O' is a sentential operator defined such that for an open sentence S, $\ulcorner OS \urcorner$ is true relative to context c and assignment I to the free occurrences of variables in S if and only if S is true relative to c and I, and S ends with the letter 'y.' Clearly then, if I assigns Cicero to both 'x' and 'y,' then the main antecedent 'y=x' is true, but its consequent false.

The (false) claim that all indiscernibility principles are true may be seen as a good illustration of the fallibility of a priori warrants: although prima facie one might reasonably have taken it to be true on the a priori grounds of the truth of Leibniz's Law, it actually turns out to be false on a priori grounds that are readily discernible, once the right instances are considered. Notice too that our ability to recognize this a priori as false is only because the meaning of 'O' is sensitive to a syntactic or orthographic feature of its complement sentence. Kazmi correctly points out that because of the existence of false indiscernibility principles, theories in semantics which imply false indiscernibility principles, controversial as these theories may be, cannot be formally faulted on that ground alone. Kazmi briefly discusses several such theories, two of which are especially relevant to our concerns.

First, it appears that the notion of logical truth generates a false indiscernibility principle. If we take the logical truths very roughly to be those true on all interpretations, then on the standard rules for interpreting individual variables and identity, 'x=x' will be logically true and 'x=y' logically false. But this suggests that what is logically true must be the (universal closure of the open) *sentence* as so interpreted, *not* simply the proposition expressed, since one might have chosen an assignment on which the values of 'x' and 'y' were the same, thus making '*x=x*' and '*x=y*' both true on that assignment. So if what is true is a proposition, what is *logically* true appears to be not a proposition but a proposition under a particular mode of presentation, or, otherwise put, a (declarative) sentence as interpreted in a particular way. Many have thought that logical truths are a priori knowable. Kazmi's argument invites us to suppose that logical truth essentially involves syntactic form. There is a syntactic/semantic *pattern* instantiated by '*x=x*' but not by '*x=y*,' recognition of which enables us to grasp a priori the truth of (the universal closure of) the former.[58]

It is directly referential terms like individual variables that bring this out. The semantic content of a directly referential expression just is its referent. There is no criterion for something being the referent of a directly referential expression other than that the expression applies to it. There is no conceptual criterion or indicator. The expression acts simply as a tag, a syntactic marker. This may be seen, if one likes, as a form of interplay between syntax and semantics: their syntax has a semantic role otherwise reserved for attributive conceptual conditions. That being the case, all distinct directly referential expressions are automatically conceptually independent of each other. This means that it is always going to take more than mere reflection on purely conceptual considerations to determine that distinct directly referential expressions are in fact co-referential. Whereas it may be purely conceptually determined that distinct occurrences of the *same* directly referential expression (within the scope of the same quantifier) will always have the same referent relative to a given assignment. The *semantic equivalence* of '*x=x*' and '*x=y*' on an assignment where '*x*' and '*y*' are coreferential is not an a priori matter. But the logical truth of '*x=x*' is. To our minds, this example works nicely as an extension to a new domain of Bigelow's 'representational' account of a priori warrants in mathematics.

---

58 The pattern includes the consideration that, relative to a given assignment, each free occurrence of '*x*' in a given open sentence picks out the same object. We take that to be a 'semantic' aspect of the pattern.

If what a logical truth *means* is simply a proposition, but what *makes it logically true* is a proposition-as-represented-in-a-particular-way, then logical truth is not simply truth by virtue of meaning — that is, it is not simply analytic truth. This conclusion accords with that of James Van Cleve (this volume). Van Cleve's main thesis is that we must distinguish the matter of the *undeniability* of the laws of logic (when the meanings of the logical constants are kept constant) from the issue of their truth. The former does not imply the latter. And since something can be analytically true — true just in virtue of meaning — only if it is true, undeniability does not imply analyticity either. So Quine is not giving up his denial that there are analytic truths when he allows that logical truths are undeniable. An interesting corollary noted by Van Cleve is that even if the truth of logical laws 'supervenes' on their meanings in the sense that for a law *L*, if *L* is true it has a meaning such that necessarily, any formula with that meaning would be true, it would not follow that true logical laws are true solely by virtue of what they mean. At most it would follow that they are true by virtue of what they mean together with whatever it is that makes the proposition they express necessary and therefore true. The latter might be something other than meanings; relations among universals, for instance. With Quine, Van Cleve here rejects conventionalism — the doctrine that all and only analytic truths are necessary, and necessary because analytic — but with the added emphasis that even necessary truths that are analytic need not be necessary *because* of this. The very same necessarily true proposition that is expressed analytically may also be expressible synthetically. Note that here propositions are once again being *distinguished* from the 'meanings' of sentences expressing them, such meanings now being construed as including conventions of use for particular expressions. While this does not get us all the way to the idea of logical truth as essentially involving structural patterns of a linguistic representation (from which, as we noted, Van Cleve's anti-conventionalism also follows), it prepares the way, by bringing expressions, syntactic entities, into the picture.

A companion doctrine to conventionalism was, of course, the linguistic theory of the a priori — that all and only analytic truths are knowable, and so knowable because analytic. Albert Casullo (this volume) can be construed as arguing (in part) against the linguistic theory, that because the adoption of linguistic conventions cannot confirm (or disconfirm), e.g. a proposition of arithmetic, such adoption cannot even help to make it knowable. So if the proposition *were* knowable a priori, this would not have anything to do with its being analytic, even if it was. If we are going to countenance a priori knowable propositions (not that Casullo suggests that we do), we might as well, therefore, countenance synthetic ones. The parallel with Van Cleve's line of argument concerning analyticity and necessity should be clear.

Returning to Kazmi, his second example of interest here is a theory of propositional attitude ascriptions according to which they may be opaque even with respect to their embedded directly referential terms. Taking proper names, this time, as directly referential, Ralph will not believe that Cicero was not Cicero, but may believe that Tully was not Cicero. Again, Kazmi argues convincingly that there is nothing formally defective about such a proposal. But (setting aside here the referential ambiguity of ordinary language proper names) surely 'Cicero is not Cicero' is knowable a priori to be false precisely because we understand the (context sensitive) semantics of such directly referential terms and therefore in particular the significance of two occurrences of the same directly referential term in the same sentential context, the same representation of a proposition.[59]

Andrew Irvine's paper can be taken as still further confirmation of the role special features of representations can play in determining a priori status. Irvine considers a number of closely related semantic paradoxes, including Curry's, Löb's, and the 'Strengthened Liar.' Let

---

59 Kazmi may actually disagree with this construal, since at one point he suggests that the theory of propositional attitude ascriptions in question is, perhaps, false on other grounds that he does not mention, and at another point he seems to link a priority more with metaphysical than with logical necessity. But then he owes us his account of a priority and its objects.

s be a declarative sentence. For (the proposition expressed by) *s* to be knowable a priori, *s* must be true. But for *s* to have a truth value at all, it seems that it must be 'grounded'; its truth value must ultimately depend on the truth value of some sentence containing no occurrence (explicit or implicit) of the truth predicate. Otherwise, said semantic 'paradoxes' — or, not to mince words, contradictions — arise from sentences containing occurrences of the truth predicate interacting with occurrences of self-referential expressions like 'this sentence.' One might well have thought that *any* sentence whose terms and predicates refer would have a truth value. One might have concluded this on a priori grounds, in view of the conceptual link between truth and reference. But such a priori warrant can only be prima facie. It is fallible. And the paradoxes in question provide persuasive a priori warrant that in fact this is *not* so. Once we see this, it seems that we can then learn to recognize ungrounded sentences a priori, simply by spotting sentences containing inappropriately interacting occurrences of the truth predicate and self-referential terms. That is, we can recognize this 'a priori' if this means something like recognizing this 'independent of experience apart from the experience required to comprehendingly scan the sentences.' To recognize an ungrounded sentence a priori enables one, armed with the paradoxes, to also recognize a priori that the sentence in question is neither true or false, indeed in an important sense fails to have truth conditions (though we can formulate its 'T-sentence').

Irvine wants to go further and claim that the ungrounded sentence is *meaningless* (see especially his n. 36). But this may take us beyond what is a priori warrantable. Not that this would bother Irvine, who is anxious to emphasize the role of empirical considerations as a corrective to 'pathological' a priori inferences. The believer in the fallible a priori *also* acknowledges the role of empirical considerations, of course, while trying at the same time to give non-empirical considerations their due.

Note the *conditional* nature of the a priori status just attributed: *given* just the experience required for understanding the sentence, that the sentence is not true can then be ascertained without further experiential ado. This recalls the conditional nature of Kitcher's account: given just any life sufficient for *X* for *p*, that *p* is true can then be ascertained without further appeals to experience. Though conditional in nature, such a priority still seems to mark off an interesting kind of warrant.

There is the following problem with it, however. One would have thought that p's having an a priori warrant gives whoever recognizes it a reason for thinking p true. But BonJour notes (this volume) that on Kant's (closely related) conditionalization of a priority this no longer holds. The truth of 'Within the bounds of experience, p' does not in itself constitute a reason for thinking that p is true. The logic of the point cannot be faulted. Truth of a conditional is no guarantee of the truth of its consequent. Still, truth of a conditional plus the truth of its antecedent does guarantee truth of its consequent. So acceptance of 'Within the bounds of experience, p' does give a reason to accept p *relative to or conditional on* the prior acceptance of the representational veracity of the innate 'formal structure' of our experiential manifold. BonJour wants and argues for more. Be that as it may, conditional reasons are already *something*; indeed, they are something which which we are all familiar on a day-to-day basis. It seems that any *empiricists* who are not skeptics must be committed to such prior acceptance. This may be closely related to De Pierris' appeal to 'juridical' deduction (see section IV above).

On the positive side, one virtue of such conditionality is to build right into the structure of the concept of the a priori the possibility of the contingent a priori. This is because a life sufficient for X for p may have to be a life in which not only analytic truths (necessary by stipulation, let us suppose) have been grasped, but also conventions of reference which are clearly contingent. For instance, dear to the hearts of some reference theorists of the late twentieth century are paradigms, similarity to which is taken to be definitive of membership in a kind or of satisfying a standard. Given the defining role, such objects are guaranteed to belong to the extension of the term, and grasping this would seem to be an a priori matter on the conception of a priority under discussion. But that a given paradigm *is* a member of the term's extension is contingent, since that very object might not have existed, or even if it did might not have had the appropriate properties. We can know a priori that

the standard meter bar in Paris is one meter long even though that very bar might have been longer or shorter. [60]
Now perhaps other (still) interesting kinds of conditional a priori warrant can be delineated by varying what is taken to be given. There is Hilary Putnam's (previously noted) proposal to make a priori warrant conditional on a background acceptance of 'rationality,' and where our theory of rationality is itself an a posteriori, evolving matter.[61] On a more modest scale, consider, e.g., a taxonomy. Given whatever experience is required to warrant its acceptance and use, we may be additionally[62] warranted without further appeals to experience in accepting certain relations between particular categories in the taxonomy. Given our (perhaps largely innate) color space, we may be thus warranted a priori in our belief that green is a color, that crimson is not burgundy, and that if something is colored then it is spatially extended, and so on. As Barry Smith observes (this volume), such relations may go beyond stereotypical analytic connections. For any taxonomy with at least two basic (undefined) categories, say F and G, there will be (conditionally) the a priori truth that if x is F then x is not G.

Finally, take an empirical theory. Typically, it is a rather complex quantitative representation of the world that, like a taxonomy, comes as a single unified package, and that projects beyond the relevant empirical evidence. Given whatever experiences we have that warrant us in accepting the theory as a whole, then, we may say that certain particular predictions made on the basis of that

---

60 Cf. e.g. Saul Kripke, *Naming and Necessity* (Cambridge, MA: Harvard University Press 1980).

61 Cf. Hilary Putnam, 'There is at Least One A Priori Truth' and 'Analyticity and A Priority': Beyond Wittgenstein and Quine' in *Realism and Reason*.

62 This qualification, here and below, signals that the warrant for the predicted result is not simply a matter of the warrant we have for accepting the taxonomy; or isn't just warrant that accrues to all our beliefs, including those that warrant us in accepting the taxonomy, by increasing coherence among all our empirically warranted beliefs and theories.

theory are additionally warranted without appeal to any further experience; that is, they are warranted a priori. This may not seem so very interesting when what the theory predicts is something that could in principle be experienced, or to which we can at least have a kind of perceptually mediated causal access. It becomes more interesting, as James Brown explores (this volume), when the theory in question is Quantum Mechanics and part of what the theory predicts is that we are precluded from having any perceptually mediated causal interaction whatsoever with the predicted phenomenon.

Brown's example also poses a dilemma for causal theories of knowledge, on the assumption that we can know via Quantum Mechanical prediction. Since there is no causally mediated interaction, yet there is empirical knowledge, either such knowledge does not require causal mediation after all and the causal theory is refuted, or such knowledge involves some kind of *nonperceptually mediated* causal interaction.[63] In a previous paper, Brown had argued that 'The moral for the causal theory is simple: it is wrong.'[64] But here he ventures the bolder hypothesis that there is a causal connection after all, mediated by abstract causal connections to abstract objects via the theory. The natural properties postulated by the theory are construed as universals; the laws of the theory are construed as relations here among such universals. Brown is adamant that these universals are *abstract*, not

---

63 Colin McGinn once proposed that we simply *define* 'a priori' truth as one that can be known without causal interaction with the subject matter of some justifying statement, and 'a posteriori' truth as one that can only be known by such causal interaction. See 'Modal Reality' in Richard Healy, ed., *Reduction, Time, and Reality* (Cambridge, MA: Cambridge University Press 1981); and also 'A Priori and A Posteriori Knowledge,' *Proceedings of the Aristotelian Society* (1976) 195-208. Such a definition would of course rule out saving the causal theory.

64 James Brown, 'π in the Sky,' in Andrew D. Irvine, ed., *Physicalism in Mathematics* (Dordrecht: Kluwer 1990), 95-120; cf. esp. 116; but also 112, n. 47, in which he hints at the position he here adopts.

concrete, apparently because, following Michael Tooley, he wants to regard them as existing even if uninstantiated (see citation in text). Be that as it may, we raise in closing two considerations, one internal and one external. First, Brown is not *forced* by his account of a priori knowledge to regard the universals as abstract, since if we are talking about knowledge of particular actual predictions of Quantum Theory, the universals in question *will*, presumably, have been instantiated. Second, concerning the notion of causal connection, the challenge Brown faces is to broaden it to accommodate causal connections to abstract objects without thereby so weakening it as to rob it of its explanatory force, which seems at this point to rest substantially on concrete paradigms.

CANADIAN JOURNAL OF PHILOSOPHY
Supplementary Volume 18

A Rationalist Manifesto

LAURENCE BONJOUR

I Justification and the A Priori

Perhaps the most pervasive conviction within the Western epistemological tradition is that in order for a belief to constitute *knowledge* it is
necessary (though not sufficient) that it be *epistemically justified*: that
the person in question have a reason or warrant which makes it at least
highly likely that the belief is *true*.[1] Historically, most epistemologists
have distinguished two main sources from which such justification

---

1 For more detailed discussion of the general conception of epistemic justification,
see my book *The Structure of Empirical Knowledge* (Cambridge, MA: Harvard
University Press 1985) [hereafter cited as *SEK*], ch. 1. Certain recent philosophers
have questioned, or seemed to question, this requirement for knowledge, arguing instead that knowledge requires only that the process leading to the acceptance of the belief in question be *reliable*, i.e., that it in fact produce or tend to
produce true beliefs, even though the person in question may have no reason of
any sort for thinking that this is so. See, e.g., Alvin Goldman, *Epistemology and
Cognition* (Cambridge, MA: Harvard University Press 1985); and Robert Nozick,
Philosophical Explanations (Cambridge, MA: Harvard University Press 1981), ch.
3. I have dealt with such views elsewhere (see *SEK*, ch. 3) and will mostly neglect
them in this essay, where my aim is to consider one crucial element of a more
traditional epistemological position.

might arise. It has seemed obvious to all but a very few that many beliefs are justified by appeal to one's *experience* of the world. But it has seemed equally obvious to most that there are other beliefs, including many of the most important ones that we have, which are justified in a way which is entirely independent of any appeal to such experience, justified, as it is usually put, a priori, by reason or pure thought alone.

In spite of its historical prominence, however, the idea of a priori epistemic justification has in recent times been the target of severe and relentless skepticism. Thus it may be useful to begin our discussion by considering briefly two closely related reasons, over and above the usual appeal to apparent examples, why this idea should still be taken seriously.

First, it is arguable that the epistemic justification of at least the vast preponderance of our knowledge must involve an indispensable a priori component — so that the only alternative to the existence of a priori justification is skepticism of a most radical kind. The argument for this conclusion is extremely straightforward and obvious, so much so that it is very hard to understand the widespread failure to acknowledge it.

The argument derives from reflecting on the relation between knowledge and observation. Though my own view of these matters is substantially more complicated, it will do well enough for present purposes to suppose that there are certain 'foundational' beliefs which are fully justified by appeal to direct or immediate observation alone. We need not pause to worry about just which beliefs these are, e.g., whether they concern ordinary physical objects or perhaps only private experiences; all that matters for present purposes is that, as will be true on any conception of direct observation that has any plausibility, such beliefs are particular rather than general in their content and are confined to situations observable at specific times. The question is then whether it is possible to infer, in a way which brings with it epistemic justification, from these foundational beliefs to beliefs whose content goes beyond direct experience: beliefs about the past, the future, and the unobserved aspects of the present, or beliefs which are general in their content or which have to do with kinds of things that are not even in principle observable.

If the answer to this question is 'no,' then the upshot is a quite deep form of skepticism (exactly how deep will depend on one's account of the foundational beliefs — perhaps even solipsism of the present moment). But if the answer is 'yes,' then such inferences must seemingly rely on either premises or principles of inference which are not justified by appeal to experience and hence must be justified at least partially a priori, if they are justified at all.[2]

Second, this argument concerning the justification of non-observational beliefs may be generalized by relating it to the most central application of the idea of a priori justification: its application to *arguments* or *reasoning*. For any argument, an issue which is closely analogous to the issue of epistemic justification for propositions can be raised: is there any reason for thinking that the conclusion of the argument will be true (or at least is likely to be true) *if* the premise is true? When such a reason exists, the argument in question may be said to be rationally cogent and the inference from the premises to the conclusion to be, in a somewhat modified sense, epistemically justified.[3]

Could an argument of any sort be entirely justified on empirical grounds? It seems clear on reflection that the answer is 'no.' Any empirical ingredient can, after all, always be formulated as an additional empirical premise. When all such premises have been explicitly formulated, either the intended conclusion will be explicitly included among them or it will not. In the former case, no inference is necessary, while in the latter case, the needed inference clearly goes beyond what can be derived from experience alone. Thus we see that the repudiation of all a priori justification is tantamount to the repudiation of

---

2 If, as I believe, there are in fact no such basic or foundational beliefs, the problem becomes even more acute, with *all* knowledge depending in part at least on a priori justification. See *SEK*, Part I, especially ch. 4, for a critique of foundationalism; and *SEK*, Part II, for what I regard as the main alternative.

3 For a particular person to be justified in accepting the conclusion of such an argument on the basis of a prior acceptance of its premises, the reason in question must, I assume, be in some way available to him.

argument or reasoning generally, thus amounting in effect to intellectual suicide. This result will be reconsidered later on, when I will consider views like those of Quine which advocate such a repudiation, but it surely constitutes at the very least a strong prima facie reason for regarding the idea of a priori justification as philosophically and intellectually indispensable.

II Rationalism and Empiricism

According to *rationalism*, a priori justification occurs when the mind directly or intuitively discerns or grasps or apprehends a necessary fact about the nature or structure of reality. Such an apprehension may of course be discursively mediated by a series of steps of the same kind, as in a deductive argument. But in the simplest cases it is allegedly direct and unmediated, incapable of being reduced to or explained by any cognitive or discursive process of a more basic sort — since any such explanation would tacitly presuppose apprehensions of this very same kind. According to the rationalist, the capacity for such direct intellectual insight into necessity is the fundamental requirement for reasoning and reflective intelligence generally. Philosophers inclined towards empiricism or materialism have often charged that there is something mysterious, perhaps even somehow occult, about the capacity in question. But from a rationalist perspective nothing could be further from the truth: the capacity for rational insight, though fundamental and irreducible, is in no way puzzling or especially in need of further explanation; indeed, without such a capacity neither puzzles nor explanations would themselves be rationally intelligible.

My thesis in this paper is that only a rationalist view of a priori justification can provide the basis for a non-skeptical account of human knowledge (with the possible exception of those parts of empirical knowledge, if any, which can be fully justified by appeal to direct experience alone). Throughout most of the history of philosophy, from Plato and Aristotle through medieval philosophy and into the modern period, rationalism was the dominant, indeed almost entirely unchallenged view of the nature of a priori justification. It is not until Hume that we find a major philosopher who clearly repudiates the rationalist account of the a priori, insisting that a priori knowledge concerns only 'relations of ideas' as opposed to 'matters of fact.' And it is a version of this suggestion that has been dominant in the twentieth century, at least in the Anglo-American world.

The underlying motivation for empiricist doubts is a deep-seated skepticism about the basic capacity for rational insight into necessity to which the rationalist appeals. To the self-proclaimed hard-headed empiricist, the idea of such a capacity, or at least of its existing in human animals, appears implausible on both metaphysical and scientific grounds, and becomes increasingly so as our knowledge of mankind and our place in the world develops. But until very recently, most empiricists have also found the existence of a priori justification and knowledge, in logic and mathematics at least, quite undeniable. It is thus incumbent on such *moderate empiricists*, as I will call them here, to offer an alternative account of a priori justification, one which is from their standpoint metaphysically and scientifically more palatable than rationalism.

Though hints can be found in various earlier authors, the main moderate empiricist view does not emerge clearly until Hume and Kant.[4] This view attempts to concede the existence of a priori justification and a priori knowledge, while in effect undermining its ultimate cognitive significance. The basic claim is that a priori epistemic justification, though genuine enough in its own way, extends only to propositions which reflect relations among our concepts or meanings or linguistic conventions, rather than saying anything substantive about the extra-conceptual world. Such propositions are at bottom trivial or tautological in character, merely *analytic* truths, and knowledge of them thus requires nothing as outlandish as the rationalist's alleged intuitive insight into necessity.

From a historical standpoint, moderate empiricism is clearly the main empiricist position on the subject of a priori knowledge; and

---

4 It is also anticipated in Locke's concept of 'trifling propositions' and in Leibniz's appeal to identical propositions to explain knowledge of necessity.

although full-dress defenses of it have been infrequent of late, it continues to be widely held. The most conspicuous recent position on the general topic of a priori knowledge, however, is a much more extreme version of empiricism. Associated mainly with W.V. Quine, this second and quite distinct version of empiricism, which I call *radical empiricism*, denies outright the very existence of a priori justification, rather than attempting to give an empiricistically acceptable account of it.

Before turning to an examination of these two versions of empiricism, however, I want to have a brief look at the rather idiosyncratic view of Kant; this is less of a digression than it might seem, for I will argue that, contrary to generally accepted classifications, Kant is at bottom a moderate empiricist, not at all a rationalist.

III Kant and the Synthetic A Priori

It is of course Kant who explicitly introduced the concept of analyticity, upon which moderate empiricist views are built. In his version, a judgment of subject-predicate form is analytic when 'the predicate B belongs to the subject A, as something which is (covertly) contained in this concept A.' In contrast, a judgment is synthetic if the predicate concept lies outside the subject concept and thus adds something to it [A6-7=B10-11].[5] Thus, for example, the proposition 'all brothers are male' is analytic in the Kantian sense, because the subject concept *brother* is equivalent to the concept *male sibling* and thus includes the predicate concept *male*.

It is important to understand clearly the epistemological significance which this concept of analyticity is supposed by Kant to have: once the proposition that all brothers are male is seen to be analytic, the epistemological problem of how I can be justified, without any appeal to experience, in believing that it is true is supposed by him to

---

5 All references to the *Critique of Pure Reason* will be to the translation by Norman Kemp Smith (London: MacMillan 1929) and will use the standard pagination.

be entirely solved. All that is required, says Kant, is to 'extract' the predicate from the subject 'in accordance with the principle of contradiction' [B12]; i.e., since the predicate concept merely repeats part of the subject concept so that the denial of the proposition would result in an immediate contradiction, anyone can see at once that such a proposition must be true.

Kant's main epistemological concern thus becomes the problem of the synthetic a priori: how there can be knowledge which is a priori in its justification and yet synthetic in its logical form? Since such knowledge could neither be justified by experience nor along the lines just sketched, how could it be justified at all? But that there is knowledge of this sort, Kant, on the surface, never questions.

It is, of course, Kant's avowed belief in the existence of synthetic a priori knowledge that makes him seem on the surface to be a rationalist. But this impression is nonetheless profoundly misleading. For Kant's acceptance of the synthetic a priori turns out to be only an apparent acceptance, one which is decisively undermined by his own answer to the question of how such knowledge is possible: It would *not* be possible, he argues, if the objects which such knowledge purports to describe were independent objects external to the knower, things-in-themselves that are part of *an sich* reality. It is only if the objects of knowledge must somehow conform to the faculties of knowledge rather than the other way around that synthetic a priori knowledge becomes possible. The idea, of course, is that the mind so shapes or structures experience as to make the propositions in question invariably come out true *within the experiential realm*. Thus synthetic a priori knowledge, according to Kant, pertains only to the realm of appearances or phenomena, not to independent reality *an sich*.

The divergence from classical versions of rationalism is already obvious enough, but it might still be thought that Kant is still a rationalist, albeit a substantially more modest one. To see why even this is mistaken, we need to explore his view more fully. Suppose that we are concerned with some specific synthetic a priori proposition P, perhaps that $7 + 5 = 12$. Kant's suggestion then is that we can know P a priori in spite of its synthetic character because the mind so operates in structuring or 'synthesizing' experience as to make *P* invariably true within the experiential realm.

The first problem with this suggestion concerns the precise identity of the proposition which is supposed to be synthetic a priori. Our pre-theoretic intuition, for which Kant is supposedly trying to account, is that it is *P* itself which has this status. But it is easy to see that Kant's position offers no reason for thinking that *P* is even *true*, let alone justifiable or knowable a priori. What would have to be true if Kant's account were correct is not the original proposition *P*, but rather the quite different proposition: *within the bounds of experience, P*; call this proposition *P'*.[6] And thus, insofar as the original intuitive datum to be accounted for is the apparent a priori status of *P* itself, Kant's explanation does not succeed.

More importantly, this first problem leads at once to a second, which concerns the status of the further proposition *P'* just formulated: is *this* proposition a priori or a posteriori, analytic or synthetic? Presumably *P'* will have the same status as the Kantian thesis from which it immediately follows, viz. the thesis that the mind so operates as to make it true. Kant cannot hold that it is a merely empirical fact that the mind so operates without abandoning any attempt to account for the original intuition that *P*, or anything resembling *P*, is knowable a priori. But if the fact that the mind so operates is knowable a priori, is it then analytic or synthetic? To say that it is synthetic, while yielding a specimen of synthetic a priori knowledge — even if not quite the one originally proposed — would create an unsolvable problem for Kant. For how would the synthetic a priori status of this new proposition

---

6 A possible response would be that *P* is meaningful only within the confines of experience, so that the specified limitation is in effect already built in and so does not alter the identity of the proposition. The argument for such a view from within Kant's philosophical position is stronger for some propositions than for others, though it is not clear that he accepts it for any. I doubt, however, whether any such contention can be made compelling on general philosophical grounds. (And if it were, the result, for reasons discussed below, would be that *P*, as long as its a priori status was capable of being accounted for by Kant's philosophy, was not synthetic after all.)

be accounted for? To offer the same account which was originally offered for P would in effect require Kant to say that the mind so operates as to make it true that: the mind so operates as to make it true that P'. It is very doubtful that this new claim even makes sense, but even if it does, the same question can be raised about it, and so on ad infinitum, thus generating a regress which is clearly vicious. The upshot is that the a priori thesis about the operation of the mind which underlies P' must seemingly be *analytic*, thus making P' itself also analytic.

The indicated conclusion is that Kant's official position on a priori knowledge, if consistently elaborated, provides no basis for even modest synthetic a priori knowledge and thus is not a rationalist position to any degree at all. The original proposition P turns out not to be knowledge of any kind and very possibly not even true, while the implicit substitute P' would turn out, if the Kantian account of the supposed synthetic a priori were successful, to be *analytic* a priori. Of course this last claim is extremely implausible, raising the possibility that if Kant had ever faced clearly the problem of the epistemological status of his own philosophical claims, he might have retreated into a more traditional rationalism.

As things stand, however, it is clear that Kant is not only not a rationalist, but, most strikingly, does not even regard rationalism as a significant option. Whereas an empiricist like Hume at least feels the need to *argue* that pure reason cannot yield knowledge of *an sich* reality, Kant does not even momentarily entertain such a possibility. On the contrary, it is for him virtually self-evident that we can have no a priori knowledge of independent reality, except that which is analytic and hence ultimately trivial.[7]

---

7 This is perhaps expressed most clearly in the B preface, but is also lurking just under the surface of the argument in many other places.

IV In Search of Moderate Empiricism

As we have seen, the moderate empiricist position on a priori knowledge holds that while such knowledge genuinely exists and has its own kind of importance, it is nonetheless merely *analytic* in character — i.e., very roughly, merely a product of human concepts, meanings, definitions, or linguistic conventions. Such knowledge thus says nothing substantive about the world, and its justification can be accounted for without appealing to anything as supposedly mysterious as the rationalist idea of rational insight into the character of *an sich* reality. It is this alleged capacity to provide an unproblematic explanation of a priori justification that constitutes the main argument for moderate empiricism, even in the face of recalcitrant rationalist counterexamples.[8] For much of this century, this general sort of position had the status of virtually unquestioned orthodoxy for most philosophers in the Anglo-American tradition; and despite the recent prominence of the radical empiricist view that will be discussed later, it seems likely that moderate empiricism continues to be the most widely held view of the nature and status of a priori knowledge.

What is profoundly misleading about the foregoing picture, however, is the suggestion that there is anything like one reasonably specific position which can be identified as moderate empiricism. On the contrary, moderate empiricism turns out to encompass a stunning diversity of distinct and not obviously compatible views, reflected in widely divergent definitions of the key term 'analytic' — views which are seemingly unified by little more than the conviction that a priori knowledge can be accounted for in *some* way which avoids rationalism and that the explanation will have *something* to do with concepts or meanings or definitions or linguistic conventions. Even more strikingly, this diversity has seldom been explicitly noticed, and it continues to be widely assumed that the divergent definitions of 'analytic'

---

8 For a clear and relatively candid expression of this outlook, see Wesley Salmon, *The Foundations of Scientific Inference* (Pittsburgh: University of Pittsburgh Press 1967), 39-40.

are all somehow getting at the same underlying idea. One consequence of this situation is that individual proponents of moderate empiricism often slide promiscuously from one such definition to another in the course of their arguments. (Indeed, it is hard to avoid the suspicion that many of those who have regarded moderate empiricism as unquestionably correct have had no very specific version in mind.)

Moderate empiricism can be understood as an attempt to defend two main theses. Formulated in terms of the concept of analyticity, these are: first, that genuine a priori justification is restricted to analytic propositions or statements; and second, that the a priori justification of analytic propositions or statements can be understood epistemologically in a way which does not require the sort of allegedly mysterious intuitive capacity advocated by rationalism and thus is epistemologically unproblematic from an empiricist standpoint. The obvious problem for the moderate empiricist is to find a univocal conception of analyticity in relation to which both of these theses can be established, and the various different conceptions of analyticity arise in this attempt.

Historically, much of the controversy between proponents of moderate empiricism and their outnumbered but persistent rationalist critics has concentrated on the first of these theses, with rationalists proposing cases of allegedly synthetic a priori knowledge and empiricists attempting to show that the propositions in question are either analytic or else not genuinely justified a priori. This discussion has tended to focus on a relatively small number of examples, such as 'Nothing can be red (all over) and green (all over) at the same time' and 'If event A is later than event B and event B is later than event C, then event A is later than event C.' But while the rationalist appeal to such examples has considerable force, it is unlikely by itself to persuade the typical moderate empiricist, who is convinced both that the rationalist account of the a priori is unacceptably mysterious and that his own account completely avoids such mystery.

Thus it is the second of the two moderate empiricist theses that is really pivotal, and it is this thesis that I want to focus on here. I will argue that, on the contrary, there is in fact no conception of analyticity which is capable of providing an adequate and complete epistemological account of all cases of a priori justification, the widespread impression to the contrary being due partly to a failure to distinguish the various divergent conceptions of analyticity and partly to a failure to grasp clearly what the central epistemological issue really is. Indeed, the ability of such conceptions to provide such an account of even a single piece of a priori knowledge will turn out to be very much in doubt. A fully adequate defense of this claim would have to canvass fully the various divergent conceptions of analyticity already alluded to. Here I will have to be content with a sampling, though one which I believe to be adequately representative.

One of the most widely accepted conceptions of analyticity, and also perhaps the clearest, is that proposed by Frege: a statement is analytic if and only if it is either (i) an instance of a logically true statement or (ii) transformable into such an instance by substituting synonyms for synonyms (or definitions for definable terms). A statement is synthetic if and only if it is not analytic.[9] I will assume, perhaps somewhat unrealistically, that just which statements count as truths of logic is clear enough for the moment; and I will also not pause to worry about the shift from judgments or propositions to linguistically formulated *statements*.

---

9 As this suggests, 'analytic' and 'synthetic' are normally construed as mutually exclusive and jointly exhaustive terms, and it is only on such a construal that the issue between rationalists and empiricists can be correctly couched in terms of whether there is synthetic a priori knowledge. Some empiricists have clouded the issue by defining 'synthetic' independently. For example, in *Language, Truth and Logic* (New York: Dover 1946), Ayer offers the following definitions:

> ... a proposition is analytic when its validity depends solely on the definitions of the symbols it contains and synthetic when its validity is determined by the facts of experience. [78]

Since the meaning of 'synthetic' seems on this definition to be simply equated with that of 'a posteriori' ('validity' presumably means the proposition's being justified), there will obviously be no synthetic a priori knowledge. Equally obviously, however, this in no way rules out the possibility of non-analytic a priori knowledge, which would be quite enough to vindicate the rationalist claim.

It is easy to see how the Fregean conception of analyticity offers a genuine, albeit modest, epistemological insight. If I am somehow justified a priori in believing that 'for any statement P, not both P and not-P' is a truth of logic, and I am able to recognize a priori that 'it is not the case that the table is both brown and not brown' is an instance of this logical truth, then I am justified a priori on that basis in believing that the latter statement is also true. But it is equally clear that this conception of analyticity is incapable of offering any epistemologically illuminating account of how the truths of logic themselves are epistemically justified or known. One can indeed insist that logical truths are themselves analytic, but this amounts to nothing more, on the present conception of analyticity, than the entirely trivial claim that logical truths are logical truths, which clearly offers no epistemological insight at all.[10]

The Fregean conception of analyticity is a paradigmatic example of what I will call a *reductive* conception of analyticity: it explains the a priori epistemic justification of some statements by appeal to that of other statements, but is thus incapable of saying anything epistemologically helpful about the a priori justification of the latter, reducing class of statements, in this case the statements of logic. Such a conception of analyticity is therefore incapable in principle of accounting for all instances of a priori justification in the way that the moderate empiricist program attempts to do, and it offers only a partial epistemological account of the instances that it does apply to.

The original Kantian conception of analyticity, discussed above, is also a reductive conception, indeed just a restricted version of the Fregean conception, though couched in terms of judgments rather than statements. A third example of a reductive conception of analyticity is that conception which defines an analytic proposition as one

10 For this reason, it would be clearer in some ways to follow Butchvarov and regard logical truths as themselves synthetic, reserving the label 'analytic' for those propositions which are reducible to logic and whose justification is thereby (partially) explained. (See Panayot Butchvarov, *The Concept of Knowledge* (Evanston, IL: Northwestern University Press 1970), 106-8.)

whose denial entails a contradiction, where what is intended is an *explicit* contradiction, a proposition of the form 'P and not-P.' That a proposition is analytic on this conception may again help to explain how it is justified and hence knowable on an a priori basis. But such an account once again presupposes and hence cannot explain the a priori justification of other propositions: of the logical truth that a proposition that is explicitly contradictory in form is always false, of the logical truths underlying the inference that any proposition that entails a false proposition is itself false, and of the propositions of logic (together, perhaps, with definitions) which are needed to derive the contradiction.[11]

Reductive conceptions of analyticity, though perhaps useful for other purposes, are thus inherently incapable of accounting for all instances of a priori epistemic justification. In addition, though the main focus of the present discussion has been on the general shape of the moderate empiricist strategy, rather than on particular recalcitrant examples, it is worth noting in passing that reductive conceptions of analyticity are almost certainly incapable of dealing adequately with all plausible examples of a priori justification.

While reductive conceptions of analyticity offer genuine, albeit partial epistemological illumination, other popular conceptions of analyticity in fact fail to do any useful epistemological work at all, despite superficial appearances to the contrary. The basic problem with these conceptions is that they tacitly equate analyticity either with a priority itself or else with necessity (while offering in the latter case no further account of how necessity itself is known). Such con-

---

11 I ignore here the fact that some of these logical ingredients would no doubt take the form of principles or rules of inference rather than theses or assertions. A principle of inference is, from an epistemological standpoint, just as much in need of epistemic justification as is an assertion, albeit in a somewhat modified sense: if one is to be epistemically justified in accepting conclusions on the basis of such a principle, one needs to have some reason for thinking that conclusions satisfying the principle will be true (or perhaps, for some kinds of principles, are likely to be true) if the corresponding premises satisfying the principle are true.

ceptions thus have the effect of obfuscating rather than advancing the essential epistemological issue.

The most widely accepted of the obfuscating conceptions of analyticity (and probably, along with the Fregean conception, one of the two most widely accepted of all) is the conception of an analytic statement as one which is 'true by virtue of meaning.' The idea is that an analytic statement is one which need only be properly understood to be recognized as true (or, equivalently, one which can only be denied if its meaning has not been fully and accurately grasped).[12]

Now it is highly plausible that many simple a priori truths have this status. To take one of the rationalist's favorite examples, it is hard to see how anyone who understands the claim that nothing can be red and green (all over) at the same time can fail to agree with it and hard to deny that such agreement is somehow justified. But the question that needs to be asked is just *how* all this is supposed to shed light on the *way* in which such a claim is justified. *How*, that is, is the appeal to one's grasp of the meaning of such a claim supposed to avoid the need for the rationalist's allegedly mysterious intuitive insight into necessity? The proponents of this conception of analyticity offer no clear answers to such questions. And without such answers, the present conception of analyticity is in fact essentially indistinguishable from the very conception that it was supposed to explain, the conception of a priori justification itself.

A second conception of analyticity that fails to offer genuine epistemological illumination defines an analytic proposition as one whose denial leads to a contradiction, differing from the verbally similar reductive conception discussed above in not demanding that the contradiction be explicit. The most extreme version of this view simply construes a contradiction as any necessarily false proposition.

---

12 Thus Quinton, in a defense of the moderate empiricist thesis, characterizes the position he is defending as the thesis that a non-derivative a priori truth is one whose 'acceptance as true is a condition of understanding the terms it contains.' See Anthony Quinton, 'The *A Priori* and the Analytic,' reprinted in Robert Sleigh, ed., *Necessary Truth* (Englewood Cliffs, NJ: Prentice-Hall 1972), 90.

But while it is undeniably true that it is self-contradictory, in this sense, to deny a genuinely necessary truth (or to accept the conclusion while rejecting the premise of a valid inference), this fact once again sheds no significant light on the epistemological issue with which we are concerned: it is obviously no easier to justify the claim that the denial of a proposition is a contradiction in this sense than it is to justify the claim that the original proposition is necessary. Other versions of this general approach move in the direction of the earlier reductive conception by counting as contradictions some more restricted class of necessarily false propositions. Such views partially inherit the defects of both the extreme conception and the reductive conception, the proportions depending on how far the class of contradictory propositions is contracted.

The final conception of analyticity that I want to look at here involves the idea that certain a priori knowable *statements*, especially the principles of logic, constitute 'implicit definitions' of the terms contained in them.[13] The problem here is to understand what the idea of an implicit definition really amounts to. In what sense are the statements in question *definitions* — and how is this status supposed to yield an account of how they can be justified a priori? It is obvious that citing the truth of such statements might help a novice to understand the terms involved, but this fact, which also holds of course for many contingent, a posteriori statements, does not seem to warrant classifying them as definitions in any more interesting sense and thus appears to be epistemologically unhelpful.

One account of the idea of implicit definition, perhaps the only clear one to be found in the literature, is offered by Butchvarov: offering a form of words as an 'implicit definition' amounts to a stipulation that any previously unknown terms it contains are to be interpreted in such a way as to make the proposition expressed under that interpretation come out true.[14] Thus, for example, one might offer the stipula-

---

13 Cf., e.g., Quinton, 101-6.

14 Butchvarov, 109-10

tion that the sentence '40 @ 8 = 5' is true, as part of an implicit definition of the symbol '@,' a way of conveying, along with other stipulations of the same kind, that '@' is to stand for the operation of long division (assuming that the other symbols in the sentence are already understood). But if this is the right account, then the justification of the proposition that forty divided by eight is equal to five (as opposed to that of the form of words '40 @ 8 = 5') is not a result of the implicit definition, but is rather presupposed by it: if I were not justified in advance, presumably a priori, in believing that forty divided by eight is equal to five, I would have no reason for interpreting '@' in the indicated way. Thus we must apparently be justified in some independent way in believing that the appropriate propositions are true if linguistic stipulations of this kind are to work, the implicit definition serving only to convey a way in which the proposition which is already believed and justified may be expressed. The upshot is that on Butchvarov's account (as he himself of course recognizes and insists upon), the idea of implicit definition has no genuine epistemological significance.

There are of course still further moderate empiricist conceptions of analyticity, but none that are any more epistemologically successful than those already considered.[15] The indicated conclusion is that the moderate version of empiricism, despite its widespread acceptance, is in fact entirely bankrupt as an account of a priori justification and thus constitutes no genuine alternative to rationalism.[16]

---

15 For discussion of some of these, see Appendix A of *SEK*.

16 It is also obvious that moderate empiricism, even if otherwise acceptable, could offer no adequate solution to the problem, discussed above in section I, of how to justify inferences that go beyond direct observation. The only way to construe such inferences as analytic would be by adopting reductive theses like phenomenalism and behaviorism. Such theses are widely regarded as untenable and would in any case only extend to part of the problem (in particular, there is no apparent reductive solution to the problem of induction). While this constitutes a further objection to moderate empiricism as an account of the a priori, the objections discussed in the text are obviously more fundamental.

V The Case for Radical Empiricism

If the moderate empiricist approach to a priori knowledge does not succeed, what alternative is then left for the empiricist? The answer is both stark and obvious: if a priori justification cannot be accommodated within the empiricist framework in the way which the moderate empiricist attempts, then it must be repudiated outright if empiricism is to be sustained. Such a view has been advocated in recent times by W.V. Quine, and it is his radical empiricist position that I want to discuss now.

As discussed briefly above, skepticism about the very possibility of a priori knowledge appears to challenge the rational cogency of reasoning and argumentation generally, thus confining epistemic justification and knowledge to the relatively few (if any) beliefs that can be justified directly by experience alone. To be sure, this result is neither acknowledged nor apparently intended by Quine; his view seems to be rather that most of science and much of common sense can be justified on a purely empirical basis. The issue of whether radical empiricism leaves room for a non-skeptical positive epistemology will be reconsidered below. For the moment, my concern is with the arguments for and against the radical empiricist thesis itself.

One thing which should be obvious at once is that radical empiricism is impervious to any direct refutation. What, after all, is such an attempted refutation to appeal to? An appeal to a priori insight or argumentation would be obviously question-begging, while no appeal to direct experience seems to have any bearing on the possibility of a priori knowledge. Thus the radical empiricist is in a very secure dialectical position, one from which he cannot be dislodged by any direct assault.

But this immunity to refutation is purchased at a rather severe price, for it makes it equally difficult to see what reason there could be in favor of radical empiricism: it is just as hard to see how the truth of radical empiricism could be supported by direct experience; while to offer an a priori argument would involve the radical empiricist in an implicit contradiction between his central claim and his manner of defending it.

Perhaps the best way to proceed in this dialectically difficult situation is to begin with a close examination of Quine's actual attempts at argument. I will start with a look at his classic paper 'Two Dogmas of Empiricism,'[17] a work which is standardly cited as containing his main arguments against the a priori.

One who approaches 'Two Dogmas of Empiricism' in search of Quine's supposedly compelling arguments against the possibility of a priori justification is faced with an immediate and severe problem, one which in fact pertains to virtually all of Quine's own writings and to those of many at least of his supporters: on the surface at least, the main target of the article is not the concept of a priori justification at all, but instead the concept of analyticity (or the analytic/synthetic distinction), with the a priori receiving very little explicit attention. Indeed, while it is reasonably clear from his subsequent writings that Quine did intend in 'Two Dogmas' to be rejecting the concept of a priori justification along with the concept of analyticity, indeed that a priori justification was ultimately his primary target, he makes almost no effort even to distinguish the two concepts from each other or from the concept of necessity, let alone to distinguish the multiple conceptions of 'analytic' from each other. Such carelessness is all the more disconcerting because Quine's major objection, at least to the concept of analyticity, is that it is *unintelligible*, an objection which is hard to take seriously when even minimal efforts at clarification have not been made.

My somewhat speculative diagnosis of this situation is that Quine's approach, here and elsewhere, is explained in part by his taking utterly for granted what is in effect a weaker, hypothetical version of the moderate empiricist thesis: roughly the thesis that *if there were* any a priori justified propositions, they would have to be analytic. If such a thesis is accepted, then showing that there are no analytic propositions would also rule out the possibility of a priori justification. But

---

17 Reprinted in Quine, *From a Logical Point of View*, 2nd ed. (Harvard: Harvard University Press 1961). Page references to this paper will use the abbreviation *TD*.

while it is easy to see how someone with Quine's strongly empiricist intellectual ancestry might find such a thesis initially plausible, it ceases to be plausible as soon as Quine's own claim that the concept of analyticity is *unintelligible* is accepted or even taken as a serious possibility. As we saw briefly above, the main appeal of moderate empiricism depends on the idea that only analyticity could provide an unmysterious account of how a priori justification is possible. Since an unintelligible or even doubtfully intelligible concept obviously cannot provide the basis for such an explanation, the effect of Quine's argument would be to destroy the main warrant for moderate empiricism, including the hypothetical version just formulated.[18]

When we restore the distinctions which Quine (along with very many others, of course) has blurred, the situation seems to be as follows. The thesis that the concept of analyticity (or the analytic/synthetic distinction) is unintelligible, which is defended in the early sections of 'Two Dogmas,' has no direct relevance to the issue of a priori justification unless something like the hypothetical version of moderate empiricism just discussed is assumed. Thus only the argument of the final two sections is relevant to our main concerns here. (It is perhaps worth mentioning in passing that I find the argument against the analytic/synthetic distinction also quite uncompelling.)

The central claim of the final two sections of 'Two Dogmas' is that 'no statement is immune to revision' [*TD* 43] or, as Quineans like to say, that any statement can be 'given up.' As Quine has made clear elsewhere,[19] 'statement' here means simply *sentence*. The idea, apparently, is that something justified or known a priori (and thus claimed to be necessary) would have to be something which could never be

---

18 And of course, even more obviously, the thesis in question would not mean in any case that the alleged unintelligibility of one of these concepts thereby extends to the other. For this to follow, Quine needs to have assumed in effect that the two terms in question are *synonymous*, a dubious assumption indeed, as we have seen — even if it were not made by one who, as we shall see, also rejects the intelligibility of the very concept of synonymy.

19 See Quine, *Philosophy of Logic* (Englewood Cliffs, NJ: Prentice-Hall 1970), 2.

revised or 'given up,' and hence that nothing has such a status. (For present purposes, I will assume that 'giving up' a previously accepted statement means rejecting it as false.)[20] Contrary to what Quine seems to think, however, what we might call the 'give-up-ability' of a *sentence* has no direct bearing on the issue of a priori knowledge. For, as Grice and Strawson have pointed out,[21] a sentence once regarded as true may be given up in two very different ways: while still possessing the same meaning or after a change in its meaning. And it is perfectly clear that the latter sort of giving up has no bearing at all on the a priori justifiability of the sentence prior to the change. It would clearly be possible for our linguistic conventions to be altered in such a way that any sentence which might presently be thought to express an a priori justifiable claim comes to express something which is obviously false. In such a situation, the *sentence* in question would no doubt be 'given up,' i.e., it would cease to be regarded as expressing a truth. But this possibility is quite irrelevant to the issue of whether this sentence in its previous meaning expresses an a priori knowable truth. Thus Quine must seemingly claim, not merely that any sentence may be given up, but that any sentence may be given up *without having changed in meaning*.

No doubt Quine himself, given his 'repudiation' of the notion of meaning, would also repudiate this way of putting the matter. But it is important to see that such a repudiation does not help to avoid the underlying problem: it remains obvious that some cases of giving up sentences, those which it is at least initially natural to describe as cases involving change of meaning, are trivial and uninteresting in relation to the issue of a priori justification. However such cases are properly to be characterized, Quine needs some way of excluding them if his claim of give-up-ability is to have any serious epistemological import — which means that Quine himself

---

20 The issue throughout obviously concerns primarily a priori justification which is direct or intuitive, not that which relies on demonstration.

21 'In Defense of a Dogma,' in Robert Sleigh, ed., *Necessary Truth* (Englewood Cliffs, NJ: Prentice-Hall 1972), 86-7

apparently needs something very much like the notion of meaning, or at least change of meaning. Since Quine's repudiation of meaning seems to me inadequately supported in any case, I will continue to speak in terms of change of meaning; but I see no reason to think that the substitution of any adequate alternative formulation would alter anything of substance.[22]

Moreover, even if cases of meaning change are somehow set aside, the bearing of Quine's claim of give-up-ability on the possibility of a priori justification remains uncertain. For it is also obvious, and something which no proponent of a priori justification need deny, that a sentence which expresses an a priori knowable proposition might be given up by a sufficiently irrational or perverse person — especially if giving up is interpreted in the behavioral way which Quine's views would suggest. Thus Quine needs at least the claim that any sentence, without having changed its meaning, can be *rationally* or *justifiably* 'given up.' And even this substantially stronger claim may still not be strong enough, for despite historical precedent to the contrary, there is, I submit, no clear reason why a proponent of a priori justification cannot admit that the putative knowledge thereby arrived at is both fallible and corrigible.

---

22 It is interesting to note that Quine himself seems to recognize in one place the possibility of change of meaning, though he avoids using that specific phrase:

By a less extraordinary coincidence, ... an eternal sentence that was true could become false because of some semantic change occurring in the continuing evolution of our own language. Here again we must view the discrepancy as a difference between two languages: English as of one date and English as of another. The string of sounds or characters in question is, and remains, an eternal sentence of earlier English, and a true one; it just happens to do duty as a falsehood in another language, later English. [*Philosophy of Logic*, 14]

But then the shift to later English does not involve 'giving up' the original sentence in any epistemologically interesting sense, and it is unclear why precisely the same thing cannot be said in the more specific case of an allegedly a priori claim. See also the discussion of deviant logics (ibid., ch. 6, esp. 74).

In any case, once the claim of give-up-ability is strengthened in this way, it is no longer very clear what the argument for it in these sections is supposed to be. One element is an appeal to an extreme version of the familiar Duhemian view that our claims about the world cannot be experientially tested one at a time, in isolation from each other, but only when taken together; nothing less than 'the whole of science,' Quine claims, can be meaningfully confronted with experience. In addition, we are presented with the familiar, closely related metaphor of the conceptual fabric or field of force, the familiar Quinean 'web of belief,' which need only be kept in agreement with experience at the edges:

> A conflict with experience at the periphery occasions readjustments in the interior of the field.... But the total field is so underdetermined by its boundary conditions, experience, that there is much latitude of choice as to what statements to reevaluate in the light of any single contrary experience. [*TD* 42-3]

The relevance of these ideas to the issue at hand is, however, quite obscure: how are they supposed to show that any sentence (with meaning unchanged) can be rationally given up?

In one of the better accounts of Quine's philosophy, Alex Orenstein offers the following summation of the point at issue:

> We are forced to recognize that from the fact that sentences cannot be tested in isolation but only as parts of systems of sentences, it follows that every sentence at all logically relevant to a test risks the danger of experimental refutation.... No sentence can be singled out as being in principle incorrigible; for in the attempt to fit theory to observation, any one sentence may become a candidate for revision. Logic and mathematics, and all other purported a priori knowledge, are parts of our system of background assumptions and are in principle open to revision. If a priori knowledge is knowledge that is justifiable independently of experience, then Quine denies that there is any....[23]

Unfortunately, though I know of no better interpretation of the argument in question, the line of reasoning suggested by Orenstein is

---

23 Alex Orenstein, *Willard Van Orman Quine* (Boston: Twayne 1977), 85-6

utterly question-begging. What follows from the Duhemian view is only that the revisions prompted by recalcitrant experience need not be confined to the observational periphery, i.e., that the demands of experience can often be satisfied equally well by revisions in the non-observational interior of the web. But to conclude from this that any sentence can rationally be given up (without having changed in meaning), it must be assumed that *epistemic rationality is concerned solely with adjusting one's beliefs to experience*: for without such an assumption, it remains possible that a particular revision, though adequate to satisfy the demands of experience, is ruled out for some other, non-experiential reason. And the whole thrust of the idea of a priori justification is precisely that there are propositions (or sentences with fixed meanings) which it is justifiable or rational to accept, and also unjustifiable or irrational to give up, for reasons which have nothing to do with adjusting to experience. Whether or not this view is finally acceptable, the Duhemian view concerning the impossibility of experientially testing individual claims in isolation does not count against it in any way.

Thus Quine's main argument in 'Two Dogmas of Empiricism' against the possibility of a priori justification and knowledge turns out to be totally lacking in force: it reaches the conclusion that there is no a priori justification only by adopting a conception of epistemic rationality which already tacitly assumes that this is so.

This is not quite the end of the story, however, for there is a further, seemingly independent, Quinean doctrine, the doctrine of the indeterminacy of translation, which is often cited to buttress the argument against the a priori.

Consider a situation of *radical translation*: a situation in which a linguist or anthropologist is attempting to translate a completely unknown language, unrelated to his own, and is therefore forced to rely solely on the observed behavior of its speakers in relation to their environment. Quine's claim, in brief, is that apart from the special cases of (i) observation sentences and (ii) truth-functional connectives, such translation is not possible in a determinate, non-arbitrary way. While translations can be found that are consistent with all possible behavioral evidence, any such possible translation will, Quine claims, be only one of indefinitely many different alternatives, all of which are equally satisfactory from a behavioral standpoint and between which only an arbitrary choice is possible.[24] Suppose that this initial thesis is granted for the sake of the argument. The natural conclusion, from an intuitive standpoint, might seem to be that the native speaker in fact determinately means one of the things suggested by the alternative translations (or some distinct further thing), that he has something definite in mind, and that the translator is merely unable to tell what that is. Quine's conclusion, however, is much more radical and intuitively paradoxical: insofar as such indeterminacy of translation exists, he claims, there is simply no right answer, no fact of the matter as to what the native speaker really means [WO 26-7, 73]. And this indeterminacy extends not only to the native speaker's meaning, but even to the state of mind of the native speaker which might be thought to embody that meaning.[25] Moreover, this conclusion is perfectly general: we ourselves can just as well be regarded as the native speakers, leading to the conclusion that our own meanings and thought contents are similarly indeterminate.

How is the thesis of the indeterminacy of translation, which we now see would be better described, but for Quinean scruples, as the thesis of the indeterminacy of meaning and belief, supposed to be relevant to the issue of a priori knowledge? Though I have been unable to find a place where Quine himself speaks very explicitly to this point, the main relevance seems to be that the indeterminacy thesis buttresses the quasi-Duhemian argument of 'Two Dogmas' in a way that makes possible a reply to the objection offered above. If sentences have no determinate meanings, if their sole significance is determined by their de facto connections with other sentences in the 'web of belief' and

---

24 The indeterminacy thesis was first developed in Quine, *Word and Object* (Cambridge, MA: MIT Press 1960), ch. 2. (This book will hereafter be cited as *WO*.) It has since been elaborated and refined in many other places. Though a full account of the thesis would involve many further details and ramifications, these are inessential for present purposes.

25 As already noted, Quine himself would not use the term 'meaning'; but I can see no reason to deprive ourselves of this useful formulation.

with experiences or stimuli, then there can be no reason why any sentence isn't as open to rational revision as any other. In particular, there is nothing on the basis of which any sentence could be recognized as necessarily true or as justified independently of experience. The effect of the indeterminacy is thus to deprive individual sentences of any isolable significance which could provide a basis for singling them out as being justified a priori.

But could the broad version of the indeterminacy thesis that extends even to thought content possibly be correct? It is very tempting to take this thesis instead as an unintended reductio ad absurdum of whatever considerations (which I have not yet attempted to specify) are supposed to generate it. For surely, the intuitive argument would go, I do normally have something definite in mind when I use a word, whether or not someone else can determine from the outside what that is, and hence any argument which leads to the denial of this obvious fact must be unsound.[26]

Moreover, the argument for these intuitively incredible results, especially as they pertain to thought itself, is obscure at best. The basic appeal seems to be to highly dubious views like behaviorism and verificationism, and perhaps ultimately to the thesis of 'naturalism': roughly the view that knowledge is confined to natural science, so construed as to be confined to claims whose justification is strictly empirical in character. But then the overall argument becomes once again question-begging, albeit in a more complicated way, when employed as an argument against the possibility of a priori justification: the argument against the isolable meanings which a priori knowledge requires depends on assuming that knowledge is confined to empirical science, so construed as to exclude both a priori justification and the sort of quasi-introspective justification which would be relevant to my grasp of my own meanings. Or, putting the matter the other way round, if a priori justification and knowledge genuinely exist, then naturalism is false and cannot support the corollaries

---

26 For an elaboration of this response, see my 'Analytic Philosophy and the Nature of Thought,' forthcoming.

needed to move from the narrow thesis of indeterminacy of translation to the broader thesis of indeterminacy of meaning and belief.
Thus Quine appears to have no non-question-begging argument
against the idea of a priori justification. He might still want to argue,
however, that this possibility should not be taken seriously because
there is no reputable cognitive endeavor which requires any sort of a
priori appeal. To assess this contention we need to examine in detail
what sort of positive epistemological position is possible within the
constraints of Quine's position.

VI Can Radical Empiricism Avoid Skepticism?

One problem that arises in assessing Quine's positive epistemology is
that it is far from clear just what status the claims that are justified by
its lights are claimed to have. One obvious question is whether a
Quinean approach can yield any reason for thinking that empirical
claims, especially those which are not strictly observational in character, are likely to be true, i.e., are epistemically justified in the sense
discussed in section I of this paper. If the answer to this question is
'no,' as argued below, then Quine is in a clear sense a skeptic about
such claims. At the same time, however, it must be acknowledged that
Quine may not intend to claim that his position yields any answer to
this sort of skepticism. Thus a full investigation of Quinean epistemology must also consider whether there is some other sense in which
some non-observational empirical claims can be rationally preferred
to others without any appeal to the a priori. As will emerge, my
answer to this second question is also negative.
What then is Quine's account of the justification of non-observational empirical knowledge? Return to the metaphor of the conceptual
fabric or web: We have already taken preliminary note of the distinction which Quine draws between observational and non-observational beliefs or sentences, i.e., between those which are at the 'edge'
of the web and those which are in the 'interior,' a distinction of which
he offers the following less metaphorical, though still rather vague
account:

> Certain statements, though *about* physical objects and not sense experience, seem peculiarly germane to sense experience — and in a selective way: some statements to some experiences, others to others. Such statements, especially germane to particular experiences, I picture as near the periphery. But in this relation of "germaneness" I envisage nothing more than a loose association reflecting the relative likelihood, in practice, of our choosing one statement rather than another for revision in the event of recalcitrant experience. [*TD* 43]

In the face of such recalcitrant experience, we revise or modify the system accordingly. The sentences which constitute principles of logic and reasoning are those which are toward the center of the web, i.e., which are 'in practice' less likely to be revised in this way. But their status is not essentially different from other elements in the system, and no sentence is entirely immune to revision. This account is elaborated and developed in many of Quine's later writings, except that talk of experience is replaced by behavioristically and 'naturalistically' respectable talk of 'sensory stimulations.'

Quine offers no clear account of the justification of observational beliefs, those at the edge of the web (assuming that it is different in principle from that of non-observational beliefs). The observational beliefs are said to be directly, or at least more directly, connected with experience (or sensory stimulations), but the precise epistemic significance of this more direct connection remains obscure. In particular, while it is clear that the justification of an observational belief can be overturned by the sorts of considerations, discussed below, that apply to non-observational beliefs, it is not clear whether the justification of observational beliefs must always appeal to such considerations or whether it is only defeasible by reference to them. Here, however, I want to focus primarily on non-observational or theoretical beliefs, those which are in the 'interior' of the web, assuming for the sake of the argument that the justification of observational claims can be accounted for in some acceptable way.

How then are the 'interior' beliefs justified? Or, to begin with a simpler question, in virtue of what is one such belief *more* justified, more reasonable to accept, than another? When faced with conflicting or recalcitrant experience, we are supposedly forced to revise our web of belief, our system of accepted sentences, but the experience itself does not fully determine which revision to make. What then does determine, or at least constrain, such revisions? Though the details are obscure, the broad outlines of Quine's answers are clear enough: he appeals to familiar scientific standards like simplicity, scope, fecundity, and explanatory adequacy, adding to them a fairly strong principle of conservatism: roughly that we make the least change possible in our overall view. Thus a system of beliefs which meets these standards to some specified degree will be more justified, by Quinean lights, than one which meets them to a lesser degree, and this difference in justification will extend to the component beliefs of such systems.[27]

There are two basic problems with this sort of response (beyond the undeniable fuzziness of the various specific standards). First, it is unclear what the connection is supposed to be between the satisfaction of such standards and *epistemic* justification, where the latter concept is understood in the way explained earlier, i.e., in terms of having a *reason* for thinking that a belief is likely to be *true*. What reason can be offered for thinking that a system of beliefs that is simpler or more conservative or explanatorily more adequate is thereby more likely to be true, i.e., that following such standards is at least conducive to finding the truth? Someone who had not rejected the very possibility of a priori justification might attempt to offer an a priori argument for the truth-conduciveness of at least some of these standards,[28] though it is doubtful whether such an attempt could have much plausibility in the case of conservatism or the general notion of simplicity. (Why, after all, should it be thought that the beliefs I happen to hold are ipso facto more likely to be true, or that the world is somehow more likely to be simple than complex?) But Quine has in any case ruled out any such a priori appeal; and it is clear at once that any attempt at an empirical argument for this sort of conclusion would be inevitably question-begging, since it would have to appeal to these same standards. Thus Quine's own strictures rule out the possibility of his having any reason for regarding his

---

27 I ignore here the problems posed by the fact that one particular belief can seemingly belong to many, indeed indefinitely many, different systems of belief.

28 For my attempt to sketch such an argument for a notion of coherence which includes the idea of explanatory adequacy as a major component, see *SEK*, ch. 8.

standards of non-observational justification as truth-conducive and hence any reason for regarding the justification they yield as epistemic justification.[29]

Second, and perhaps even more damagingly, it is unclear why these standards impose any real constraint at all on possible revisions. After all, any such standard, since it cannot on Quinean grounds be justified or shown to be epistemically relevant independently of considerations of adjustment to experience, is itself merely one more strand in the web, itself equally open to revision.[30] Thus in any situation in which one possible revision of one's system of beliefs might seem to be more justified than another by appeal to such standards, one need only revise or abandon the standards themselves to make the alternative revision at least as acceptable.

The Quinean response would presumably be that such wholesale revision of one's epistemic standards, though possible, is itself less likely to be justified or epistemically reasonable — that in terms of the metaphor, such standards are, as is also claimed for the principles of logic, closer to the center of the web and hence more insulated from the impact of experience. But it is impossible to find any adequate rationale for such a view within the resources of the Quinean position.

---

29 It is important to be clear that the issue here is not merely a verbal issue concerning the proper understanding of the term 'justification' as it occurs in epistemic contexts. What has been shown is that a Quinean epistemological view can offer no (non-question-begging) reason for thinking that the beliefs it sanctions are even likely to be true. And that is enough to make such a position a very strong version of skepticism, one which is unable to vindicate the ordinary claims of science and common sense — no matter what use is made of the term 'justification.'

30 It is less than clear just how such epistemic standards are to be represented in a Quinean framework. It is more natural to take them as principles or rules rather than as beliefs, i.e., in linguistic terms, roughly as imperative sentences rather than declarative ones. Quine has little to say about this issue, however, and I shall not worry about it here. It is clear at least that such standards, however they may best be represented, cannot for a Quinean be construed as immune to the possibility of revision.

Construed as a mere psychological claim about what we are in fact disposed to revise, such a picture might well be correct; but there is no apparent basis for claiming that it has any *epistemic* significance, that frequent and wholesale revision of one's epistemic standards is in any way epistemically unreasonable or less likely to lead to the truth. To appeal to the very standards themselves, e.g., to the principle of conservatism in order to defend the reluctance to revise the principle of conservatism, is obviously circular; while any further standard, even a meta-standard having to do with the revision of first-level standards, will itself be equally open to revision.[31]

Moreover, it is important to see that this problem arises not only for relatively abstruse standards like conservatism and simplicity, but also for simpler and seemingly less problematic logical standards such as even the principle of consistency or non-contradiction itself. If there are any constraints at all according to which some revisions of the system of beliefs in the face of recalcitrant experience are more justified than others, it seems clear that they must include the idea that a system which is free of contradiction is preferable, at least where other things are equal, to one which contains contradictions. But Quine can apparently offer no reason at all why the principle of non-contradiction should not be as freely revised or abandoned as any other part of the system.

Thus even apart from worries about their relevance to epistemic justification, the Quinean constraints on justified revision of the one's system of beliefs come to very little. At best, they make some total systems (including epistemic principles and principles of logic) less justified than others. But for any less global issue, any question of

---

31 As Harman points out, 'Quine's theory of evidence may also be thought of as a coherence theory of evidence: a person attempts to make his total conceptual scheme as coherent as possible ...,' where the various standards mentioned above constitute the components of the idea of coherence ('Quine on Meaning and Existence II,' *Review of Metaphysics* **21** (1967-68), 351). In these terms, the point being made in the text is the familiar one that the epistemic authority of coherence cannot itself be established by appeal to coherence. For more discussion, see *SEK*, 108-10.

common sense fact or scientific theory which does not extend to the specification of such principles, it will seemingly always be possible to find a revision of one's system of beliefs containing any answer one likes (together with appropriately adjusted epistemic and logical principles) which is as justified on Quinean grounds as any alternative revision. The inescapable conclusion is that all such specific answers are equally justified from a Quinean standpoint, which can only mean that none is in fact justified at all.

Moreover, even this bleak picture is more optimistic than the radical empiricist view really warrants. I have been conceding for the sake of the argument that revision of at least some non-obervational beliefs, which might include epistemic or logical principles, is sometimes required in the face of 'recalcitrant experience.' But in fact the Quinean position can ultimately offer no reason at all why *any* revisions are *ever* required. Remember that for Quine the elements of the system are merely *sentences*, having no meanings beyond their roles in the system, and also that there is no a priori background logic which connects and relates such sentences. (The set of sentences of course includes sentences of logic, but these are only further elements of the system.) Thus the basis for any supposed incompatibility within any set of sentences (reflecting a need for revision in the face of experience) can apparently only be some further sentence in the system which says explicitly that the acceptance of such a set is objectionable. But if we now consider the enlarged set of sentences which includes that one, the same situation repeats itself: that set of sentences can only be unacceptable by virtue of some still further sentence, and so on, thus generating an infinite demand for further sentences if the incompatibility is to be genuine. But since the total set of sentences is presumably finite, this regressive demand will eventually fail to be satisfied, meaning that the alleged incompatibility or need for revision does not exist after all. The upshot is that even the revision of one's epistemic or logical principles discussed earlier turns out not to be necessary, since at some level there will inevitably fail to be a further sentence saying that the total set of sentences which includes that principle and which seems intuitively to be incompatible really is incompatible. This means that any non-observational sentence or set of such sentences can always be retained, even without revising one's epistemic or logical principles. This point is sufficiently tricky to make a simple illustration desirable. Suppose then that I find myself in the following situation: I accept some sentence *P* and also, perhaps as a result of observation, its intuitive denial not-*P*, and in addition I accept some third sentence *PNC* which is intuitively a formulation of the principle of non-contradiction. From a rationalist standpoint, I can know a priori that *P* and not-*P* cannot both be true, and hence that the chance that my set of beliefs is true will be enhanced if one of them is rejected; if my concern is finding the truth, I therefore revise accordingly. But Quine rejects such a view and instead apparently must hold the view that one of *P* and not-*P* must be given up solely because I accept the further sentence *PNC*, where this sentence, though not unrevisable, is claimed to have a status which makes it less reasonable to revise it in at least most cases than to give up one of the other sentences. The point made earlier was that he has and can have no epistemic reason for assigning such a status to *PNC*, and hence that the option of rejecting *PNC* while retaining both *P* and not-*P* is for him just as reasonable as giving up one of the latter. But the present point is that once meaning and a priori logic are excluded, there is nothing about the sentences *P*, not-*P*, and *PNC*, taken by themselves, which makes them incompatible or demanding of revision. Thus a genuine incompatibility requires at least that the system contain a further sentence, *MPNC* (a meta-principle of non-contradiction), which says explicitly that the other three sentences are incompatible. And now the problem repeats itself: for *P*, not-*P*, *PNC*, and *MPNC* to be incompatible will require a further sentence *MMPNC*, etc., and eventually the further sentence will simply not be present.[32]

---

32 Ironically enough, the point here is similar to an argument which Quine, and Harman following him, offers against the moderate empiricist appeal to convention: just as the logical force of the conventionalist's conventions cannot derive from the conventions themselves, so also the logical force of the sentences of the web cannot be given merely by other sentences in the web. Hence, if those

In fact, the picture just presented is oversimplified in one obvious but ultimately unimportant respect. What actually happens, of course, is that at one of these stages, perhaps the one including *PNC* but more likely the one including only *P* and not-*P*, our actual cognitive *practice* is such as to treat the sentences in question as incompatible: when we realize that we have accepted such a set of sentences, we in fact revise. But of course practices are, for Quine, no more sacrosanct or unrevisable and no more justifiable a priori than are sentences; and he can hardly claim that the presence of such a practice is essential to the meaning of *PNC*. Thus the question of why such a practice cannot be freely revised or abandoned cannot be avoided, and once again Quine has no resources available to answer it. For this reason, the presence of such a practice, though undeniable as a matter of psychology, cannot be used to show that revision is rationally required.

One upshot of this last point is that the familiar Quinean metaphor of the cognitive web or fabric is in fact deeply inappropriate. What we have on a Quinean view is just a set or bundle of sentences, sentences which are not connected by any background of logic and which turn out to be incapable of somehow connecting themselves.

Thus the skepticism which seemed almost total from our earlier perspective turns out to be utterly complete: from a Quinean perspective, there is not only no reason for thinking that any non-observational belief is true, but also no reason why we cannot accept or retain any set of non-obervational sentences at all, no matter how seemingly contradictory or incoherent and no matter what sentences seemingly expressing epistemic or logical standards it may contain. Any such set is as justified as any other, which means of course that none is justified at all. And the immediate point, to repeat once more, is not that such an extreme skepticism might not, for all we have seen so far, be correct, but only that it surely precludes Quineans from arguing that the

---

sentences are all there is, they lose all logical force and the need for revision collapses (except, possibly, for sentences which are strictly observational, if there are any of these).

possibility of a priori justification, even if not otherwise ruled out, need not be taken seriously because no clearly reputable epistemic goal requires it. In this way, both Quinean epistemology and the Quinean case against the a priori come to nothing.

In concluding, I want to mention briefly one further possible move which Quine or Quineans might want to make, though I know of no place where Quine himself says anything very close to it. It might be possible to avoid the extreme skeptical outcome while retaining something approaching a Quinean view by adopting an *externalist* theory of epistemic justification, according to which epistemic justification or warrant need not involve the possession by the believer of anything like a *reason* for thinking that his belief is true. On the most common version of such a view, a belief is justified if it is produced or caused in a reliable way — whether or not the believer has any reason to think that this is so.[33] The basic difficulty with this suggestion is that externalism seems to simply change the subject without really speaking to the issues which an adequate epistemology must address: whatever account externalists offer for concepts like knowledge or justification, there is still a plain and undeniable sense in which if externalism is the final story, we have no reason to think that any of our beliefs are true, and this result amounts by itself to a very strong version of skepticism. And this in turn is enough to show that an externalist view does no better than Quine's own in showing that the possibility of a priori justification can safely be dismissed.

VII Conclusion

My conclusion is simple: Neither moderate empiricism nor radical empiricism can provide an adequate, non-skeptical epistemology. A priori justification can neither be accommodated within empiricism, as the moderate empiricist tries to do, nor eschewed entirely, along the lines proposed by radical empiricism. Thus if we are to have any

---

33 See *SEK*, ch. 3, and the references offered there.

knowledge or justification that extends beyond the bounds of immediate experience, narrowly construed, or, more generally, if we are to
be capable of epistemically justified reasoning at all, there must be a
priori justification that fits the original rationalist conception: i.e., the
human mind must have the capacity to directly discern necessary
facts and connections pertaining to independent reality. But having
said that much, it must be admitted that, due in large part to two and
one-half centuries of empiricist evasion, the task of giving a really
perspicuous account of such justification has hardly been begun.[34]

---

34 Versions of this paper were presented at Western Washington University and at
the University of Nebraska. I am grateful to the audiences there for many useful
comments and suggestions. Ann Baker was a constant source of advice and
encouragement.

Analyticity, Undeniability, and Truth

JAMES VAN CLEVE

In his 1970 book *Philosophy of Logic*, Quine propounds what he calls 'the deviant logician's predicament': when a reformist logician tries to deny a law of classical logic, he succeeds only in changing the subject.[1] This position, summed up in the aphorisms 'deny the doctrine and change the subject' and 'an illogical culture is a mistranslated one,' has struck many of Quine's readers as backsliding.[2] The old Quine denied that any statements whatever are analytic in the sense of being true solely in virtue of what they mean; the new Quine holds that certain laws of logic cannot be denied without changing the meanings of the logical connectives.[3] Does not the position of the new

---

1 W.V. Quine, *Philosophy of Logic* (Englewood Cliffs, NJ: Prentice-Hall 1970), ch. 6

2 Hilary Putnam, '"Two Dogmas" Revisited,' in *Realism and Reason* (Cambridge: Cambridge University Press 1983), 87-97, at 92; Susan Haack, *Deviant Logic* (Cambridge: Cambridge University Press 1974), 15; Michael Dummett, 'Is Logic Empirical?' in *Truth and Other Enigmas* (Cambridge, MA: Harvard University Press 1978), 269-89, at 270

3 The 'old Quine' is of course the Quine of 'Two Dogmas of Empiricism,' first published in 1951 and reprinted in *From a Logical Point of View* (New York: Harper Torchbooks 1963), 20-46. The views of the 'new Quine' (as Adam Morton points out in 'Denying the Doctrine and Changing the Subject,' *The Journal of*

James Van Cleve

Quine invest logical laws precisely with the status 'true solely in virtue of what they mean'?

I shall argue here that the answer is no. My concern is not so much to render Quine's overall position consistent[4] as it is to cast doubt on whether logical laws — or any statements at all, for that matter — are in any significant sense true solely in virtue of what they mean.

I

To soften us up for the view he advocates in *Philosophy of Logic*, Quine starts us off with an extreme case:

> Suppose someone were to propound a heterodox logic in which all the laws which have up to now been taken to govern alternation were made to govern conjunction instead, and vice versa. Clearly we would regard his deviation merely as notational and phonetic. For obscure reasons, if any, he has taken to writing "and" in place of "or" and vice versa. (81)

He then turns to a less extreme but still 'far out' case:

> To turn to a popular extravaganza, what if someone were to reject the law of non-contradiction and so accept an occasional sentence and its negation both as true? ... [Those who do so] think they are talking about negation, "~," "not"; but surely the notation ceased to be recognizable as negation when they took to regarding some conjunctions of the form "p & ~p" as true.... Here, evidently, is the deviant logician's predicament: when he tries to deny the doctrine he only changes the subject. (81)

Philosophy **70** [1973] 503-10) actually go back at least to 1954. See Quine's 'Carnap and Logical Truth' in *The Ways of Paradox* (New York: Random House 1966), 100-25, esp. 102 and 105.

4   There does appear to be at least one respect in which Quine has reversed himself. The Quine of 'Two Dogmas' held that no statement is immune to revision, not even the law of excluded middle. The Quine to be discussed here holds that the laws of classical logic cannot be rejected without changing their meanings, and that makes them unrevisable in the only relevant sense of 'revision.'

90

In short, any signs that mean the same as our '&' and '~' must obey the same laws that they do, and that appears to make those laws true by virtue of their meaning. In this section, I wish to address an apparent gap between what is shown by Quine's two cases. What is illustrated by the first case is evidently this: any concept that obeyed all the same laws as conjunction would *be* conjunction, and similarly for disjunction; that is why there cannot be a logic in which the two concepts exchange functions. Otherwise put, any sign in any system that obeyed all the same laws as a given sign of ours, say '&,' would be synonymous with '&.' For short:

(A) Same laws → same meaning.

In Quine's second example, we do not envisage anything so drastic as junking all of a connective's laws and replacing them by the laws of another; we simply drop one or two laws and the theorems that depend on them. The interesting historical cases are of this less drastic sort. For example, proponents of intuitionist propositional logic drop only excluded middle, double negation elimination, and the theorems that depend on them; proponents of quantum logic recommend giving up only the distribution laws for conjunction and disjunction. In both cases, a strong complement of classical laws is retained.[5] In ruling that these deviant logicians have changed the subject just as surely as the more thoroughgoing reformers of the first example, Quine can no longer be relying merely on principle A above. Instead, he appears to need the following principle: any sign in any system that is to have the same meaning as a given sign of ours, say '&,' must obey all of its laws. For short:

---

5 The retained laws include the standard introduction and elimination rules for the logical constants, which in the opinion of some philosophers are the only laws that are essential to the meanings of the logical constants. See, for example, Hilary Putnam, 'The Logic of Quantum Mechanics,' in *Mathematics, Matter, and Method* (Cambridge: Cambridge University Press 1975), 174-97, and Neil Tennant, *Anti-Realism and Logic* (Oxford: Clarendon Press 1987), ch. 9.

(B) Same meaning → same laws

Between A and B there is all the difference between a statement and its converse. How are we supposed to get from A to B — or otherwise justify principle B?

   The following occurs to me as an argument by which one might try to show that if we accept A, we must also accept B. Suppose we reject B, holding that there could be a deviant logic DL1 containing a sign '#' that means the same as our '&,' yet without obeying all the same laws. It obeys many of them, let us say, but not commutation. If this could happen at all, then presumably it could equally well happen that there was a deviant logic DL2 containing a sign '#' with the same features as in DL1 and also containing another sign '@' that *did* obey all the same laws as '&.' According to A, '@' would be synonymous with '&' and hence (by transitivity of synonymy) with '#,' since by hypothesis '#' is synonymous with '&.' But now we have reached an impossible result: '@' and '#' cannot be synonymous within DL2, since we have supposed that one is commutative and the other not. So if we accept A, we cannot reject B without generating an absurdity.

   In the foregoing argument, we advance from A to B with the help of three auxiliary assumptions. One of the assumptions is the intra-systemic version of B, which is weaker than B itself: it says that two signs that are synonymous *within the same system* must obey the same laws. This is weaker than B itself, which is meant to apply *across* systems, so it is a fair premise to use in the present context. Another of the assumptions is the transitivity of synonymy, whether within systems or across them. Since by 'synonymy' we mean full sameness of meaning (not some attenuated relation of 'meaning the same for the most part'), this is well-nigh incontestable. (If there is ever a case in which denying a doctrine changes the subject, then surely denying transitivity changes the subject to something other than synonymy!) Finally, there is an assumption to the effect that the mere addition of new vocabulary does not alter the meaning of the old. To be precise: if there could be a deviant logic DL1 in which some sign '#' had the same meaning as our '&,' yet did not obey all its laws, then there could also be a deviant logic DL2 in which (i) '#' occurred as before, having the same meaning as our '&' but not obeying all its laws, and (ii) there also occurred some other sign '@' that *did* obey all the laws of '&.' This assumption seems to me to have at least a modicum of plausibility. We could obtain DL2 from DL1 merely by adding a new sign and some new laws, not adding or subtracting in the bargain any laws couched in the vocabulary of DL1; so if '#' as it occurs in DL1 means the same as our '&,' why should the same not be true of '#' as it occurs in DL2?

Nonetheless, I anticipate that some readers will question the third assumption. Perhaps they will want to say something like this: a sign in another system, to be synonymous with our '&,' must be the *closest counterpart* in that system to our '&' (or at least a counterpart than which none is closer). Once we add '@,' '#' is no longer the closest counterpart to '&,' so it loses its claim to be synonymous with '&.'

I do not advocate the closest counterpart approach to synonymy. One thing against it is that the relation of closest counterparthood is not transitive, so we would have to give up the intersystemic transitivity of synonymy after all. Nonetheless, since the argument from A to B may remain controversial, I will not rest anything upon it.[6]

Here is another way to establish principle B, this time without relying on principle A. 'Same meaning, same laws' — is that not a simple consequence of the principle that synonyms should be substitutable for one another (at least in extensional contexts) salva veritate? Suppose L(s) is a law governing sign s, and suppose further that s is synonymous with t. Then L(t), a law obtained by substituting t for s in L(s), should also be a true law. We already appealed to this above in the intra-systemic case (where s and t are signs in the same logical system), but should it not hold in the intersystemic case for just the same reason? If so, principle B is swiftly secured, and the deviant logician apparently ensnared in his predicament.

---

6 In conversation, Felicia Ackerman has objected to principle A on the ground that there are logical and arithmetical operations that are equivalent (hence subject to the same laws), yet different in cognitive meaning, such as single and triple negation, subtracting a number and adding the corresponding negative number, etc.

I believe the argument of the last paragraph is flawed. Before I can say what is wrong with it, however, I need to say more about my main topic.

II

Quine's position in *Philosophy of Logic*, whether established by any of the foregoing considerations or not, is that no one can deny a law of classical logic without changing the meanings of the connectives. It may appear to follow from this that those laws are true by virtue of what they mean. For if we say that a sign has the same meaning as our '&' only if it obeys the same laws as our '&,' are we not saying that the laws for '&' supervene on its meaning? And is this not to say in turn that those laws hold in virtue of what '&' means?

Be that as it may, Quine continues to repudiate any suggestion that logical laws are true by meaning. In this section I will consider three ways in which one might try to keep Quine's views in *Philosophy of Logic* from reinstating truth in virtue of meaning. All three strategies have been discussed in an interesting article by Michael Levin, who puts the issue this way: how can we square Quine's 'empirical' view of logic — rather than being true by meaning, laws of logic could be shown false — with his 'mistranslation' view — anyone who apparently denies a logical law has been mistranslated?[7]

1. Levin first raises the possibility that Quine's position on deviant logicians (or illogical cultures) may be the analog of Hume's position on miracles. Hume did not hold that miracles are impossible, but only that it could never be reasonable to believe in one (on the basis of testimonial evidence, at any rate). Similarly, perhaps Quine does not reject illogical cultures as impossible, but only counsels that it could never be reasonable to believe that we had found one.

---

7 Michael Levin, 'Quine's View(s) on Logical Truth,' in *Essays on the Philosophy of W.V. Quine*, R.W. Shahan and C. Swoyer, eds. (Norman, OK: University of Oklahoma Press 1979), 45-67

We should always 'reject the greater miracle,' assuming that apparent deviance from a logical law reflects difference in meaning rather than genuine dissent from it. There are occasional hints in Quine that his mistranslation thesis should indeed be given this Humean form, for example: 'One's interlocutor's silliness, beyond a certain point, is less likely than bad translation.'[8] If this is all Quine has in mind, he is no backslider.[9]

As Levin points out, however, it usually appears that Quine does have something more in mind. He does not content himself with saying, 'When the deviant logician tries to deny the doctrine, he *probably* changes the subject.' Nor does he even settle for 'It would always be more rational to believe that he has changed the subject.' He appears to hold that genuine dissent from a logical law is impossible.

2. We come next to one of Quine's own explicit grounds for disowning commitment to truth by meaning. According to Quine, the mistranslation view is merely an instance of the methodological injunction to *save the obvious*.[10] It would bid us equally to save 'grass is green' and 'there is a nose on my face,' sentences no one thinks true by meaning.

Levin dismisses this strategy only because he does not distinguish it from the first strategy.[11] He appears to think that if logic is merely obvious (i.e., obvious but not true by meaning), then finding someone who rejects it is merely improbable, not impossible. But couldn't someone hold that it is impossible to deny the merely obvious? If so, we need a separate response to strategy 2.

One possible misgiving with strategy 2 is the following: if all we are told is that the mistranslation view is a consequence of 'save the

---

8 W.V. Quine, *Word and Object* (Cambridge, MA: MIT Press 1960), 59

9 I am setting aside here any verificationist doctrine that would admit no distance between 'it could never be rational to believe *p*' and '*p* could not be true.'

10 See *Philosophy of Logic*, 82 and 96-7.

11 He considers them under the same heading on 51-3 of 'Quine's View(s).'

obvious,' we do not know whether to demote logic to the status of the merely obvious (Quine's own preference) or declare everything obvious true by meaning. The latter alternative seems dictated by the argument given in the first paragraph of this section. Perhaps the point about obviousness shows that something is wrong with that argument, but it does not show what. If nothing else, strategy 2 requires supplementation.

3. We come finally to the reconciliation Levin favors, the key to which is the distinction between what *cannot be denied* and what *must be affirmed*. The deviant logician cannot deny our laws, but he can drop them from his system altogether, provided he also drops their component concepts. The only *must* is a conditional *must*: if you use our concepts, you must accept our laws. For example, anyone who uses the classical concept of negation must accept excluded middle, but the intuitionist is free to put his own concept of negation with its own laws in its place. As Levin notes, 83-7 of *Philosophy of Logic* strongly suggest that this is Quine's view, and in a reply to Levin, Quine has endorsed it.[12]

It should be noted that this reconciliation works only by weakening the empirical view. It is no longer permitted that logical laws might come to be *rejected*; it is only permitted that they be *abandoned*, or missing from the start in certain systems.

I have two reservations about this strategy. First, if logical laws are obvious, as Quine says, isn't refusing to affirm them almost as bad as outright denying them? In place of Levin's distinction, perhaps we need a threefold distinction: denial, refusal to affirm, and mere failure to affirm. Failing to affirm an obvious logical law is understandable, in so far as one may never have thought of it; but refusing to affirm

---

12 See W.V. Quine, 'Replies to Eleven Essays,' *Philosophical Topics* **12** (1981), esp. 231-3. At 232 Quine says, 'The reconciliation, as I see it, is as Levin suggests. In conformity with the empirical view we may in an extremity rescind a logical principle, and in so doing we do not contravene the mistranslation view as long as we do not adopt a contrary principle.'

an obvious law (as deviant logicians appear to do) seems as problematic as denying it.[13]

Second, the present strategy does nothing to undo the prima facie impression that Quine is committed to a kind of truth by meaning. For all that has been said, the truths that go unexpressed in deviant systems are true by virtue of their meanings in the systems where they occur at all. So the third strategy, like the second, cannot stand alone.

III

My own suggestion for reconciling 'there are some sentences you cannot deny without changing their meanings' and 'there are no sentences that are true in virtue of their meanings' differs from any of those canvassed above. It turns on distinguishing two senses of 'denial' as it occurs in formulas such as 'anyone who denies sentence S must be changing its meaning,' 'S cannot be denied by anyone who means by it what we do,' etc. On the one hand, 'cannot be denied' can mean 'cannot be the object of the attitude of denial'; on the other, it can mean 'cannot have a negation sign affixed to it truly.' Corresponding to these two senses, there are two things that can be meant by the formulas:

1. Necessarily: anyone who denies one of our laws (e.g., 'p v ~p') does not mean what we do by all the signs occurring in it.

2. Necessarily: if 'p v ~p' is not true (as used by others), it does not mean for them what it means for us.

Contraposing, formula 1 tells us that anyone who means what we do by 'v' and '~' must not deny the law of excluded middle. Formula 2 tells us that any string of symbols that has the same meaning as our

---

13 Morton suggests that Quine wishes to oppose weak deviance (refusing to assent to a classical law) as well as strong deviance (assenting to its negation).

law of excluded middle must be true. More generally, the idea behind formula 1 is that if your signs are to mean what ours do, you must observe our laws; the idea behind formula 2 is that these laws must be true.[14]

My suggestion is this: we do not have 'truth in virtue of meaning' unless we at least have *truth*, and formula 1 does not guarantee truth. It is only formula 2 that would take us back to analyticity in the sense of truth by meaning; yet it is only formula 1 that emerges from Quine's strictures against deviant logicians and pre-logical mentalities.

The distinction I am urging may seem starkly obvious, yet I believe it is often overlooked (or perhaps rejected on principle). Quine himself either misses or rejects it when he observes that the following questions are 'in close harmony' and 'almost ... two forms of a single question':

> Is logic a compendium of the broadest traits of reality, or is it just an effect of linguistic convention? Must all right-minded men agree on logic, or is it every language for itself?[15]

The first question is the question what makes logic *true* — reality or convention? The second question, for Quine, is the question whether logic is built into translation, i.e., whether we must count others as holding true (or at least not dissenting from) our own logical laws. To

---

14 'Observing our laws' is ambiguous; it can mean affirming them, manipulating symbols in accordance with them, or simply not denying them. The differences among these three do not matter for the present point, which is that none of them guarantees that the laws in question are true.

Incidentally, some readers may wonder how Quine, the repudiator of modality, can affirm either 1 or 2 given that each contains a 'necessarily.' I suspect the answer is that he cannot, in which case to get a consistent Quine we would have to retreat all the way back to Levin's first reconciliation, back to the Humean version of the mistranslation thesis that merely says it is improbable that anyone should take exception to our logical principles. As we saw, however, Quine gives every impression of wanting to say something stronger — something not properly expressible without using modal operators.

15 *Philosophy of Logic*, 96

run these questions together is evidently to conflate what everyone must agree upon with what must be true.[16]

Levin appears to make a similar conflation. He takes the mistranslation thesis to imply a battery of conditionals such as the following, called by him *crucial conditionals*: 'If you use a term translatable as "not," you must accept "p v ~p."' He characterizes *conventionalism* as the view that the antecedents of the crucial conditionals explain their consequents, thereby explaining *why necessary truths are true* (his words). He then objects to conventionalism on the following ground alone: that the crucial conditionals are *bare tautologies*, their antecedents and consequents too close in meaning for one to explain the other. He does not question the idea that if you *did* explain via crucial conditionals why certain laws must be accepted, you would thereby explain why they are true. He thus packs together precisely what I am trying to keep apart: 'must be accepted' and 'must be true.'

I will cite one more author in whom the conflation I am highlighting is explicit. Arthur Pap gives the following as 'the criterion for necessary propositions': 'If the proposition *p* expressed by *S* is necessary, then anybody who honestly denied *S* would not interpret *S* to mean *p*.'[17] Later he gives us the converse: 'For if from the fact that so-and-so denies *S* it follows that so-and-so has changed the usual meaning of *S*, then it follows that the proposition usually expressed by *S* is necessary.'[18]

---

16 If you think the phrase 'right-minded' deflects my point, note that the translation argument makes the phrase redundant: a wrong-minded man would be a misunderstood one.

17 Arthur Pap, *Semantics and Necessary Truth* (New Haven: Yale University Press 1958), 123

18 Pap, 169. I venture to suggest that the conflation I am targeting may also be made by those writers who gloss Quine's challenge to the analytic-synthetic distinction as a challenge to the distinction between change of meaning and change of belief. For how is the latter challenge supposed to be tantamount to the former? Evidently, those who equate the challenges are presupposing that a sentence *S* is analytic for a person *J* iff no person *K* (who could be a different person or *J* himself at a later time) could deny *S* without attaching to it a different meaning

IV

As noted above, those who fail to honor the distinction I am urging may not be simply failing to notice it; they may be rejecting it on principle. In this section I will consider three arguments for not allowing a wedge to enter between 'must be accepted' or 'cannot be denied' on the one hand and 'must be true' on the other. (The differences between 'must be accepted' and 'cannot be denied' will no longer be crucial.)

First argument: pragmatic paradox. The first argument is that anyone who suggests that an undeniable doctrine might be false falls into a pragmatic paradox. Suppose I grant that anyone who denied doctrine D would be changing the subject. Then how can I raise the possibility that D might be false for all that? 'If someone says D is false, he is not denying *my* doctrine.' If I say that, how can I go on to entertain the possibility that D (rather than some other doctrine expressed in the same words) might turn out to be false? In short, it seems that I cannot put anything in the category 'undeniable but possibly false' without changing the subject myself, or in some illicit way 'stepping outside my conceptual scheme.'[19]

Reply: To deal with this objection, we must distinguish between saying of a *particular* undeniable doctrine that it might turn out to be false and saying that it might turn out that *some undeniable doctrine or other* is false. Perhaps if I say of some particular doctrine that it might be false despite its undeniability, I am changing the subject;[20] but I need not change the subject if I merely say

---

from that which *J* gives it. If (as many contend) there is no saying whether a difference in the verdicts *K* and *J* offer on *S* represents a difference in belief or a difference in meaning, it would then follow that there is no saying whether *S* is analytic. My point in the text is that the connection between analyticity in this sense and analyticity in the sense of '*truth* by virtue of meaning' is problematic.

19 I find at least a hint of this objection in the first note appended to Hilary Putnam's 'There is at Least One A Priori Truth,' in *Realism and Reason* (Cambridge: Cambridge University Press 1983), 98-114, at 110-11.

> Possibly, for some L, (L is undeniable & L is false)

which is all I am committed to in holding that undeniability does not entail truth.[21] My situation here is structurally similar to that of Descartes, who could not entertain the falsehood of any particular proposition of which he had a present clear and distinct perception, but who (before he had attained knowledge of God's existence and veracity) could nonetheless suppose

> Possibly, for some *P*, (I have a clear and distinct perception of *P* & *P* is false).

Second argument: meaning as use. My supposition that there is a gap between 'anyone who denies/refuses to affirm sentence *S* does not mean by it what we do' and '*S* is true' will no doubt be challenged by those who equate meaning and use. They might say that the laws in accordance with which a sign is manipulated are ipso facto the laws it obeys: for example, that if it is part of our practice to infer *Q* from '*P* & *Q*,' then it is part of the meaning of '&' that this can be done. There is accordingly no room for the suggestion that a law that must be adhered to as part of its meaning might be false.

We might also make this point by saying that in the case of logical principles, to *hold* them true is to *make* them true. We could then offer the following syllogism:

---

20 This assumes that if asserting 'not-*p*' changes the subject, so does asserting 'possibly, not-*p*.'

21 A referee has raised the following objection: suppose one held that every law of logic is undeniable and also that every law of logic is possibly false. Then one would have to say of any particular doctrine that one recognized as a law of logic (excluded middle, let us say) that it is both undeniable and possibly false, thus falling into precisely the paradox I am discussing. Reply: Perhaps *Quine* holds that every law of logic is possibly false, but I do not; I only hold that undeniability does not entail truth.

1. Anyone who means what we do by *S* holds it true.

2. For anyone who holds *S* true, it *is* true.

3. Therefore, *S* cannot mean for anyone what it does for us without being true.

Reply: Every teacher of beginning philosophy knows that some students are prone to commit certain basic fallacies, e.g., denying the antecedent. Is it really plausible that these students are making the right moves with their own brand of conditional, rather than the wrong moves with ours? Yet that is what the 'meaning is use' doctrine would oblige us to say.

As a further point against the second premise in the above syllogism, we may cite A.N. Prior's discussion of the connective 'tonk,' imagined by him to obey the rules 'from *A*, infer *A* tonk *B*' and 'from *A* tonk *B*, infer *B*.'[22] If holding logical principles true could make them true, these principles could be true; but if they were true, contradictions could be derived from any premise.

Third argument: the omniscient interpreter. Donald Davidson's 'omniscient interpreter' argument, though not advanced by him in connection with the present issue, is easily adapted to address it. Here is one of Davidson's presentations of the argument:

> It may seem that the argument so far shows only that good interpretation breeds concurrence, while leaving quite open the question whether what is agreed upon is true.... But now it is plain why massive error about the world is simply unintelligible, for to suppose it intelligible is to suppose there could be an interpreter (the omniscient one) who correctly interpreted someone else as being massively mistaken, and this we have shown to be impossible.[23]

---

22 A.N. Prior, 'The Runabout Inference Ticket,' *Analysis* **21** (1960)

23 Donald Davidson, 'The Method of Truth in Metaphysics,' reprinted in *Inquiries into Truth and Interpretation* (Oxford: Clarendon Press 1984), 199-214, at 200-1. There is another presentation of the argument in 'A Coherence Theory of Truth and Knowledge,' reprinted in *Truth and Interpretation*, Ernest LePore, ed. (Oxford: Basil Blackwell 1984), 307-19, at 317.

Davidson offers us a way of closing the gap between 'their beliefs must mostly agree with ours' and 'our beliefs must mostly be true.' If his strategy works, perhaps we can use something similar to close the gap between 'their logic must agree with ours' and 'our logic must be true.'

It is clear that what Davidson's argument needs to invoke is the possibility of an interpreter who is not only omniscient (believing or knowing whatever is true), but also infallible (believing nothing that is false). With this understood, we might reconstruct his argument as follows:

1. Assumption for reductio: it is possible that most of our beliefs (or anyone else's) are false.

2. Necessarily: anyone who correctly interprets anyone else's utterances must share most of his beliefs.

3. Necessarily: it is possible that anyone's utterances be correctly interpreted by an omniscient and infallible interpreter.[24]

From assumptions 1 and 3 we may conclude that there is a world w in which (a) most of our beliefs are false and (b) our utterances are correctly interpreted by an omniscient interpreter J. From (b) and assumption 2 we have it that (c) most of our beliefs are shared by J. Finally, from (a) and (c) via a proportional syllogism we may conclude

---

24 Note the nested modalities in this formulation. Quantifying over possible worlds, we would put it this way: given any world w in which a person S has a system of beliefs, there is a world w' in which S's beliefs are as before and an omniscient and infallible interpreter interprets his utterances. We need not suppose that $w' = w$; that is, we need not suppose that every world, or every world with believers, contains an omniscient interpreter. (Thus we may give a negative answer to the title question of Richard Foley and Richard Fumerton's 'Davidson's Theism?' *Philosophical Studies* **48** [1985] 83-9.) We *do* need to suppose, however, that the contents, truth values, and linguistic hook-ups of S's beliefs are the same in w' as in w; otherwise, we would not be capturing Davidson's claim that anyone's beliefs and utterances must be interpretable *such as they are.*

that at least one of *J*'s beliefs in *w* is false, thus contradicting the supposition that *J* was infallible. We have thereby reduced assumption 1 (or one of the assumptions, at any rate) to absurdity. (For a finer-grained analysis of this argument, see the Appendix.)

In the analog of Davidson's argument I wish to consider, instead of talking about the majority of all our beliefs, we talk about the entirety of a privileged subset of them, namely, those expressed by logical laws. The argument goes like this:

1. Assumption for reductio: it is possible that one of our logical laws is false (despite being so obvious as to be built into translation).

2. Necessarily: anyone who correctly interprets one of our laws must believe it himself.

3. Necessarily: anyone's utterances could be correctly interpreted by an omniscient and infallible interpreter.

From this trio as from the last, we may deduce that in some possible world an infallible interpreter believes a falsehood.[25] We thereby reduce to absurdity the assumption that what is built into translation (or interpretation) could be false.[26]

Reply: Faced with the original version of Davidson's argument, I think many would wish to question premise 2. Why *can't* one person

---

25 From 1 and 3, it follows that there is a world *w* in which a law *L* is false, but correctly interpreted by infallible interpreter *J*; adding 2, we have it that in *w J* believes *L*; so *J* believes a falsehood.

26 It may appear that this argument works only if logical laws enjoy necessity of acceptance. What if, as in Levin's reading of Quine, their only privilege is impossibility of denial? The answer is that we can still reach an absurdity, though not the same one as before. The contradiction is no longer that an infallible interpreter believes something false, but that an omniscient interpreter is debarred from believing something true (viz., that law *L* is false). Alternatively, the contradiction is that *J* knows *L* to be false (because *L* is false and *J* is omniscient), yet cannot believe *L* to be false (because *L* is undeniable).

correctly interpret the utterances of another as expressing beliefs that the interpreter thinks mostly false — especially if the interpreter has a good explanation of how the other's erroneous beliefs have come about?[27] In the adapted version, however, it is not open to us to challenge premise 2, since for the sake of argument we are now assuming with Quine that logic is a matter on which everyone must agree. Anyone who interprets one of our logical laws correctly (i.e., anyone who does not change the subject) must accept it.[28]

What, then, of premise 3? One might be inclined to dismiss this premise as gratuitous verificationism. Does it not amount to the assumption that there can be no facts about what people mean and believe unless these facts are knowable, and knowable to boot on the strength of the data and methods available to a radical interpreter? Such verificationism may well be involved in Davidson's original version of the argument. As far as I can see, however, it is not an essential ingredient in the adapted version. On closer inspection, it appears that the argument would work just as well if for premise 3 we substituted the following weaker version of it:

3'. Necessarily: anyone's utterances could be correctly interpreted by an interpreter who believed nothing false.

Here we are not insisting that facts about what people mean and believe be knowable on the basis of any circumscribed evidence base; we are only insisting on the possibility of true beliefs (on the part of a de facto infallible being) with regard to such facts. Any why should this not be possible? Why could it not happen, if only by luck, that

---

27 On this point, see Richard Grandy, 'Reference, Meaning, and Belief,' *The Journal of Philosophy* **70** (1973) 439-52.

28 If this point is not clear, consider the following syllogism: anyone who interprets our law L correctly takes it to mean what we mean by it (tautology); anyone who takes L to mean what we mean by it accepts it (Quine); therefore, anyone who interprets L correctly accepts it. If we substitute 'does not deny' for 'accepts,' the rest of the argument must proceed as in note 26, above.

someone managed to hit upon the correct interpretation of all of our sentences and believed nothing false in the bargain? — Well, it could not happen if, as now envisioned, among our sentences was a false law with the property that anyone who correctly interpreted it had to affirm it.

The weakened premise 3' is plausible, I must admit. Nonetheless, if we are already accepting 2, I believe we should reject 3'. For is it not clear that something is wrong with their joint result — that necessity of acceptance (by all who understand correctly) is a guarantee of truth? If so, we must declare, perhaps surprisingly, that some possible worlds are off limits to infallible interpreters.[29]

V

It is time to return to two matters left dangling above. The first is the salva veritate argument of section I. I ended that section with the thought that simply by appealing to the principle that synonyms are substitutable for one another salva veritate, we could arrive at the result that if two signs are synonymous, then for every true law involving one there is a corresponding true law involving the other. In other words: same meaning, same laws. But if we establish that, I asked, have we not thereby established the deviant logician's predicament?

We are now in a position to see that the answer is no. What is established by the salva veritate argument is 'same meaning, same laws *true*'; and from this we cannot derive 'same meaning, same laws *held* true.' So we have not shown by this argument that the deviant logician cannot deny (in the purely attitudinal sense) any of our laws.

It might be thought that we *can* show something much more interesting: that the deviant logician cannot deny any of our laws truly. But

---

29 Somewhat more accurately: there are worlds w such that worlds like w except for containing infallible interpreters are impossible.

this does not follow, either. For all that the salva veritate argument shows, it may be that we are the ones espousing false laws. This brings us to the second matter. At the beginning of section II, I presented (if only rhetorically) the following argument:

> If we say that a sign has the same meaning as our '&' only if it obeys the same laws as our '&,' are we not saying that the laws for '&' supervene on its meaning? And is this not to say in turn that those laws hold in virtue of what '&' means?

At the time we had not yet distinguished between saying that a sign that means what our '&' does must be *held* to obey the same laws and saying that such a sign must be *truly* governed by those laws. If we now say explicitly that any sign translatable as '&' must be *truly* governed by whatever laws truly govern our '&,' do we not have the makings of a good argument that logical laws, if true, are true in virtue of what they mean?

I think not. Though perhaps superficially more promising than the argument based on 'deny the doctrine, change the subject,' the foregoing argument breaks down on closer examination.

When we say that the truth of certain laws supervenes on their meanings (or the meanings of their constituent signs), all that the salva veritate principle entitles us to mean by this is the following: two laws that are alike in meaning in any world must also be alike in truth value in that world. (This is an instance of what Kim calls 'weak supervenience.'[30]) It does not follow that either law is true; nor, if they are true, does it follow that they are analytic in the sense of being true in virtue of what they mean. *Any* two sentences that are alike in meaning in a given world must share the same truth value in that world,[31] but that scarcely suffices to make either of them analytic. For example, if the

---

30 Jaegwon Kim, 'Concepts of Supervenience,' *Philosophy and Phenomenological Research* 45 (1984) 153-76

31 If it is held that indexical terms can be alike in meaning yet different in their reference, then what I just said must be restricted to indexical-free sentences.

sentence 'there are maple trees in Rhode Island' is true in a world w, no other sentence can mean in w what that sentence means without being true in w; but the sentence is synthetic nonetheless.

Suppose we were in a position to say that the truth of logical laws supervenes on their meanings in the following stronger sense: for any law L, if L is true, it has a meaning such that necessarily, any formula with that meaning would be true.[32] This thesis goes beyond the thesis of the last paragraph; it lets us say, given any law L that holds in our world, that no formula *in any other world* could mean what L does in our world without being true in that other world. I maintain that even if this were the case (as it may well be, despite not following from the salva veritate considerations), it would be a further question whether logical laws are, in any interesting sense, true solely in virtue of what they mean.

Here's why. Let C be any class of sentences all of which (in the actual world) express necessary truths, and let S be a member of C that expresses p. Any sentence S' in any world w that means in w what S does in the actual world will be true in w. That is because in w S' expresses p (we are assuming) and p, being necessary, holds in all worlds. *Whatever* the source of the necessity of p (logic, meanings, relations of universals, or what have you), it will be the case that any sentence in any world meaning what S does in the actual world is true. So the truth of sentences in C supervenes in the indicated stronger sense on their meanings. Yet it seems altogether too facile to say that those sentences are true *solely* in virtue of their meanings. Surely there is room to insist that the sentences in C are true in virtue of *two* things: (i) what they mean (i.e., which propositions they express) and (ii) the fact that the propositions they express are necessary.

Admittedly, there is also room to insist that the sentences in C are true in virtue of factor (i) alone. This could be on the ground that the only *contingent* fact one need cite in explaining why a sentence in C is true is that it has the meaning it does. The facts under (ii), being

---

32 This is not quite Kim's 'strong supervenience,' for which we would need to put another 'necessarily' in front of the entire thesis just stated.

necessary truths, could be regarded as redundant elements in any explanation.[33] Nonetheless, I hope this much will be clear: in saying that some of our sentences are in the foregoing sense true solely in virtue of what they mean, one goes no distance at all toward providing a conventionalist or meaning-based account of necessary truth. By convention we can indeed make certain sentences true — we can contrive, through definitions or otherwise, to have them express necessary truths. But the necessity of what is expressed is not made by our meanings.

To summarize the main points of this paper, the following two theses must be distinguished:

1. Anyone who means what we do by L must affirm (cannot deny) it.

2. Any sentence that means the same as our L must be true.

The Quinean dictum 'deny the doctrine and change the subject' only gives us Thesis 1. It does not imply that L is true by virtue of its meaning, because it does not imply that L is true at all. Thesis 2, on the other hand, does imply that L is true; and if you like, it even implies that L is true solely in virtue of what it means. But in just the same sense, any sentence whatsoever that expresses a necessary truth is true solely in virtue of what it means. This result can be accepted by the hardiest of believers in the synthetic a priori.[34]

---

33 Two modal assumptions come into play here: (1) what is necessary is necessarily necessary, and (2) if p and q together entail r and q is necessary, then p by itself entails r.

34 I wish to thank Felicia Ackerman, Anthony Appiah, Carl Posy, Ernest Sosa, and two referees for helpful comments and criticisms.

Appendix

According to Davidson, correctly interpreting someone else as being mostly mistaken is impossible — that is one version of his Principle of Charity. In the text, I rendered this principle as (2): *J* correctly interprets *S* only if most of the beliefs *S* holds are beliefs *J* holds, too. But there is also another way of taking the principle, namely, as (2'): *J* correctly interprets *S* only if most of the beliefs *J* attributes to *S* are beliefs *J* holds, too. (2') is probably a better rendition of the principle. After all, I do not 'interpret *S* as mistaken' simply because I reject what he *in fact* believes; I interpret him as mistaken only if I reject what I *take him* to believe. How should the omniscient interpreter argument proceed if the Principle of Charity is taken as (2') rather than (2)?

One possible line of reasoning is the following. From (1) and (3) we conclude as before that there is a world *w* in which (a) most of *S*'s beliefs are false and (b) *S* is correctly interpreted by omniscient *J*. From the new premise (2') and (b) we now infer not (c), but (c'): most of the things *J* takes *S* to believe are things *J* believes himself. Somehow or other we must now try to reach (c), that most of the things *S* in fact believes are things *J* believes himself. We could try adding the premise (d), that most (or even all) of the things *S* believes are things that *J* takes *S* to believe. We might then conclude from (c') and (d) to the original (c): most of the things *S* believes are things *J* believes himself. From (c) and (a) we could then conclude, as in the text, that *J* has at least one false belief.

The trouble with this line of reasoning is that (c) does not follow from (c') and (d). The pattern of argument 'All (or most) Fs are Gs, most Gs are Hs, therefore most Fs are Hs' is simply invalid, as one may see by considering the following instance of it: all elephants are living things, most living things are microorganisms, therefore most elephants are microorganisms.

A valid argument may perhaps be obtained if we remember that Davidson's omniscient interpreter is also infallible. That is, *J* takes *S* to believe all *and only* the things *S* does in fact believe, so that the class $\{p:SBp\}$ = the class $\{p:JBSBp\}$. We may now reason as follows. By assumption (1) (the assumption of massive error), we have it that most members of $\{p:SBp\}$ are false. By assumption (2') (the revised Principle of charity), we have it that most members of {p:$JBSBp$} are also members of {p:JBp}. By this and the class identity assumption, we have it that most members of {p:SBp} are members of {p:JBp}. Therefore (by proportional syllogism) at least one member of {p:JBp} is false. That contradicts J's infallibility and completes the reductio.

I think it rather doubtful, however, that the foregoing argument can be what Davidson intended. I take it that J's omniscience and infallibility are not supposed to extend to S's beliefs directly, but only to the nonsemantic and nonintentional facts about the world. (Otherwise, there would be no need for J to use Davidson's methods of interpretation.) We can therefore affirm the class identity used above, {p:SBp} = {p:$JBSBp$}, only if we know that the method of radical interpretation, when applied to correct and comprehensive data, is guaranteed to produce uniquely correct results. I doubt that Davidson believes that all interpreters who are omniscient in his sense must reach the same interpretations from the same data.

CANADIAN JOURNAL OF PHILOSOPHY
Supplementary Volume 18

Analyticity and the A Priori

ALBERT CASULLO

The analytic/synthetic distinction has played a central role in discussions of a priori knowledge throughout the twentieth century. One of the primary reasons for the prominence of this distinction is the widespread influence of the tradition of logical empiricism which endorsed the following principles:

(LE1) All analytic propositions are knowable a priori[1]

and

(LE2) All propositions knowable a priori are analytic.

---

1 This formulation of (LE1) might be regarded as implausible since it entails that *all* analytic propositions are knowable. Some have claimed, for example, that it is possible that some analytic propositions are too complex for human comprehension and, hence, not knowable. Such claims raise issues about how to understand the modality in (LE1) which I will not address in this paper. I propose to grant that all analytic propositions are knowable and to focus exclusively on the issue of whether there is any good reason to suppose that they are knowable *a priori*. If one finds this concession troubling, one can understand the subject of (LE1) to involve an implicit restriction to *knowable* analytic propositions. The same point applies to the related principles (LE4) and (LE1*).

Albert Casullo

Hence, proponents of the a priori often argue in support of the contention that the propositions of a particular discipline, say mathematics or logic, are knowable a priori by arguing that it consists solely of analytic propositions. On the other hand, detractors of the a priori often reject such knowledge on the grounds that the analytic/synthetic distinction is not cogent. My primary goal in this paper is to challenge the prevalent acceptance of (LE1).[2]

I Preliminary Clarifications and Outline of the Argument

Discussion of (LE1) is complicated by the fact that there is no fully articulated and generally accepted characterization of either of its key concepts. Hence, some initial clarification is necessary. The distinction between a priori and a posteriori knowledge is *epistemic*. Although it is notoriously difficult to provide a philosophically adequate account of the distinction, two points are uncontroversial: (a) that the *basis* of the distinction is the type of *justification* one has, or could have, for believing a proposition; and (b) that one's justification for believing a proposition is a priori just in case it is independent of experiential evidence. The problems arise when one attempts to articulate precisely the relevant senses of 'independent' and 'experiential.'[3] For our purposes, the rough characterization provided by (b) is sufficient.

---

2 Hilary Putnam, in 'There Is At Least One A Priori Truth,' in *Philosophical Papers*, Vol. 3 (Cambridge: Cambridge University Press 1983), and Philip Kitcher, in *The Nature of Mathematical Knowledge* (Oxford: Oxford University Press 1983), ch. 4, both challenge (LE1) on the grounds that (1) if *p* is knowable a priori then *p* is rationally unrevisable, and (2) analytic propositions are rationally revisable. I do not find this challenge compelling since (1) is extremely implausible. For a defense of this claim, see my 'Revisability, Reliabilism, and A Priori Knowledge,' *Philosophy and Phenomenological Research* **49** (1988) 187-213.

3 For a discussion of these problems, see A. Casullo, 'A Priori/A Posteriori,' in J. Dancy and E. Sosa, eds., *A Companion to Epistemology* (Oxford: Basil Blackwell forthcoming).

The distinction between analytic and synthetic propositions, however, is *not* epistemic but *semantic*. This distinction is more difficult to characterize in a noncontroversial manner since there are numerous ostensibly different characterizations available in the literature. Anthony Quinton, for example, has isolated four different senses of this term which have figured in recent discussions:

(i) An analytic statement is one true in virtue of the meanings of the terms it contains;

(ii) An analytic statement is an instance of the law of identity whose denial is an explicit contradiction;

(iii) An analytic statement is one that is true in virtue of the conventions of language;

(iv) An analytic statement is a truth of logic or reducible to one with the help of definitions.[4]

What is common to all of these accounts is the central role, either implicit or explicit, of semantic notions such as linguistic convention, definition, or meaning.

In assessing (LE1) and (LE2), two points are relevant. Since the concept of a priori knowledge is *epistemic* while the concept of analyticity is *semantic*, it cannot be assumed, without further argument, that they are coextensive or connected in some other significant manner.[5]

---

4 Anthony Quinton, 'The A Priori and the Analytic,' in R.C. Sleigh, Jr., ed., *Necessary Truth* (Englewood Cliffs, NJ: Prentice-Hall 1972), 90-1. For a lucid and more comprehensive discussion of this concept, see Panayot Butchvarov, *The Concept of Knowledge* (Evanston: Northwestern University Press 1970), ch. 2.

5 Saul Kripke, in *Naming and Necessity* (Cambridge: Harvard University Press 1980) and 'Identity and Necessity,' in M.K. Munitz, ed., *Identity and Individuation* (New York: New York University Press 1971), makes a similar point with respect to the concepts of a priori knowledge and necessary truth. For a critical discussion of Kripke's view on the relationship between the a priori and the necessary, see my 'Kripke on the A Priori and the Necessary,' *Analysis* **37** (1977) 152-9,

Furthermore, any argument offered in support of (LE1) or (LE2) must take as its starting point a characterization of the a priori/a posteriori distinction which is *epistemic* and a characterization of the analytic/synthetic distinction which is *semantic*. To offer an argument which either characterizes the a priori in terms of analyticity or characterizes analyticity in terms of the a priori is to trivialize the principle being defended.[6]

Proponents of logical empiricism typically focused their efforts on rejecting the synthetic a priori. They argued either that the alleged examples of such propositions are analytic or that they are knowable only a posteriori. Such arguments, if cogent, would be sufficient to reject the contention of their rationalist opponents and to support (LE2). They would not, however, be sufficient to support (LE1). But since (LE1) was accepted by their rationalist opponents, it was not necessary to address it in resolving their dispute. Hence, (LE1) was generally accepted without argument.

My primary goal is to show that their acceptance of (LE1) was a mistake and, furthermore, that the reason why it was a mistake can be found in the work of two of the movement's leading figures. I proceed by first examining the views of Carl Hempel and A.J. Ayer regarding the status of mathematics.[7] These authors are significant because, in addition to arguing for the *semantic* thesis

---

reprinted in P. Moser, ed., *A Priori Knowledge* (Oxford: Oxford University Press 1987). Some related issues are discussed in my 'Actuality and the A Priori,' *Australasian Journal of Philosophy* **66** (1988) 390-402.

6 It is somewhat ironic that in *Naming and Necessity*, Kripke makes it a matter of stipulation that '... an analytic statement is, in some sense, true by virtue of its meaning and true in all possible worlds by virtue of its meaning. Then something which is analytically true will be both necessary and a priori' (39). Clearly, on this account, it is trivially true that all analytic statements are necessary. It is not clear, however, why Kripke thinks that it follows from this stipulation that analytic statements are a priori.

7 A.J. Ayer, *Language, Truth and Logic*, 2nd ed., (London: Gollancz 1946), ch. 4; and Carl Hempel, 'On the Nature of Mathematical Truth,' in R.C. Sleigh, Jr., ed., *Necessary Truth*

(LE3) All mathematical propositions are analytic

they also argue explicitly for the *epistemic* thesis

(LE4) All mathematical propositions are knowable only a priori.

Hence, they are defending a close relative of (LE1)

(LE1*) All mathematical analytic propositions are knowable only a priori.

(LE1*) is both stronger and weaker than (LE1). It is weaker in that it makes a claim about all *mathematical* analytic propositions rather than *all* analytic propositions. It is stronger in that it precludes the possibility that such propositions are knowable a posteriori as well as a priori. My examination of logical empiricism falls into two parts. In sections II and III, I argue that the primary argument offered by Hempel and Ayer in support of (LE4) fails. In sections IV, V, and VI, I maintain that this argument can be reformulated to show that the *semantic* thesis (LE3) does not support the *weak epistemic* thesis that mathematical propositions are *knowable* a priori, let alone the *stronger epistemic* thesis (LE4). Hence, the logical empiricists' treatment of mathematics undermines their acceptance of (LE1). Finally, in section VII, I go on to examine the arguments of several later writers who explicitly defend (LE1). There I show that each attempt ultimately trivializes the principle because it essentially involves a *nonepistemic* characterization of the a priori. My conclusion is that although (LE1) is generally accepted, convincing arguments in support of it are difficult to come by.

II The Rejection of Inductivism: The Irrefutability Argument

A.J. Ayer and Carl Hempel both attempt to establish that mathematical propositions are analytic and knowable only a priori. They are, in effect, defending (LE1*). Neither Ayer nor Hempel employs a *direct* argument in support of (LE1*). A *direct* argument for (LE1*) utilizes the claim that mathematical propositions are analytic as a *premise* in support of the conclusion that mathematical propositions are knowable a priori. Such an argument shows that the a priority of mathematics is a *consequence* of its analyticity. Instead, both Ayer and Hempel offer an *indirect* argument for (LE1*). An *indirect* argument for (LE1*) consists of two independent arguments, one which establishes that mathematical propositions are knowable only a priori and one which establishes that mathematical propositions are analytic. The arguments are independent in the sense that neither uses the conclusion of the other as a premise.

The structure of Ayer's and Hempel's argument can be put as follows:

(1) Mathematical skepticism is false.

(2) Mathematical propositions are knowable either a priori or a posteriori.[8]

(3) No mathematical proposition can be known on the basis of experience.

(4) Therefore, all mathematical propositions are knowable only a priori.

(5) All mathematical propositions are analytic.

---

8 Hempel entertains a third option, that mathematical propositions require no justification because they are self-evident, which he quickly rejects as too subjective. He may be viewing this option as a version of rationalism.

(LE1*) Therefore, all mathematical analytic propositions are knowable only a priori.

Several points are worth noting about this argument. First, both Hempel and Ayer take for granted that most individuals possess at least some mathematical knowledge. Mathematical skepticism is not seriously considered. Furthermore, neither endorses a mitigated skepticism which restricts such knowledge to specialists with some advanced training in mathematics or logic. Second, both Hempel and Ayer support (3) by arguing against *pure inductivist* accounts of mathematical knowledge. Pure inductivism maintains that *all* mathematical knowledge is acquired by inductive generalization from experienced cases. Neither, however, considers a *pure theoretical* account which maintains all knowledge of mathematical propositions is acquired in a manner analogous to knowledge of the more theoretical propositions of empirical science. Neither considers a *hybrid empiricist* account on which some mathematical propositions are known by induction from experienced cases while others are known abductively on the basis of those known inductively. Furthermore, in supporting (3), neither considers the possibility that mathematical propositions are knowable on the basis of the testimony of experts or some other external reliable source such as a computing machine. They are concerned exclusively with *primary* mathematical knowledge, i.e., mathematical knowledge whose justification does not depend on having justified mathematical beliefs from some *other* source. They would not have regarded mathematical knowledge obtained from a reliable external source as primary since they would have taken for granted that (1) in order to know a mathematical proposition on the basis of an external source, one must be justified in believing that the source is reliable; (2) in order to be justified in believing that the source is reliable, one must have inductive justification that its pronouncements are generally true; but (3) in order to have inductive justification that its pronouncements are generally true, one must have justified mathematical beliefs from a different source. Finally, Ayer and Hempel differ in their accounts of the analyticity of mathematics and, as a result, offer different arguments in support of (5). Hempel takes mathematics to be analytic in Quinton's sense (iv) and defends a version of logicism. Ayer, however, takes mathematics to be analytic in Quinton's sense (iii) and defends a version of conventionalism.

In this and the subsequent section of the paper, I assess the argument Ayer and Hempel offer in support of (4). Since I have no disagreement with (1) and view (2) as uncontroversial, the assessment focuses on (3). Both offer virtually the same argument against inductivism. Hence, I consider here only Hempel's version. My primary goal is to show that an inductivist account of mathematical knowledge can be articulated in a manner which survives their criticism.

Hempel presents the following argument in support of (3):

> From a hypothesis which is empirical in character — such as, for example, Newton's law of gravitation — it is possible to derive predictions to the effect that under certain specified conditions certain specified observable phenomena will occur. The actual occurrence of these phenomena constitutes confirming evidence, their non-occurrence disconfirming evidence for the hypothesis. It follows in particular that an empirical hypothesis is theoretically disconfirmable; that is, it is possible to indicate what kind of evidence if actually encountered, would disconfirm the hypothesis. In the light of this remark, consider now a simple "hypothesis" from arithmetic: 3 + 2 = 5. If this is actually an empirical generalization of past experiences, then it must be possible to state what kind of evidence would oblige us to concede the hypothesis was not generally true after all.[9]

Two interesting points emerge in this passage. First of all, Hempel begins by pointing out that if inductivism is true then it should be possible to state observable phenomena that constitute *confirming* evidence for mathematical propositions as well as observable phenomena that constitute *disconfirming* evidence. On the face of it, the inductivist can provide a list of confirming instances for the mathematical proposition '3 + 2 = 5.' There are many examples from every-

---

9 Hempel, 35-6. See Ayer, 75-6, for a similar argument. Ayer's argument is critically evaluated in my 'Necessity, Certainty, and the A Priori,' *Canadian Journal of Philosophy* **18** (1988) 43-66.

day experience where one has counted a group of objects which totaled two, a second group which totaled three, combined the two groups, recounted, and discovered that they totaled five. One may think that such experiences do not constitute *genuine* confirming evidence for a mathematical proposition. But one cannot dismiss them as providing *only apparent* confirming evidence without offering an argument. To do so would beg the question against the inductivist. Hempel, however, does not address the issue of apparent experiential *confirming* evidence for mathematical propositions. Instead, his discussion focuses exclusively on the issue of apparent *disconfirming* experiential evidence for such propositions. Second, Hempel's discussion of apparent disconfirming experiential evidence for mathematical propositions does not include a consideration of the most obvious cases of such disconfirmation. For example, he does not consider cases such as counting two apples, counting two pears, and, finally, counting four pieces of fruit as disconfirming the proposition '2 + 2 = 5.' More generally, he does not consider the wealth of cases where experience appears to provide disconfirming evidence for mathematical propositions which *we reject as false*. Instead, he focuses exclusively on the question of whether experiential evidence could *disconfirm* a mathematical proposition such as '2 + 3 = 5' which *we accept as true*. On the basis of a negative answer to this question he draws the conclusion that experience does not *confirm any* mathematical propositions. Consequently, if we are to understand Hempel's rejection of inductivism, two issues need to be addressed: (1) On what grounds does he discount the experiential evidence which inductivists claim provides *genuine* confirmation for the mathematical propositions which we accept as true as providing *only apparent* confirmation? (2) How does he move from the claim that experience cannot confirm those mathematical propositions which *we accept as true* to the more general claim that experience cannot confirm *any* mathematical propositions?

I want to suggest that there are two underlying principles involved in this argument against inductivism. The first is relevant to distinguishing between *genuine* as opposed to *only apparent* confirming evidence. Inductivists typically support their position by providing examples of experiential evidence which yield results in accordance with our accepted mathematical beliefs. Since these results accord with our accepted beliefs, the conclusion is drawn that they are evidentially relevant to our acceptance of these propositions. Hempel's gambit is to maintain that the fact that some experiences yield results which accord with our accepted mathematical beliefs is not sufficient to establish that such experiences confirm those beliefs. In order to sustain this gambit it is necessary to introduce a means of distinguishing between experiences which genuinely confirm and those which do not.

Hempel's proposal is to focus attention on the connection between confirming and disconfirming evidence for a proposition and to utilize that connection to provide a *necessary* condition of *genuine* confirming evidence. The principle can be stated as follows:

(GCE) Evidence of type E (genuinely) confirms a mathematical proposition that p only if evidence of type E can disconfirm the proposition that p.

The plausibility of (GCE) can be seen by considering the position of one who rejects it. According to the inductivist, a mathematical proposition, such as that $2 + 3 = 5$, is a general proposition which can be confirmed by the observation of instances of it. Among the confirming instances are cases where one counts a group of objects which is a combination of two groups of objects, one of which consists of two objects and the other of which consists of three objects, and arrives at the result that it consists of five objects. Now suppose that the inductivist rejects (GCE) and maintains that alternative results, such as arriving at the result that such a group consists of four objects, do *not* disconfirm that $2 + 3 = 5$. Such an inductivist must also reject the following necessary condition of correct inductive reasoning: infer that all As are B only if no observed A has been determined to lack B. Since rejecting this condition is completely implausible, the inductivist is not in a position to reject (GCE).[10]

———————

10 Analogous considerations establish the implausibility of rejecting (GCE) for other types of evidence. For example, if a proof of a mathematical proposition

(GCE) can now be conjoined with Hempel's claim that experience cannot disconfirm the 'hypothesis' that 2 + 3 = 5 to establish that experiential evidence does not *genuinely* confirm such propositions:

(1') Experiential evidence cannot disconfirm any mathematical proposition which is accepted as true.

(2') If experiential evidence cannot disconfirm a mathematical proposition then it cannot confirm such a proposition.

(3') Therefore, experiential evidence cannot confirm any mathematical proposition which is accepted as true.

This argument, which I shall call the *Irrefutability Argument* (IA), provides the core of Hempel's rejection of inductivism.

IA, however, does not yet have the requisite generality sought by Hempel. For, ideally, he would like to establish

(4') Therefore, experiential evidence cannot confirm *any* mathematical proposition.

Before turning to the question of whether the conclusion can be generalized, let us first note that IA, as it stands, is sufficient to blunt the standard argument provided by inductivists in support of their position. For that argument consists in the observation that numerous experiences yield results in conformity with our accepted mathematical beliefs. IA establishes that this observation is *not* sufficient to show that such experiences confirm accepted mathematical propositions. Returning to the question of whether (3') can

---

that *p* from a certain set of axioms confirms that *p*, it would be implausible to maintain that a proof of not-*p* from the same set of axioms does *not* disconfirm that *p*. Similarly, if it is maintained that one's seeming to remember that one last revised this paper on Thursday confirms the proposition that one last revised this paper on Thursday, it would be implausible to also maintain that one's seeming to remember that one last revised this paper on Wednesday does *not* disconfirm that proposition.

be generalized, there is a plausible epistemic principle which sanctions the inference from (3') to (4'):

(EU) If evidence of type *E* is alleged to confirm propositions of type *T*, then if *p* is a proposition of type *T* which does not differ in any epistemically relevant way from other propositions of type *T* and there is evidence of type *E* for *p* and that evidence does *not* confirm p, then evidence of type *E* does not confirm *any* proposition of type *T*.

(EU) is, in effect, a principle of *evidential universalizability*. If a type of evidence, say perceptual, is alleged to confirm a type of proposition, say medium-sized physical object, then it confirms *all* propositions of that type for which such evidence is forthcoming. One cannot maintain, for example, that perceiving physical object O_1 in circumstances *C* confirms the proposition 'O_1 is present before me,' but perceiving physical object O_2 in circumstances *C* does *not* confirm the proposition 'O_2 is present before me,' without some principled account of the difference between the two cases. Similarly, it would be blatantly ad hoc for the inductivist to maintain that, although available experiential evidence cannot confirm accepted mathematical propositions, such as that $2 + 3 = 5$, it can confirm others without providing some account of the epistemically relevant differences between the two cases. Given that no plausible account of such differences appears to be forthcoming, Hempel's observations about disconfirmation together with (GCE) and (EU) are sufficient to establish (4').

III The Inductivist Rejoinder to the Irrefutability Argument

Let us now turn to the evaluation of Hempel's case against inductivism. Given the plausibility of (EU), the case stands or falls with the soundness of IA. IA is clearly valid and we have also provided support for (2'). The only remaining question is whether (1') can be sustained. Hempel offers the following defense of (1'):

> We place some microbes on a slide, putting down first three of them and then another two. Afterwards we count all the microbes to test whether in this instance 3 and 2 actually added up to 5. Suppose now that we counted 6 microbes altogether. Would we consider this as an empirical disconfirmation of the given

proposition, or at least as a proof that it does not apply to microbes? Clearly not; rather, we would assume we had made a mistake in counting or that one of the microbes had split in two between the first and the second count.[11]

This defense is not convincing because it is based on a very weak case of apparent experiential disconfirmation. The case is weak for several reasons: (1) it does not take into account whether there are confirming instances of the proposition in question; (2) it involves only a single disconfirming instance of the proposition; and (3) the hypotheses which are invoked to explain away the apparent disconfirming instance are not subjected to independent empirical test. The case would be considerably stronger if the following revisions were made: (1) the number of apparent disconfirming instances is increased so that it is very large relative to the number of confirming instances; and (2) the hypotheses which are invoked to explain away the apparent disconfirming instances are subjected to independent investigation and found to be unsupported. Given these revisions, the proponent of IA can continue to endorse (1') only at the expense of either divorcing mathematics from its empirical applications or holding empirical beliefs which are at odds with the available evidence.

This point can be brought out more clearly by considering the following set of propositions:

(a) The mathematical proposition that $2 + 3 = 5$ is applicable to microbes;

(b) The empirical procedure of counting microbes provides *only apparent* disconfirming evidence for the proposition that $2 + 3 = 5$;

(c) The results of independent empirical investigation do not support the auxiliary hypotheses introduced to explain away the disconfirming evidence as only apparent.

---

11 Hempel, 36. Ayer offers a similar defense.

Although (c) does not entail not-(b), it does provide strong grounds for rejecting (b). Clearly, the proponent of IA cannot simply assert (b). For to simply assert (b) without independent support is to beg the question against the inductivist. But (c) establishes that the independent reasons offered in support of (b) are unfounded. Hence, (b) must be rejected. The proponent of IA, however, cannot accept both (a) and not-(b). For if the disconfirming evidence provided by the procedure of counting microbes is *not* merely apparent then it is genuine. So only two alternatives remain: either (i) reject (a) and hold that mathematics is not applicable to microbes or (ii) continue to hold (b) despite (c). Neither alternative is palatable. For (i) effectively divorces mathematics from its empirical applications, while (ii) puts one in a position of holding a belief which is counter to one's available evidence. The most plausible alternative is to accept (a) and reject (b).[12] But to reject (b) is to reject premise (1') of IA. Hence, the argument against inductivism falls short of its mark.

One might attempt to defend Hempel at this point by maintaining that he has a stronger argument for (1') which has been overlooked. For the passage quoted above continues in the following manner:

> But under no circumstances could the phenomenon just described invalidate the arithmetical proposition in question; for the latter asserts nothing whatever about the behavior of microbes; it merely states that any set consisting of 3 + 2 objects may also be said to consist of 5 objects. And this is so because the symbols "3 + 2" and "5" denote the same number: They are synonymous by virtue of the fact that the symbols "2," "3," "5," and "+" are *defined* (or tacitly understood) in such a way that the above identity holds as a consequence of the meaning attached to the concepts involved in it.[13]

12 This claim is defended in more detail in my 'Necessity, Certainty, and the A Priori.'

13 Hempel, 36. Mark Steiner, in 'Mathematics, Explanation, and Scientific Knowledge,' *Nous* **12** (1975) 17-28, defends the view that all arithmetical identities follow from stipulations and maintains that any apparent empirical disconfirmation of such an identity statement should be attributed to '... the failure of a certain physical procedure to determine the number in the union of two disjoint sets' (25). He does not, however, consider the point stressed in the text that claims

This passage is difficult to interpret but the structure of the argument appears to be as follows:

(6) The identity '2 + 3 = 5' holds as a consequence of the meaning attached to the symbols involved in it.

(7) Therefore, '2 + 3 = 5' asserts nothing whatever about the behavior of microbes.

(8) Therefore, the observation of microbes cannot invalidate the arithmetical proposition that 2 + 3 = 5.

(8), of course, provides direct support for (1').

This proposed defense is not very promising for two reasons. First, although Hempel endorses (7), he also endorses

(a) The mathematical proposition that 2 + 3 = 5 is applicable to microbes.

What is the relationship between (7) and (a)? Either not-(7) is a logically necessary condition of (a) or it is not. In other words, either it is a logically necessary condition of the *applicability* of mathematics to microbes that mathematical propositions *assert something* about microbes or it is not. If it is, then Hempel can accept (7) only at the expense of rejecting (a). If it is not, then he can consistently accept *both* (7) and (a). But can he accept both (a) and (8)? If it is granted that mathematical propositions are applicable to microbes, then in order to maintain that the observation of microbes cannot invalidate that 2 + 3 = 5, he must also endorse

_____

to the effect that certain empirical procedures fail to determine the number of objects in a set are themselves subject to empirical confirmation or disconfirmation.

(b) The empirical procedure of counting microbes provides *only apparent* disconfirming evidence for the proposition that $2 + 3 = 5$.

Hence, the proposed defense leaves Hempel faced with the same dilemma posed earlier: either hold that mathematics is not applicable to microbes, or continue to endorse (b) despite evidence to the contrary.

Second, the proposed defense would significantly alter the structure of the logical empiricist argument in support of (LE1*). That argument, as originally formulated (see above), is an *indirect* argument since it does not utilize the *semantic* thesis that mathematical propositions are analytic to support the *epistemic* thesis that mathematical propositions are knowable only a priori. But (6), which is the leading premise of the proposed defense, is an alternative formulation of the *semantic* thesis that '$2 + 3 = 5$' is an analytic proposition. Hence, to invoke (6) in support of (1') is to invoke the *semantic* thesis that mathematical propositions are analytic to support the *epistemic* thesis that mathematical propositions are knowable only a priori. This, in effect, is to attribute to the logical empiricists a *direct* argument for (LE1*) and would require the following reformulation of their argument:

(5) All mathematical propositions are analytic.

(4) Therefore, all mathematical propositions are knowable only a priori.

(LE1*) Therefore, all mathematical analytic propositions are knowable only a priori.

The reformulated argument, however, is *circular* unless it can be shown that (5) supports (4) without invoking (LE1*).

IV The Rejection of the Epistemic Import of Logicism: The New Irrefutability Argument

Section III established two main conclusions: (1) that the *indirect* argument for (LE1*) fails because IA does not establish that mathematical propositions are knowable only a priori; and (2) that the *direct* argument for (LE1*) is circular in the absence of an independent argument which shows that (5) supports (4). These two results, however, do *not* show that (5) does *not* support (4). Therefore, it will be argued in Sections IV, V, and VI that a successful demonstration of the analyticity of mathematics would *not* support the *weak* epistemic thesis that mathematical propositions are knowable a priori, let alone the *stronger* epistemic thesis that they are knowable *only* a priori.

Assessing the epistemic significance of a successful demonstration of the analyticity of mathematics is complicated by the fact that proponents of the position employ differing accounts of analyticity. Hempel's account is scrutinized in Section IV and V; Ayer's account is scrutinized in Section VI. In both cases, it is argued that considerations similar to those articulated in IA can be used to show that a successful demonstration of the analyticity of mathematics would be of little epistemic significance. Section VII examines some general arguments which purport to establish a significant connection between the a priori and the analytic. Here it is shown that these arguments trivialize the thesis being defended.

Hempel's defense of the analyticity of mathematics consists in an endorsement of logicism. The goal of logicism was to (1) devise a logical language sufficiently rich to represent all mathematical propositions; (2) define the primitive mathematical concepts in terms of the logical concepts; and (3) demonstrate that the transcribed mathematical propositions can be derived from the primitive logical principles. There are important technical problems associated with each of these goals. The first raises the question of the demarcation of logic and the status of principles such as the axiom of infinity and the axiom of choice.[14] The second raises questions about the sorts of definitions which are permissible and, in particular, the permissibility of impre-

---

14 For a discussion of these issues, see W.V. Quine, *Philosophy of Logic* (Englewood Cliffs, NJ: Prentice-Hall 1970), ch. 5; Hilary Putnam, 'Philosophy of Logic,' sect. III, in *Philosophical Papers, Vol. II* (Cambridge: Cambridge University Press 1979); and Mark Steiner, *Mathematical Knowledge* (Ithaca: Cornell University Press 1975), ch. 2.

dicative definitions.[15] Finally, the third runs up against the Gödel incompleteness proof.[16] For our purposes, we will skip over these technical difficulties, not because they are unimportant, but because they detract from the primary issue at stake: would the success of the logicist program offer any support for the epistemic thesis that mathematical knowledge is a priori?

There are two reasons for thinking that it would not. The first is the familiar point that logicism does not offer an account of mathematical knowledge. At best, it reduces the epistemology of mathematics to the epistemology of logic. But the very same issue which we raised with respect to mathematical knowledge arises at the level of logical knowledge: is there any compelling reason to believe that knowledge of logical principles is a priori? In the absence of such a reason, the fact that one can derive mathematical propositions from logical principles provides little support for the thesis that mathematical knowledge is a priori.

Clearly, a proponent of logicism cannot respond that such knowledge is a priori because logical principles are analytic in sense (iv) without trivializing the position. For, by (iv), it is simply true by stipulation that logical truths are analytic. Hence, a substantive defense of the claim that logical truths are a priori because analytic requires that a sense of the term 'analytic' other than (iv) be adopted and that it be shown that propositions which are analytic in this sense are knowable a priori. This project falls outside the scope of the logicist program. Hence, logicism can establish that mathematical knowledge is a priori only if it can offer some independent argument for the claim that logical truths are knowable a priori.[17]

---

15 For a discussion of this issue, see Charles Parsons, 'Frege's Theory of Number,' in Max Black, ed., *Philosophy in America* (Ithaca: Cornell University Press 1965); and Steiner, ch. 1.

16 See Hempel, 41, for a discussion of this issue.

17 It might be thought that since some proponents of logicism held that logical truths are constitutive of every linguistic framework or, more generally, all rational thought, the question of their justification does not arise. But this is a

The second reason is more fundamental and is directed at the basic conception of the program. The logicist claims that the derivation of an accepted mathematical proposition from some basic logical principles using suitable derivation rules and definitions provides confirmation or, to use Hempel's expression, validation of that proposition. Hence, the logicists' strategy for establishing that logicist derivations confirm mathematical propositions exactly parallels the inductivists' strategy for establishing that experiential evidence confirms mathematical propositions. Both attempt to show that their preferred account of confirmation yields results which are in accord with our accepted mathematical beliefs. But, as we saw earlier, Hempel is not willing to concede that merely showing that a particular account of evidence yields results which accord with our accepted beliefs is sufficient to establish that the evidence cited in the account is *genuine* as opposed to *merely apparent* confirming evidence. Principle (GCE) is introduced to identify merely apparent confirming evidence. It will now be argued that (GCE) can be marshalled to establish that logicist derivations do *not* provide genuine confirming evidence for mathematical propositions.

The connection between mathematics and logic is provided by the logicist definitions of mathematical concepts. Unfortunately, proponents of logicism are not fully explicit about the conditions which a satisfactory definition of a mathematical concept must satisfy. Furthermore, the rudimentary remarks on this issue offered by different proponents of logicism often are at odds with one another. This considerably complicates the project of providing a conclusive assessment of the epistemic implications of logicism. Nevertheless, it is the role of such definitions and, in particular, the criteria of adequacy for a proposed logicist definition which is the focus of our investigation.

_____

mistake. Even if one of these accounts is correct, a person still could believe a logical truth for *bad reasons* and, hence, *not* be justified in holding that belief. For example, if p is a logical truth but my only reason for believing that p is the testimony of an individual whom I know to be unreliable on such matters, then I am not justified in believing that p.

Albert Casullo

Hempel is explicit about one feature of the definitions he favors. They are not purely stipulative but provide an analysis of our customary mathematical concepts. An adequate definition of a mathematical term must capture the *customary meaning* of that term:

> The Peano system permits of many different interpretations, whereas in everyday as well as in scientific language, we attach one specific meaning to the concepts of arithmetic. Thus, for example, in scientific and in everyday discourse, the concept 2 is understood in such a way that from the statement "Mr. Brown as well as Mr. Cope, but no one else is in the office, and Mr. Brown is not the same person as Mr. Cope," the conclusion "Exactly two persons are in the office" may be validly inferred. But the stipulations laid down in Peano's system for the natural numbers, and for the number 2 in particular, do not enable us to draw this conclusion; they do not "implicitly determine" the customary meaning of the concept 2 or of the other arithmetical concepts.[18]

These remarks are not entirely satisfactory for they do not provide a general statement of the necessary and sufficient conditions an interpretation of the Peano axioms must satisfy in order to capture the customary meaning of mathematical terms.

Even if we restrict attention to the particular example cited by Hempel, we have, at best, a necessary but not a sufficient condition for the customary meaning of the term 'two.' For example, the concept designated by the term 'two' in everyday discourse in such that

(9) There are exactly two people in the office

entails

(10) There is a person x and a person y such that x and y are in the office, x is not identical with y, and no one else is in the office

but not

---

18 Hempel, 42-3

(11) Mr. Brown as well as Mr. Cope, but no one else is in the office, and Mr. Brown is not the same person as Mr. Cope

and (10), as well as (11), entails (9). Furthermore, the concept designated by the term 'two' is such that the following propositions are true:

(12) Every water molecule contains two hydrogen atoms;

(13) Every positive real number has exactly two real square roots;

and the following are false:

(14) There are two primary colors;

(15) Every natural number is the sum of two distinct prime numbers.

But surely any adequate definition of the customary concept *two* must preserve the truth value of these propositions.

This suggests the following *necessary* condition for a logicist definition to capture the customary meaning of a mathematical term:

(CM) All propositions involving a customary mathematical concept which are accepted as true (false) remain true (false) when the concept is replaced by the proposed definition.

This condition has the virtue of eliminating interpretations of the Peano axioms such as defining '0' as the origin of a ray and the remaining numerals as successive points on the ray or defining '0' as 10 and the remaining numerals as successors of 10. Furthermore, any definition which does not satisfy this condition will fail to preserve the mutual entailment of propositions such as (9) and (10). It might be suggested that although this is a plausible *necessary* condition, it is not *sufficient* since it does not insure that the definition captures what people have in mind when they use mathematical concepts. Hempel, however, explicitly rejects this condition on the grounds that he is concerned with the logical rather than psychological sense of meaning.[19] Hence, it appears that for Hempel (CM) is both necessary and sufficient for an adequate definition of a customary mathematical concept.[20] For our purposes, it is not important whether (CM) provides a plausible *sufficient* condition for an adequate definition of a customary mathematical concept. Our concern is with the implications of its being a plausible *necessary* condition.

Hempel's claim that a logicist definition must provide an adequate definition of our customary mathematical concepts together with the further claim that (CM) provides a plausible necessary condition for an adequate definition provides the basis for our argument against the epistemic import of logicist derivations. Since this argument draws its inspiration from the Irrefutability Argument, I shall refer to it as the *New Irrefutability Argument* (NIA):

> (1*) A logicist derivation cannot disconfirm any mathematical proposition involving customary mathematical concepts which is accepted as true.

> (2*) If a logicist derivation cannot disconfirm a mathematical proposition then it cannot confirm such a proposition.

> (3*) Therefore, a logicist derivation cannot confirm any mathematical proposition involving customary mathematical concepts which is accepted as true.

---

19 Ibid., 44-5, note

20 W.V. Quine proposes and defends a similar account of necessary and sufficient conditions for a definition to conform to customary meaning: 'For such conformity [to traditional usage] it is necessary and sufficient that every context of the sign which was true and every context which was false under traditional usage be construed by the definition as an abbreviation of some other statement which is correspondingly true or false under the established meanings of its signs' (see 'Truth by Convention,' in *The Ways of Paradox* [Cambridge: Harvard University Press 1976], 79).

NIA has the same logical structure as IA. Furthermore, both share a common second premise or, more accurately, the second premise of each argument is an instance of (GCE). Hence, NIA is also valid and its second premise uncontroversial. (3*) also can be generalized to the stronger conclusion

(4*) A logicist derivation cannot confirm any mathematical proposition

by invoking principle (EU). Hence, NIA establishes that logicist derivations of mathematical propositions are of no epistemic significance provided that (1*) is true.

It was argued in Section III that IA fails because (1') is false. The question which remains to be addressed is whether a proponent of logicism can reject premise (1*) of NIA in a manner analogous to that in which (1') of IA was rejected. (1') was rejected by considering a hypothetical situation in which (a) there appeared to be a very large number of disconfirming instances of a mathematical proposition accepted as true; and (b) attempts to explain away these disconfirming instances as apparent were not supported by independent investigation. Now suppose that we attempt to reject (1*) along similar lines. We envisage that (a) there are many putative examples of logicist derivations of the negations of mathematical propositions involving customary mathematical concepts which are accepted as true; and (b) attempts to explain away this disconfirming evidence as merely apparent on grounds such as (i) failure to correctly translate the mathematical propositions into the primitive logical vocabulary, or (ii) flaws in the derivations of the logicist counterparts of the mathematical propositions, are unsupported by independent investigation. Would such a scenario constitute disconfirmation of mathematical principles presently regarded as true? No. Given (a) Hempel's claim that logicist definitions must capture their customary meaning and (b) (CM), this scenario would establish only that the logicist definitions of the mathematical concepts were incorrect.

V Two Logicist Rejoinders to the New Irrefutability Argument

The proponent of logicism has two options at this point. The first is to agree with Hempel that the logicist definitions must provide an analysis of our customary mathematical concepts but deny that (CM) is a necessary condition for so doing. The second is to reject the contention that these definitions analyze our customary mathematical concepts. One might exercise the first option by suggesting that (1) the logicist is providing an *explication* of our customary mathematical concepts; and (2) given the vague and unsystematic nature of everyday discourse, an explication of a concept which is useful for theoretical purposes may deviate from the customary concept. Carnap, for example, points out that whales and seals are excluded from the scientific concept *fish* despite the fact that they were subsumed under the prescientific concept *fish* which the former explicates. More generally, he maintains that considerable differences between explicandum and explicatum are permissible provided that this deviation is justified by the exactness and fruitfulness of the explicatum.[21] Hence (CM) is not a necessary condition for an adequate explication of a concept.

Carnap's rejection of (CM) appears to provide him with the latitude to reject (1*) of NIA. For he maintains that (1) the logicist definitions of mathematical concepts *explicate* those concepts; and (2) it is *not* in general the case that given some true proposition, P_1, involving the explicandum, the proposition, P_2, which results from replacing the explicandum in P_1 by its explicatum, is also true. For example, the proposition 'Whales are fish' is true given the prescientific concept *fish*. But the proposition which results by replacing this prescientific concept with its scientific explicatum is false. This appears to leave open the possibility that a situation might arise in which (1) there is a mathematical proposition, P_1, which is true given our customary

---

21 See Rudolf Carnap, *Logical Foundations of Probability*, 2nd ed. (Chicago: University of Chicago Press 1962), 5-8, for a discussion of the requirements for an adequate explication.

mathematical concepts, and (2) the proposition, P_2, which results from replacing the customary mathematical concepts in P_1 by their logicist counterparts, is false.

Although rejecting (1*) is compatible with Carnap's *general* requirements for an adequate explication of a concept, it is *not* compatible with his *specific* views about *mathematical* concepts. Carnap maintains that the explication of a concept sometimes proceeds in two stages: (1) the *formalization* of the terms of a theory; and (2) the *interpretation* of the primitive terms of the formalized theory. In the case of arithmetic the process of formalization has a long history which culminates in Peano's axioms:

> The prescientific terms of this field are the numerals "one," "two," etc. (or the corresponding figures) and terms for arithmetical operations like "plus" (previously "and"), "times," etc., as they are used in everyday language for counting things and for calculating with numbers applied to things. Preliminary steps toward a systematization of the theory and an explication of the terms have been made for several thousand years in the form of rules of calculation. The first axiom system for arithmetic which satisfies modern requirements as to the exactness of formulation is the famous axiom system of G. *Peano*.[22]

Two features of this process are significant. First, the rules of calculation employed in everyday life, which are codified in sentences such as '2 + 3 = 5,' are part of the process of explicating mathematical concepts. Furthermore, the Peano axioms, which culminate the first stage of the process of explication, impose a constraint on any satisfactory interpretation of the mathematical terms. A necessary condition of a satisfactory interpretation is that they insure the truth of the axioms. Since the codified rules of calculation are logical consequences of these axioms, any satisfactory interpretation must also insure their truth.

Not any interpretation which satisfies the Peano axioms, however, will yield an acceptable explication. Carnap, like Hempel, maintains that '... we have to give an explication for the terms "one," "two," etc.,

---

22 Ibid., 16

as they are meant when we apply them in everyday life.'[23] After endorsing the logicist interpretation provided by Frege and later by Russell, Carnap concludes his discussion with the following remark:

> It is a historically and psychologically surprising fact that this explication was such a difficult task and was achieved so late, although the explicanda, the elementary concepts of arithmetic, are understood and correctly applied by every child and have been successfully applied and to some extent also systematized for thousands of years.[24]

Since Carnap maintains that a satisfactory interpretation must capture the meaning of mathematical terms as they are applied in everyday life and he also maintains that they have been understood and correctly applied prior to any logicist interpretation of them, it follows that any satisfactory interpretation must not be at variance with those correct applications.

These observations on the process of formalizing and interpreting mathematical terms undercut the significance of Carnap's earlier remarks regarding the *general* requirements of an adequate explication. For, on the one hand, if the everyday mathematical sentences which codify rules of calculation are part of the explication of mathematical concepts, they cannot be viewed as prescientific sentences which are potential candidates for replacement. Since these sentences are all consequences of the Peano axioms, whose truth any satisfactory explication must guarantee, any satisfactory explication must also guarantee their truth.[25] On the other hand, if the elementary concepts

---

23 Ibid., 17

24 Ibid.

25 Although Carnap maintains that '... in spite of practical skill in usage, people in general, and even mathematicians before Frege, were not completely clear about the meaning of numerical words ...' he, nevertheless, also maintains that 'To demonstrate the adequacy of his explications, he [Frege] had to show that the numerals and the other arithmetical signs, as defined by him, had the properties customarily ascribed to them in arithmetic.' See Rudolf Carnap, 'Replies and Systematic Expositions,' in P.A. Schilpp, ed., *The Philosophy of Rudolf Carnap*

of mathematics are correctly and successfully applied, then any adequate explication of them must also conform to those correct applications. For example, the truth of the proposition expressed by 'The number of fingers on my right hand is 5' must be preserved by any acceptable interpretation of the primitive mathematical terms. Hence, the conditions Carnap imposes on a satisfactory explication of a *mathematical* concept are identical to those formulated in (CM) and do not provide the logicist with the latitude to reject (1*).

The second option open to the logicist is to deny that the definitions of mathematical concepts are explicative. Mark Steiner, for example, argues that these definitions are *purely stipulative*. On the face of it, this claim appears implausible since mathematical symbols have a preexisting use. They are not just arbitrarily defined by the logicist. Steiner replies to this charge by distinguishing between (1) what logicism *claims* regarding mathematical knowledge; and (2) how the logicist demonstrates the *correctness* of this claim. The logicist *claims* that one can know mathematics a priori by knowing (a) the axioms and rules of logic; and (b) various stipulative definitions. To demonstrate the *correctness* of this claim, the logicist must show that the proposed definitions explicate the customary usage of mathematical terms. Steiner puts his point as follows:

> Indeed, the logicist, in demonstrating the correctness of his philosophy, must explicate familiar mathematical concepts in terms of logic.... He must capture the ordinary usage of the numeric discourse, so far as ordinary usage is worth preserving — and, by and large, it is.... The philosopher, the logicist, must make do with the preexisting use of mathematical terminology, the "preexisting synonymies."
>
> But none of this enters into what logicism is about, what logicism says.... Logicism claims that a mathematician can learn mathematics from scratch, knowing only logic to begin with. From that mathematician's point of view, definitions such as
>
> $x + y = S^y(x)(Df.)$

(LaSalle: Open Court 1963), 935 and 939. For a more extensive discussion of the role of criteria of adequacy in Carnap's method of explication, see Arthur Pap, *Semantics and Necessary Truth* (New Haven: Yale University Press 1958), ch. 14.

> may be pure stipulation, even if the framer of the system chose the definition for stipulation on the basis of established usages.... Such a mathematician, the claim goes, need not know the established usage of "+."[26]

Steiner's primary epistemic claim is that a mathematician who treats the logicist definitions of mathematical terms as purely stipulative can acquire mathematical knowledge without needing to know the customary meaning of those terms. But does this claim, if correct, provide the logicist with the latitude to reject (1*) of NIA?

Consider a mathematician who introduces the following stipulative definition of '+':

$$x + y = S(S^y(x)) \ (Df.^*)$$

Would such a mathematician be justified in believing that $2 + 3 = 6$? Clearly, not. For Steiner maintains that a necessary condition for the *correctness* of logicism is that it explicate the customary meaning of mathematical terms. So, even if the mathematician need not *know* the customary meaning of the mathematical terms which are stipulatively defined, these definitions must conform to their customary meanings. Logicists, however, have traditionally maintained that Peano's axiom system provides a partial explication of the customary meaning of mathematical terms and that a complete explication of them must satisfy its axioms and definitions. (Df.*), of course, is incompatible with Peano's system. Furthermore, rejecting any other mathematical proposition generally accepted as true requires rejecting some axiom or definition of Peano arithmetic. Hence, the stipulative logicist can reject (1*) only at the expense of revising the Peano system.

Steiner, however, does not take seriously this possibility:

> Can we be sure we will not need a new definition of addition in order to prove arithmetic theorems as yet undiscovered? ... Yes we can.... For whatever we learn about addition, we will never *change* these two basic truths:

---

26 Steiner, 62-3

$$x + 0 = x$$
$$x + Sy = S(x + y)$$

both of which are provable via set theory from our definition of addition, assuming some standard definition of "S."[27]

Two points are worth noting in this passage. The first concerns the *order* of justification. Steiner's confidence regarding the logicist stipulative definition of '+' is based on the fact that the two basic truths enshrined in Peano's definition of addition are derivable from it. He does *not* base his confidence that these basic truths are unrevisable on the fact that they can be derived from the definition. This indicates that these basic truths are epistemically prior to the logicist definition from which they are derived. Second, since Steiner regards these truths as unrevisable, any logicist definition of '+' from which they cannot be derived, such as (Df.*), would be rejected as incorrect. Therefore, a proponent of logicism who regards logicist definitions of mathematical terms as stipulative is in no better position to reject (1*) of NIA than one who regards them as explicative.

Let us briefly summarize the results of Sections IV and V. We began by drawing attention to the central role of definitions of mathematical concepts in the logicist program. It was then argued that, given plausible criteria of adequacy for such definitions, logicism is open to NIA. The conclusion of NIA is that a logicist derivation of a mathematical proposition does not confirm or validate that proposition. We explored two alternative accounts of definitions to see whether they provide the logicist with the latitude to reject premise (1*) of NIA and argued that neither does so. Hence, we can now conclude that the *semantic* thesis that mathematics is analytic in sense (iv) does not support the *epistemic* thesis that mathematical knowledge is a priori.

---

27 Ibid., 66

VI The Rejection of the Epistemic Import of Conventionalism: The New Irrefutability Argument Extended

The considerations invoked in Section V to argue against the epistemic significance of stipulative logicism can be extended to the view that mathematical propositions are analytic in sense (iii). Ayer, for example, claims that the truths of mathematics are analytic propositions and that

> ... a proposition is analytic when its validity depends solely on the definitions of the symbols it contains and synthetic when its validity is determined by the facts of experience.[28]

Ayer's use of the term 'validity' in this context is unorthodox and I assume that it can be replaced by 'truth.' If we make the further assumption that the definitions Ayer has in mind are conventionally established linguistic definitions as opposed to objective relations holding among abstract meanings, then he is maintaining that mathematical propositions are analytic in sense (iii).[29]

The primary difference between the view that mathematical truths are analytic in sense (iii) as opposed to the view that they are analytic in sense (iv) can be brought out by considering the role of definitions in each view. On the latter view, definitions are utilized only to establish that mathematical truths are abbreviated logical truths. They are not used to provide a characterization of the nature of logical truth. On the former view, both the truths of mathematics and logic are characterized as true by convention. Furthermore, on this view, the reducibility of mathematics to logic is not regarded as a necessary condition for establishing that mathematical truths are analytic.

---

28 Ayer, 78

29 I do not consider here the view that analytic propositions are true in virtue of *abstract* meanings. Such platonist accounts of mathematical truth, or of necessary truth in general, raise their own distinctive epistemic problems. I discuss some of these in 'Causality, Reliabilism, and Mathematical Knowledge,' *Philosophy and Phenomenological Research* **52** (1992) 557-84.

Our primary concern is with the epistemic implications of Ayer's claim that mathematical truths are analytic. Does this contention support the conclusion that such truths are knowable a priori? Ayer offers the following argument:

> Thus, the proposition "There are ants which have established a system of slavery" is a synthetic proposition. For we cannot tell whether it is true or false merely by considering the definitions of the symbols which constitute it. We have to resort to actual observation of the behavior of ants. On the other hand, the proposition "Either some ants are parasitic or none are" is an analytic proposition. For one need not resort to observation to discover that there either are or are not ants which are parasitic. If one knows what is the function of the words "either," "or," and "not," then one can see that any proposition of the form "Either *p* is true or *p* is not true" is valid, independently of experience. Accordingly, all such propositions are analytic.[30]

Ayer's central epistemic claim is that one can discover the truth of an analytic proposition merely by considering the definitions of the words used to express it. Since one can know such propositions without resorting to observation, they are knowable a priori. Three observations are crucial in assessing Ayer's argument. First, he supports the *semantic* thesis that the proposition 'Either some ants are parasitic or none are' is analytic by appealing to the *epistemic* premise that one need not resort to observation to discover that the proposition is true. This argument, however, simply assumes that only analytic propositions are knowable a priori. Second, the epistemic premise is left unsupported. Finally, since Ayer has supported the *semantic* thesis that certain propositions are analytic by appealing to the *epistemic* premise that they can be known without resorting to observation, he cannot appeal to the alleged analyticity of such propositions in defending the epistemic premise that they are knowable a priori. Hence, Ayer is not in a position to offer a *noncircular* argument in support of the claim that analytic propositions are knowable a priori.

---

30 Ayer, 78-9

Furthermore, NIA provides good reason to believe that no such argument is forthcoming. Suppose we grant that analytic propositions are true by linguistic convention or definition. Now let us consider a mathematical proposition such as '1 + 2 = 3.' Presumably, a proponent of (iii) would maintain that the following linguistic conventions are relevant to its justification:

(D1) $1 = S(0)$

(D2) $2 = S(1)$

(D3) $3 = S(2)$

(D4) $x + y = S^y(x)$.

If our *only* justification for believing that $1 + 2 = 3$ is the adoption of these stipulative definitions, then the adoption of alternative definitions should provide us with as much justification for believing alternative mathematical propositions. For example, adopting alternative definitions of '+' such as

(D5) $x + y = S(S^y(x))$

(D6) $x + y = S(S(S^y(x)))$

along with

(D7) $4 = S(3)$

(D8) $5 = S(4)$

should provide equal justification for believing, respectively, the propositions that $1 + 2 = 4$ and that $1 + 2 = 5$. Given that there is equal justification for believing either '1 + 2 = 3' or '1 + 2 = 4' or '1 + 2 = 5,' on what grounds can a proponent of this position maintain that it provides an account of our justification for believing that $1 + 2 = 3$?

The only response available is to maintain that (D4) alone captures the customary meaning of '+' and, hence, (D5) and (D6) are irrelevant to the justification of the proposition that $1 + 2 = 3$. This response, however, leaves the position vulnerable to the NIA. For the respondent is claiming that it is only definitions or conventions which conform to customary usage that justify us in accepting or rejecting mathematical propositions. But, any definition of '+,' such as (D5) or (D6), which yields the result that a proposition such as '1 + 2 = 3,' which we accept as true, is false will be rejected as not conforming to the customary meaning of '+.' Hence, it follows that

(1**) The adoption of a set of linguistic conventions cannot disconfirm a mathematical proposition which is accepted as true.

But if we add to this conclusion a suitable version of (GCE):

(2**) If the adoption of a set of linguistic conventions cannot disconfirm a mathematical proposition then it cannot confirm such a proposition.

we arrive at the further conclusion that

(3**) Therefore, the adoption of a set of linguistic conventions cannot confirm a mathematical proposition which is accepted as true.

Hence, NIA establishes that neither Hempel's nor Ayer's account of the analyticity of mathematics can support the epistemic thesis that mathematical propositions are knowable a priori.

VII Two Circular Arguments

Our examination of Ayer's argument revealed a tendency to *assume* a significant relationship between the a priori and the analytic in the course of *defending* the claim that such a relationship exists. We conclude by examining briefly the arguments of two more recent writers who exhibit a similar tendency. Both defend the view that there exists some significant relationship between the a priori and the analytic. It is shown, however, that both defenses beg the interesting epistemic issues by defining the a priori in terms of either necessity or analyticity. This result underscores the difficulty of finding nontrivial defenses of the epistemic thesis that all knowledge of analytic propositions is a priori.

According to Anthony Quinton, '"A priori" means either, widely, "non-empirical" or, narrowly, following Kant, "necessary".'[31] His primary goal is to defend the thesis that

(Q) All a priori statements are analytic

when 'a priori' is understood narrowly and 'analytic' is understood in any of the four sense presented earlier. But, on the narrow reading of 'a priori,' it is true by stipulation that

(K) All a priori statements are necessary.[32]

Hence, Quinton devotes his efforts exclusively to arguing that the categories of the necessary and the analytic coincide on all four readings of 'analytic.'

Three points are worth noting here. First of all, even if Quinton succeeds in providing a substantive defense of the coextensiveness of the categories of the analytic and the necessary, he has not provided a substantive defense of the *epistemic* thesis that there exists a significant relationship between the a priori and either the analytic or the necessary. For the entire burden of his epistemic argument rests on stipulating that 'a priori' means 'necessary.' Second, although Quinton is correct in maintaining that Kant endorses (K), Kant does not do so on the basis of a stipulative definition. Instead, he maintains that necessity is a 'criterion' of the a priori and offers a supporting argu-

---

31 Quinton, 90

32 It is also true by stipulation on the narrow reading of 'a priori' that
    (K*) All necessary statements are a priori.
    (K*), together with Quinton's further claim that the categories of the necessary and the analytic are coextensive, entails
    (Q*) All analytic statements are a priori.

ment for this position.[33] Furthermore, this argument does not depend on either defining the a priori in terms of the necessary or defining the necessary in terms of the a priori. Hence, Kant has addressed, rather than begged, the epistemic issues. Finally, Quinton's account does not fare any better on the wider reading of 'a priori.' For he maintains that 'The idea of the empirical is a development or elucidation of the idea of the contingent.'[34] If this claim is granted, then the empirical is also a *metaphysical* concept and its connection with the *epistemic* concept of the a priori has been established by stipulation.

R.G. Swinburne offers an account of the a priori which, like Quinton's, draws its inspiration from Kant. Swinburne, however, is aware of some of the pitfalls of Quinton's account and begins his own discussion by making a number of sound observations:

> Modern philosophers who have been so prolific in their definitions of "analytic" have not in general attempted rival definitions of "a priori" to Kant's. They have usually used the term in a somewhat Kantian sense without precise definition, or they have simply equated "a priori" with "necessary" — an equation which appears to beg interesting questions in this field. Writers who have made this equation have appealed to the text of Kant as justification for doing so. Quinton writes that one meaning of "a priori" is "following Kant, necessary." I do not myself find this equation in the text, at any rate the text of the Introduction to the *Critique of Pure Reason* in the second edition. There are there arguments to show that if we know a necessary truth we know it a priori.[35]

---

33 For a critical discussion of Kant's argument, see my 'Necessity, Certainty, and the A Priori.'

34 Quinton, 92. Quinton considers a challenge to the assumption that all contingent statements are empirical which is based on employing conclusive falsifiability by experience as an *epistemic* criterion of the empirical. In response to it, he drops the wider notion of the a priori from further consideration and maintains that '... the essential content of the thesis [Q] is that all *necessary* truths are analytic' (93).

35 R.G. Swinburne,'Analyticity, Necessity, and Apriority,' in P. Moser, ed., *A Priori Knowledge*, 184

There are several important points articulated in this passage: (1) Kant provides an *epistemic* characterization of a priori knowledge; (2) a definition of 'a priori' which simply equates it with 'necessary' begs interesting questions; and (3) Kant does not make this equation but provides an *argument* to show that if we know a necessary truth we know it a priori, i.e., independently of experience.

Given these initial observations, it is surprising that Swinburne later endorses the following characterization of the a priori:

(c) A proposition is a priori if and only if it is necessary and can be known to be necessary[36]

and defends it by appealing to Kant:

> What Kant meant by "knowledge absolutely independent of all experience" is knowledge which comes to us through experience but is not contributed by experience.... But how are we to recognize the knowledge that is not contributed by experience? Kant's answer is that "necessity and strict universality are ... sure criteria of a priori knowledge, and are inseparable from one another." In effect he proposes my definition (c), and this seems to me a definition which will have the consequence of classifying as a priori the propositions which most philosophers would judge to be a priori.[37]

It will suffice here to reiterate Swinburne's three original points in criticism of his account: (1) Kant's characterization of a priori knowledge is not a *metaphysical* characterization in terms of the concept of *necessity* but an *epistemic* characterization in terms of the concept of independence of experience; (2) an account which stipulates that a priori knowledge is restricted to necessary propositions as well as maintaining that all knowledge of necessary propositions is a priori begs interesting questions; and (3) Kant argued for the thesis that all knowledge of necessity is a priori rather than stipulating that it is true.

---

36 Ibid., 185
37 Ibid., 186

Matters get even worse, however, since Swinburne goes on to maintain that the term 'necessary' in (c) is to be taken in the following sense:

(A) A proposition is necessary if and only if it is analytic

yielding the following fully articulated definition:

(S) A proposition is a priori if and only if it is analytic and can be known to be such.[38]

So, in the end, Swinburne defines the *epistemic* concept of the a priori in terms of the *semantic* concept of the analytic with the result that the coextensiveness of the analytic and the a priori is a trivial consequence of the definition.

VIII Conclusion

It generally has been taken for granted by those who do not dispute the coherence of the analytic/synthetic distinction that there is some close relationship between the a priori and the analytic. Although there has been disagreement about the status of synthetic a priori propositions, few have disputed the thesis that all analytic propositions are knowable a priori. Consequently, one standard strategy for demonstrating that a particular theory is knowable a priori is to maintain that it consists solely of analytic propositions. My primary goal has been to argue that this strategy is mistaken. The argument proceeded at two different levels. The first consisted in arguing that some standard conceptions of the analyticity of mathematics do not support the conclusion that mathematical propositions are knowable a priori. The second consisted in showing that several recent arguments purporting to establish some significant relationship between

---

38 Ibid., 187

the a priori and the analytic do so only at the expense of trivializing the principle in question. Since there are many competing conceptions of analyticity and our investigation has not been exhaustive, we cannot claim to have established that there is *no* significant relationship between the a priori and the analytic. Enough has been done, however, to establish that such a relationship cannot be taken for granted.[39]

---

39 I would like to thank Robert Audi, Panayot Butchvarov, Philip Hanson, Philip Hugly, Bruce Hunter, Michael Jubien, Penelope Maddy and Joseph Mendola for their helpful comments on earlier versions of this paper.

CANADIAN JOURNAL OF PHILOSOPHY
Supplementary Volume 18

The Doubtful A Priori

JOHN BIGELOW

Mathematics has become so sophisticated that it is easy to lose touch with the mathematical realities out of which it arises. Many nowadays think of mathematics as complicated games with forests of symbols. Yet this is an image which could not have got a grip on the ancient mathematicians, like those of the Pythagorean brotherhood, who stood nearer to the roots of those forests. Now we are lost in the higher branches of mathematics, and we sometimes forget that all these growing branches are nourished ultimately by roots far below in down-to-earth reality.

The early Pythagoreans discovered things which are thus and so, and which could not have been otherwise. Yet although these things could not have been otherwise, the Pythagoreans who discovered them could have done otherwise. Hence the truths which the Pythagoreans discovered are things which would still have been so even if no one had ever discovered them.

In the minds (and so in the brains) of the mathematicians there were perceptions or conceptions. It was contingent that these occurred in the minds they did occur in, or indeed in any minds at all. Yet in virtue of having these contingent perceptions or conceptions, mathematicians came to recognize that certain things are thus and so, and that these things could not have been otherwise. These mathematicians

151

used words and gestures, scratched patterns in the sand, assembled arrays of pebbles, and did a wide variety of things to convey their perceptions and conceptions to one another. The fierce formalisms of modern mathematics emerged from communicative activities of this sort. Symbols emerged, together with rules for their use, and games people played with them; yet these symbols were not mere counters in a self-contained game that had nothing to do with anything beyond itself. The symbols did refer to things beyond themselves. They expressed perceptions or conceptions in the minds of those who used them. And those perceptions or conceptions, in turn, constituted the recognition of necessary truths. Hence symbols and the perceptions and conceptions they express both correspond to things which would still have been so even if there had been no one to discover that these things are so, or to tell anyone about their discoveries.

Mathematical inquiry yields a priori knowledge of necessary truths about intangible things. Any adequate philosophy of mathematics must allow mathematics a subject matter, and it must allow that necessary truths may be known a priori about this subject matter. How is this possible? That is Kant's problem of the synthetic a priori. Kant offered an Idealist theory; I urge a Realist theory.

The Realist theory I offer aims to grant mathematics all three of its most distinctive characteristics: its epistemic status as a priori, its semantic status as comprising truths which are unconditional necessities, and its metaphysical status as concerning a subject matter other than that of localized, concrete, historical particularities.

Mathematical truths can be established without any essential dependence on inferences from premises which cite contingent facts about who has experienced what and when: that is, mathematical truths can be known a priori.

Mathematical truths are also necessary: not only are these things so, but they could not possibly have been otherwise.

And mathematical truths concern matters which have a distinctive kind of universality, and this makes it impossible to locate any particular concrete things which could be deemed to constitute the distinctive subject matter of mathematics.

These three features give the empiricists the creeps in three different ways: epistemically, semantically, and ontologically. Empiricists believe that all knowledge comes from experience. Because of this, it is hard for them to allow mathematics to be at the same time a priori, and necessary, and having an unlocalized, unhistorical subject matter. If knowledge comes from experience, how can anything be known a priori? How can anything be known which is necessary, and hence not contingent on experience? And how can anything be known about a subject matter which is not perceived in any particular place at any particular time? Some empiricists have managed to allow mathematics one or two of its traditional characteristics; but it is very hard for empiricists to allow mathematics all three.

Early in the twentieth century, some empiricists were logical positivists, and these empiricists did allow mathematics its a priori necessities. Yet they did this at the cost of denying mathematics any subject matter. They construed mathematics as consisting of nothing but merely verbal truths, just games with symbols, played according to conventions which are settled by social consensus.

Quine was a positivist who restored a subject matter to mathematics: the hierarchy of pure sets. Quine took mathematics to be a theory about the empty set, and about sets which may be built up in an iterative hierarchy from the empty set. Yet although Quine gave mathematics a subject matter, he did this under a kind of empiricism which denied mathematics its distinctive modal and epistemic character. Quine failed to capture the necessity of mathematical truths, and the a priori forms of proof by which these truths are justified.

Armstrong is an empiricist of another stripe. His theory of universals, a posteriori realism, offers a much better subject matter for mathematics, in my opinion. Armstrong's metaphysics allows mathematics to be about universals — physical properties and relations — rather than sets. Yet Armstrong's theory, like Quine's, runs the severe risk of misconstruing mathematics as merely contingent and a posteriori. Armstrong and Quine fail to adequately explain how mathematical truths can be necessary and can be known a priori.

I offer a Platonist, or better, a Pythagorean theory of the a priori necessities of mathematics. This is a theory which grants mathematics all three of its distinctive characteristics: it allows mathematics to be a priori and necessary and yet also to consist of truths about a nonlocal and yet nevertheless real and existent subject matter. If the theory I offer is not recognizably an empiricist one, so much the worse for empiricism in my opinion. If the only theory which does justice to mathematics is one which fits more comfortably under the label 'rationalism,' then call me a rationalist.

Mathematics is the study of patterns. These patterns are not particular individuals which can be located and dated. They do not have birthdays and they do not grow older as time passes. They can be instantiated in many places at the same time — or at least most of them are like this, although I do not think all patterns are capable of multiple realization. Patterns are, or include, properties and relations. The important ones, the ones we find instantiated in the actual world, are in my opinion all ones which I would call 'physical' properties and relations. In traditional terminology, they are universals rather than particulars. Mathematics is the theory of universals.

One pattern can be part of another pattern. The theory of relations of part to whole is called 'mereology.' I offer a theory which I call mereological Platonism.

When one pattern contains another pattern as one of its constituents, this part-whole relationship is not an accidental, inessential matter. The more inclusive pattern would not be the pattern that it is, if it did not contain the constituent that it does contain. Hence whenever the more inclusive pattern is instantiated, this necessarily implies the instantiation of the constituent pattern. This is the source of the necessity of mathematical truths.

Sometimes, when we are lucky, these necessities in the world are reflected in the minds of the agents who are seeking to understand that world. When we perceive or conceive a pattern, there will be patterned activity in the brain. This pattern in the brain will represent a pattern in the world. Sometimes this pattern in the brain will also contain another pattern as one of its constituents. And sometimes this constituent pattern will in its turn be one which represents some further pattern in the world. Then we will have two patterns in the brain representing two patterns in the world. In that case, when a person has the more complex perception or conception instantiated in the brain, this will necessarily imply that they have the constituent perception or conception too. There will be a necessary link between the patterns in the brain which constitute representations of reality.

In some cases, this necessary link between representations may then mirror a necessary link in the world, between the things which they represent. This harmony between representations and things represented is the source of the a priori character of mathematical knowledge.

In a priori knowledge, necessities in the world are represented in such a way that the force of these necessities in the world is reflected in parallel necessities in the representations. In perceiving or conceiving the more inclusive pattern, a person necessarily also perceives or conceives the constituent pattern that it contains. It is not possible to conceive the one pattern in that way without also conceiving the other. So not only does the person represent those two patterns, but the person also registers the necessary connection between them. To perceive the necessary connection simply is for there to be a parallel necessary connection between the perceptions themselves.

Nothing in this account guarantees infallibility of a person's judgments about which of their knowledge claims are a priori. A person may think some item of knowledge is a priori when it is not. A person may think that the part-whole relation between representations mirrors a part-whole relation between the things represented, and yet no matter how confident they are that this is so, there is no guarantee that they are right. There is no reason why their judgment should be taken to be beyond all reasonable doubt. Yet it is important not to conflate the a priori with the indubitable. I may have doubts, even reasonable doubts, about whether relations between given representations mirror relations between the things represented. Yet it may nevertheless be true that the representations do mirror the things represented in that way. And if they do, then they constitute a priori knowledge. It is possible to know something, even if you have reasonable doubts about whether you know it.

Consider an illustration. Nine pebbles can be arranged in a square grid — a pattern with as many rows as columns, with the same number of pebbles in each row and in each column. Ten pebbles cannot be arranged to make a square grid like that. Sixteen pebbles can. Twenty-five pebbles can. And so on. Let us begin to list the so-called square numbers in order; the list begins:

4, 9, 16, 25 ....

(I omit 0 and 1 because it is arguably anachronistic to include them as numbers, when we are trying to recapture Pythagorean ideas; and besides, I hold a theory that endorses Aristotle's claim that the natural numbers begin at 2, 0 and 1 being mere notational conveniences.)

Now list the differences between each square number and the one which follows — the difference between 4 and 9 is 5, between 9 and 16 is 7, between 16 and 25 is 9, and so on. This list of differences begins:

5, 7, 9 ....

Note that each of these differences is two greater than the one before, or at least, so it seems when we survey the first few steps in the series. The question arises whether this pattern will continue indefinitely as we climb along the endless list of square numbers. Will the differences always increase by twos? I will return to this plea for a proof. But first I will illustrate the nature and importance of the pattern that the Pythagoreans had discovered.

The pattern which we have seen instantiated by pebbles is one which can also be instantiated by things which look superficially very different from pebbles. Consider a falling object. In a unit of time, suppose it to be moving at a given average speed, so that it covers a given distance. In the next unit of time, suppose that the object naturally preserves its previous speed, in virtue of which it would fall the same distance as in the previous interval; but in addition to preserving its previous speed, it receives an additional increment of speed — the force of gravity gives it a little tug. Due to the extra increment of speed it falls further than it would have fallen if it had merely preserved its previous speed. So it falls further than it fell during the previous interval. Rescale units of distance so that the distance travelled in the second interval of time is two units of distance greater than the distance travelled in the first unit of time.

Suppose now that this pattern is repeated in succeeding units of time. In the third unit of time, the object retains all the speed it had in the second unit of time, but again gravity gives it a little tug, so that it acquires another increment of speed. Suppose that this results in the object falling two units of distance further in the third unit of time than it did in the second unit of time. Again the distance fallen is two units greater than the one before.

If this pattern continues, then the distance fallen in each interval of time will be two distance units more than that fallen in the previous interval. The Pythagorean discovery about square arrays of pebbles showed that when you keep adding two more than you added last time, you make bigger and bigger square numbers. This leads to the conclusion that the distance fallen by an object is proportional to the square of the time during which it falls. That is Galileo's law of free fall. And the way Galileo himself articulated this law referred explicitly to the arithmetic fact, discovered by Pythagoreans, that a sum of numbers which increase by twos will be a square number.

The Pythagoreans discovered truths about pebbles. But they also discovered truths about the patterns which those pebbles instantiated, and these same patterns can be instantiated not only by pluralities of pebbles laid out in square grids, but also by a single pebble as it falls under the influence of the constant force of gravity.

The Pythagoreans noticed that if you add 5 to the square number 4 then you get another square number, 9. If you now add two more than you added last time, you get another square number, 16. If you again add two more than you added last time, you get yet another square number, 25. Does this pattern continue indefinitely? If you keep adding two more than you added last time, will you always keep getting larger and larger square numbers? Yes you will. But how can we know this to be so? Not by testing infinitely many cases, one at a time. We can know a priori that the pattern will continue. If you think about it in the right way, you can just *see* that the pattern *must* continue in this way.

Imagine a square number of pebbles, say nine:

o o o
o o o
o o o

To make the next number, we need to add a row and a column:

```
o o o o
o
o
o
```

This added row-and-column makes a Γ-shape which the Greeks called a *gnomon*. Every time you add a gnomon to a square, you get the next larger square. And each added gnomon has to have two more pebbles in it than the one before: one extra pebble to make the row one pebble longer, and the other to make the column one pebble longer. This is why the differences between square numbers must always increase by twos.

When you think about square patterns made with pebbles, necessary truths leap out at you from time to time, and catch you by surprise. Yet what is it that leaps out at you? Not language games you could play with symbols. Not introspective insights into the workings of our own minds. When you think about arrays of pebbles, you are not thinking about your own mind, or about anyone else's. You are finding out things about pebbles; and beyond the pebbles, you are finding things about the patterns which the pebbles instantiate.

Thus, what the ancient mathematicians discovered were truths about patterns, not truths about words or thoughts. Necessary truths are truths about these patterns. More specifically, they are truths about how one complex pattern contains another simpler pattern as a constituent. When a large pattern contains a constituent pattern, then this is not an accidental, contingent matter. The larger pattern would not have been the pattern that it is, had it contained a different constituent pattern. The constituent pattern is an essential part of the pattern which contains it.

Consider for instance a square array of pebbles. This pattern contains gnomons; indeed it is constituted entirely of a series of gnomons added onto a single initial pebble; and each of these gnomons contains exactly the pattern of the gnomon before it but with one extra pebble added to each end. The distinctive necessity of the Pythagoreans' discovery arises from the containment of one pattern in another.

I conjecture that this containment of one pattern in another is the source of all necessities in mathematics. I conjecture also that this theory recaptures some of the spirit of Pythagorean doctrines about number and nature. Pythagoreans were realists about mathematics; but unlike later Platonists, they were not transcendent realists. They saw mathematical truths in the physical world, not in some other world. It is difficult to justify such sweeping statements about what the early Pythagoreans thought. They lived a long time ago, and it is said that they took a vow of secrecy. There is a severe risk of distortion when we describe their thoughts using words which are currently fashionable, like the word 'realism.' Yet I am willing to take this risk. The imminent mathematical realism implicit in Pythagoreanism is what lies at the heart of the scientific advances of such great modern minds as those of Galileo, Kepler, and Newton.

Mathematics has a subject matter: namely, patterns. And it discovers truths, indeed necessary truths, about this subject matter. When mathematicians discover these truths about patterns, there is a distinctive way in which they set about justifying their opinions about these patterns. Mathematics not only has a distinctive subject matter, it also has a distinctive methodology. The characteristic form of justification found in mathematics is one which has traditionally been called a priori. A mathematical opinion is supported, not by assembling sensory observations, but by proofs which do not make any appeal to any contingent observations that anyone happens to have made. Such proofs are said to be a priori because the order of justification begins without ('prior to') any assumptions about any experiences of any agents. Experiences will be required to help someone understand a proof; but no assertions about those experiences feature as premises in the proof. Different people have different experiences which lead them to understand the proof; but it is the very same proof that they come to understand.

One of the key ideas in Pythagoreanism is that of a harmony between the patterns in the world around us, and the patterns in the mind of the inquirer who seeks to understand this world. Music is the model; beauty arises from a match between mathematical patterns in the world, and mathematical patterns in the mind. It is this harmony between the microcosm and the macrocosm that holds the key to the distinctive a priori status of mathematical justifications.

When a person perceives or imagines or in any way thinks of a pattern, there will be some pattern in the person's mind or brain. For instance, when people represent to themselves a square grid of pebbles, there will be something structured inside them which serves to represent this square grid. And when they represent to themselves a gnomon of pebbles, there will be something structured inside them which represents this gnomon. One thing which can sometimes happen, then, is that the pattern which represents the gnomon is contained within the pattern which represents the square grid. It may happen that the part-whole relation which holds between the square and the gnomon in the world is mirrored in the mind of the inquirer, and the representations stand in the same part-whole relation as the things they represent.

Part-whole relations among representations recall the Kantian idea of *analytic* truths. Kant defined analytic truths in the special case of simple subject-predicate judgments. An analytic truth, Kant said, is a proposition in which the concept corresponding to the predicate is already contained in the concept of the subject. Representations are, in fact, complex structures; and one representation can contain another quite literally as a part. The Kantian idea is worth giving a run for its money. It is a point in its favor, that it offers some promise of capturing the distinctive 'Aha!' of recognition which accompanies the proofs of simple mathematical truths like those discovered by the early Pythagoreans. When you get clear and distinct representations of a complex pattern, and of one of its constituent patterns, then you can just *see* that one necessarily contains the other: in fact, you can just *see* one pattern *as* containing the other.

Caution is called for, however. History has taught us some hard lessons. Again and again people have taken truths to be self evident which turned out, in the course of time, to be far from self evident. Some things people thought to be self evident turned out in the end not to be truths at all. The a priori status of mathematical justifications should not be conflated with anything like certainty. People can be quite certain about things which are not true. And people can be uncertain about things which are in fact necessarily true. It can be quite rational for a person to be uncertain about something even if it is in fact a necessary truth. It can be rational for a person to be uncertain about *whether* something is a necessary truth. Hence a priori justifications should not be misconstrued as providing infallible proofs in any epistemic sense. An a priori justification may support a proposition which is in fact not only true but necessary: something which could not have been otherwise. In this case there is a sense in which a belief in this proposition is one which 'could not have been mistaken.' Yet despite this, it may be a belief which could *for all we know* have been mistaken. It may be rational to hold some degree of doubt about it.

History has taught us to be wary of any pretensions to infallibility. Yet this should not mislead us into denying the existence of a priori justifications in mathematics. It is right and proper to reserve a degree of doubt about any claims we might make about *which* justifications really are a priori. Something may seem to be a priori and yet may not be. Nevertheless, the fallibility of judgments about what is a priori does not establish the nonexistence of anything a priori. Mathematical justifications often do have a distinctive status, even if they do not establish their conclusions beyond all reasonable doubt. We need a name for the distinctive kinds of justifications which we find in mathematics; and 'a priori' is the name which best fits. However epistemically fallible mathematics may be, its justifications are nevertheless a priori.

What makes a mathematical justification a priori, I propose, is the way in which the part-whole relations which constitute the necessities in nature are reflected in part-whole relations among the representations in the mind or in language. This proposal gains credibility from the imaginative exercise of recreating the early discoveries of the simplest mathematical necessities in nature. Most rival, contemporary philosophies of mathematics do not score very well at all, by comparison, when they are held up against simple mathematical discoveries of the earliest mathematicians.

The programme I offer is sketchy, and so it is hard to back it up by proofs. What I propose to do is, rather, to undermine complacency about current orthodoxies, and hence to stimulate a sense of urgency about searching for new theories. In this, I am continuing useful initiatives taken by Maddy in her book *Realism in Mathematics*.

John Bigelow

The recent philosophies of mathematics which are most deeply informed by mathematics itself all fall within the tradition of logical positivism. One way these philosophies can be sustained is by keeping your mind on the most rarefied and abstract branches of contemporary mathematics, and by keeping your thoughts from dwelling too long upon the mathematicians who stood at the dawn of all mathematical discoveries. Yet it counts quite heavily against positivist philosophies of mathematics, that if they are held up against simple, primordial mathematical discoveries, it takes a great deal of double talk to convince yourself that there is no incompatibility between theory and history.

Logical positivists work under the shadow of empiricism. They assume that all knowledge of the world around us must come from contingent experience. Hence no necessary truths could be truths about the world. Early positivists acknowledged that mathematical truths are necessary truths; but they granted their necessity only at the cost of denying them any subject matter. Mathematical truths were said to be *analytic,* and this not in Kant's sense, but in the sense that they were made true merely by conventions of language, and not because any things in the world really are the way the mathematicians say they are.

It is hard to refute a schematic theory of this kind. Yet its plausibility drains away if you seriously immerse yourself in a simple mathematical discovery such as those the early Greeks were so excited about. A historical exercise in empathy does not constitute a logically compelling refutation; yet it is a rhetorical technique which is not without some degree of legitimacy of its own. It is a point in favor of any rival to the early positivist theory, if it can grant mathematics a subject matter.

Under the hand of Quine, logical positivism took a significant change of course. A subject matter was restored to mathematics; and this was a step in the right direction. Yet the subject matter which Quine offered for mathematics was nothing but the infinite hierarchy of pure sets. Quine even toyed with a wild metaphysical theory which he called Pythagoreanism, a theory in which nothing is said to exist, nothing is 'quantified over,' but sets.

162

And yet it is far from plausible to suppose that the subject matter studied by the ancient Pythagoreans consisted of the infinite hierarchy of pure sets. Quine's principal reason for taking sets to comprise the subject matter of mathematics is one which is historically bound tightly to the twentieth century. Our current understanding of the world rests critically on physics, and physics draws heavily and essentially on the differential and integral calculus. It turns out that the equations which are needed in physics would all get the right truth values if they were interpreted as assertions about sets. So Quine urges us to take mathematics to consist of truths about sets. Our justification for believing in the truth of these propositions runs as follows. Sophisticated modern physics requires the assertion of equations of the calculus; and these would be assertible if they were assertions about (quantifying over) sets. We are currently justified in believing anything which would generate the theories of current physics. Hence we are currently justified in taking mathematics to consist of truths about sets.

None of the Quinean story, however, gives any reason at all for thinking that the ancient Pythagoreans were thinking or talking about sets. We might grant that the utility of set theory in modern physical theory does give us some reason to believe in the existence of sets. So suppose there are such things as sets. We are left with the question whether it is likely that these things came continually to the forefront of the attention of ancient mathematicians over two thousand years ago. I say they did not.

Quine mischaracterises the subject matter of mathematics. He also misdescribes the necessity of mathematical truths. Physics uses mathematics, he notes; so he concludes that if you were to change mathematics then this would have far-reaching effects on physics. This, Quine urges, makes it reasonable for us to be reluctant to tinker with mathematical propositions which are deeply embedded in physical theory. And this is, he suggests, why mathematics seems to have a different status from other disciplines, a greater immunity to refutation from recalcitrant experience, and so a status which often prompts us to call its propositions necessary truths.

And yet, for Quine we have no reason for believing mathematical propositions to be true, except insofar as these propositions enter into explanatorily productive theories in physics. So if experimental evidence were to mount which failed to fit current physics, then we would lose the only justification we currently have for believing mathematical propositions to be true. Hence there is an obvious sense in which the Quinean theory portrays mathematics as contingent, and its alleged necessities as mere illusions.

None of this, however, makes much sense when held up alongside the simple mathematical discoveries of the ancient Greeks. There is no reason to think that they derived the illusion of necessity from the anticipation that changes in their mathematical beliefs would carry in train far-reaching revisions of other beliefs, revisions which it was reasonable of them to resist making as long as they could avoid doing so. It is much more plausible, I urge, to propose that the idea of mathematical necessity arose from a recognition that one pattern is contained in another pattern.

Does contemporary mathematical knowledge have the same grounding as ancient mathematics? Not necessarily. In an important book entitled *Mathematical Knowledge*, Kitcher gives a plausible story of the recursive, cumulative history of mathematics. How do I know that a minus times a minus makes a plus? I know it because I was told by someone who knew. That person knew because they were told by someone who knew. And so on back into the mists of time. This is the kind of grounding most of us have for most of our mathematical knowledge. What needs to be explained, in addition to this social transmission, are the additions which are made to mathematical knowledge from time to time. Special cases of such additions will be those which occur at the very early stages of the growth of mathematics, those in which some mathematical knowledge is added to the almost nonexistent prior mathematical knowledge. This is a place where my account of a priori knowledge may get a grip.

It could be objected, however, that my account of a priori knowledge has little direct relevance to current mathematical knowledge, since we now stand so far from the early discoveries which kicked off the whole historical growth. I reply that mathematics is continually regrounded in ways which recreate the processes of the earliest discoveries in mathematics. Applied mathematics continually draws us into perceptions of mathematical patterns in physical things. Sometimes we may blindly apply equations and get the right answers, without much real understanding of what we are doing. Yet sometimes we get flashes of insight, in which understanding dawns on us. When this happens, we do have a priori knowledge. This knowledge does not rest only on the authority of history, or on the indirect utility of mathematics in physics, but in direct perceptions which are bound up with the consciousness of necessities. This direct consciousness of necessities is, I argue, grounded in the direct perception of part-whole relations among patterns. Quine mischaracterizes the necessity of mathematics. He also mischaracterizes its epistemology. It is simply not true that our only reason for believing mathematical propositions to be true is that they enter into explanatory physical theories. No one can think this while bringing themselves face to face with a simple mathematical proof like the ones the Pythagoreans discovered long ago. It is much more plausible to suppose that the essence of mathematical proof lies in the achievement of representations, in the mind or in language, which mirror the structures of the patterns they represent.

The ancient Greeks were filled with a touching optimism. Their a priori proofs were often accompanied by a degree of confidence which it is not rational for us to share. Yet it is a mistake to conflate fallibility with contingency. Mathematical truths are necessary, not contingent; and mathematical justifications are, characteristically, a priori not experimental. We must not allow the overwhelming sophistication of modern mathematics to fog our vision. We must not lose sight of the harmonies between representations and the patterns which they represent. These harmonies are the source of the necessary truths and the a priori justifications which lie at the heart of mathematics.

References

Armstrong, D.M. *A Combinatorial Theory of Possibility* (New York: Cambridge University Press 1989)

Benacerraf, P. and H. Putnam. *Philosophy of Mathematics: Selected Readings* (Cambridge: Cambridge University Press 1983)

Bigelow, J.C. 'Real Possibilities,' *Philosophical Studies* **52** (1987) 85-112

John Bigelow

Bigelow, J.C. *The Reality of Numbers* (Oxford: Oxford University Press 1988)

Bigelow, J.C. and R.J. Pargetter. *Science and Necessity* (London: Cambridge University Press 1990)

Burkert, W. *Lore and Science in Ancient Pythagoreanism* (Cambridge, MA: Harvard University Press 1972)

Forrest, P. and D.M. Armstrong. 'The Nature of Number,' *Philosophical Papers* **16** (1987) 165-86

Galileo, Galilei. *Dialogues Concerning Two New Sciences*. H. Crew and A. de Salvio, trans. (New York: Dover 1954)

Guthrie, K.S. *The Pythagorean Sourcebook* (Grand Rapids, MI: Phanes Press 1987)

Heath, T.L. *A History of Greek Mathematics I. From Thales to Euclid* (Oxford: Oxford University Press 1921)

Irving, A.D., ed. *Physicalism in Mathematics* (Dordrecht: Kluwer 1990)

Kitcher, P. *The Nature of Mathematical Knowledge* (Oxford: Oxford University Press 1983)

Kline, M. *Mathematics and the Physical World* (New York: Dover 1959)

Lewis, D.K. *Parts of Classes* (Oxford: Basil Blackwell 1991)

Maddy, P. *Realism in Mathematics* (Oxford: Clarendon 1990)

Quine, W.V. *From a Logical Point of View*, 2nd ed. (New York: Harper and Row 1961)

CANADIAN JOURNAL OF PHILOSOPHY
Supplementary Volume 18

Some Remarks on Indiscernibility[1]

ALI KAZMI

I

If α and α' are distinct variables and ϕ and ϕ' are open sentences of some language, where ϕ' is the result of replacing one or more free occurrences of α in ϕ with free occurrences of α' in ϕ', then a universal closure of $\ulcorner(\alpha = \alpha' \to (\phi \to \phi'))\urcorner$ is an indiscernibility principle of that language. For instance, (1) is an indiscernibility principle.

(1) $\forall x \forall y (x = y \to (x = \text{Cicero} \to y = \text{Cicero}))$.

The existence of opaque constructions falsifies the familiar unrestricted principle of substitution which affirms that co-referential expressions are intersubstitutable in all contexts without change of truth-value. But indiscernibility principles are another matter. Not every counter-example to the unrestricted principle of substitution is

---

1 Earlier versions of this paper were read at the Alberta Philosophy Conference at Banff, 1987 and at the Ninth International Congress of Logic, Methodology, and Philosophy of Science at Uppsala, 1991.

a counter-example to some indiscernibility principle. Indeed, it is likely to be thought that there is no counter-example to any indiscernibility principle, and that the semantics of variables and objectual quantification ensures that all indiscernibility principles are true. Quine[2] advocates this view in *Word and Object*, and more recently, David Kaplan[3] and Richard Cartwright[4] have argued in its defence. In this paper, I examine these arguments, and some examples of apparently false indiscernibility principles, and I try to show that notwithstanding these arguments, the semantics of objectual quantification is compatible with the falsity of some indiscernibility principles.[5]

II

Examples of false indiscernibility principles are readily obtained by reflection upon those sentential operators which are sensitive to the orthographic features of their complement sentences. For a simple example of this kind, suppose that the vocabulary of an interpreted first-order language is augmented with a one-place sentential operator O which is characterized as follows:

> (i) if S is a closed sentence, then $\ulcorner OS \urcorner$ is true relative to a context c just in case S is true relative to c and S ends with the letter 'y,' and

---

2 W.V. Quine, *Word and Object* (Cambridge, MA: The MIT Press 1960), 167-8

3 David Kaplan, 'Opacity' in L.E. Hahn and P.A. Schilpp, eds., *The Philosophy of W.V. Quine* (La Salle, IL: Open Court 1986), 274-5

4 Richard Cartwright, 'Indiscernibility Principles' in his *Philosophical Essays* (Cambridge, MA: The MIT Press 1987), 200-15

5 Mark Richard also defends this view in his 'Quantification and Leibniz's Law,' *Philosophical Review* **96** 555-78, and in his *Propositional Attitudes* (Cambridge: Cambridge University Press 1990), 199-208.

(ii) if S is an open sentence, then $\ulcorner OS \urcorner$ is true relative to a context c and an assignment I to the free occurrences of variables in S just in case S is true relative to c and I and S ends with the letter 'y.'

Given this characterization and the assumption that 'Cicero = Tully' and 'Tully = Cicero' are true sentences of this language, 'O Cicero = Tully' is true, but 'O Tully = Cicero' is not true. Likewise, according to this characterization and the assumption that 'Cicero = y' and 'Cicero = x' are open sentences of this language, 'O Cicero = y' is true relative to the assignment of Cicero to 'y,' but 'O Cicero = x' is not true relative to the assignment of Cicero to 'x.' But then (2) is a false indiscernibility principle.

(2) $\forall x \forall y \ (y = x \rightarrow (O \ Cicero = y \rightarrow O \ Cicero = x))$.

Let us say that a singular term is directly referential just in case its semantic content relative to an assignment and a context is its referent relative to that assignment and context. Objectual quantification supports the view that variables are directly referential. One might think that the direct referentiality of variables ensures that all indiscernibility principles are true. This thought is apparently founded on the idea that the semantic content of an expression relative to a context and an assignment is what that expression contributes to the semantic content relative to that context and assignment of any complex expression in which it occurs. But this idea is mistaken. Quotational constructions provide counter-examples to it. Moreover, there is no good reason to think that if an expression contains an occurrence of a variable which is accessible to quantification from outside of that expression, then relative to any assignment and context what this variable contributes to the semantic content of that expression is its semantic content. On the contrary, the characterization of O illustrates that since 'O Cicero = x' and 'O Cicero = y' disagree in truth-value relative to the assignment of Cicero to both 'x' and 'y,' if variables are directly referential, then relative to this assignment not both 'x' and 'y' contribute their semantic content to the semantic contents of the corresponding open sentences. This suggests that whether an occurrence of a variable in an expression is accessible to quantification from outside of that expression is not decided by what contribution the variable makes to the semantic content of that expression relative to a context and an assignment, but depends instead on other syntactic and semantic features of that expression.

III

In defense of indiscernibility principles Kaplan writes:

> Several authors, seemingly emboldened by their awareness that substitutivity does not hold in general in opaque contexts, have announced formalisms in which they casually reject instances of the second law of identity, especially those of the form:
>
> 1D2 $\forall x \forall y(x = y \rightarrow (\ulcorner xx \leftrightarrow \ulcorner xy))$
>
> with the variables occurring within an opaque context in $\ulcorner$. (Their thought seems to be that distinct variables can carry the same individual off in different directions. It is they whom Quine justly accuses of wantonness. However, it is possible to reformulate the second law of identity so that it is no longer a principle of substitutivity. By this I mean that the second law need not involve any replacements of one variable by another within the context $\ulcorner$. Let v_1 and v_2 be any distinct variables, and let $\ulcorner$ be any formula having free occurrences of at least v_1. ($\ulcorner$ may also have free occurrences of v_2 and other variables as well.) The following along with the first law of Identity: "$\forall xx = x$" (reflexivity), suffices to axiomatize identity theory.
>
> 1D2* $\forall v_2[\exists v_1(v_1 = v_2 \& \ulcorner) \rightarrow \forall v_1(v_1 = v_2 \rightarrow \ulcorner)]$.
>
> I call 1D2* the "why not take all of me" principle.... If 1D2 is derivable from reflexivity and 1D2*, what does it mean for a system to defy 1D2 but satisfy reflexivity and 1D2*? It means that something entirely independent of identity has gone wrong in the sentential or quantificational part of the system.[6]

Cartwright also argues in defense of indiscernibility principles. He writes:

---

6 Kaplan, 274-5. I have modified the notation to conform with the style of this essay.

This reasoning ... can be put to use in direct support of any indiscernibility principle. Consider just one example. If it is suggested that, although x is identical with y, something z is a friend of x but not of y, then x, y, and z will be such that

$\forall w(w = y \leftrightarrow w = x)$ & z is a friend of x

and

$\forall w(w = y \leftrightarrow w = y)$ & –z is a friend of y.

Hence y and z will be such that

$\exists u(\forall w(w = y \leftrightarrow w = u)$ & z is a friend of u)

and

$\exists u(\forall w(w = y \leftrightarrow w = u)$ & –z is a friend of u).

But then consider the thing that is y. Is z a friend of it? There will be no saying.... Indeed, any indiscernibility principles can be defended in the same manner.[7]

(3) and (4) are obtained by making uniform substitution in Kaplan's schemas 1D2 and 1D2* respectively.

(3) $\forall x \forall y[x = y \to (-O\, x = x \leftrightarrow -O\, x = y)]$.

(4) $\forall x[\exists y(y = x \,\&\, -O\, x = y) \to \forall y(y = x \to -O\, x = y)]$.

But given the characterization of O, whereas (4) is true, (3) is false. Therefore, any derivation of 1D2 from 1D2* must employ a rule of inference or a principle which is not in general truth-preserving. Kaplan's suggested derivation of 1D2 from 1D2* and reflexivity apparently assumes a principle P_1 which licenses the inference of a sentence of the form: $\forall v_1 \lceil (v_1, v_1)$ from another sentence of the form: $\forall v_1 \forall v_2 \lceil (v_1, v_2)$. Since (5) is true, but (6) is false, P_1 is falsified by O.

(5) $\forall x \forall y[(y = x \,\&\, -O\, x = y) \to \forall y(y = x \to -O\, x = y)]$.

(6) $\forall x[(x = x \,\&\, -O\, x = x) \to \forall y(y = x \to -O\, x = y)]$.

It might appear that P_1 is a principle of pure quantification theory and independent of indiscernibility principles, and that any formalism

---

7 Cartwright, 212-13. I have modified the notation to conform with the style of this essay.

which contains operators such as O which violate P_1 could be rejected on the grounds of quantification theory alone. But that would not be correct. P_1 licenses substitution of variables in the scope of $\ulcorner$ which cannot be justified without ultimately appealing to the corresponding indiscernibility principles. Therefore, not only P_1 cannot be defended by the principles of quantification theory alone, but also any derivation of 1D2 from 1D2* which itself rests on P_1 cannot be used in defense of those indiscernibility principles. That a justification of P_1 requires more than the principles of quantification theory alone may be appreciated by contrasting it with another principle P_2 which licenses the inference of a sentence of the form: $\forall v_1 \lambda v_3 \lambda v_4 \ulcorner (v_3, v_4)] v_1 v_1$ from another sentence of the form: $\forall v_1 \forall v_2 \lambda v_3 \lambda v_4 \ulcorner (v_3, v_4)] v_1 v_2$. Unlike P_1, P_2 doesn't license substitution of variables in the scope of $\ulcorner$, and unlike P_1, P_2 is not falsified by O. P_2 does not support the derivation of 1D2 from 1D2*.

In Cartwright's argument the transition from

$$\forall w(w = y \leftrightarrow w = x) \ \& \ z \text{ is a friend of } x$$

to

$$\exists u(\forall w(w = y \leftrightarrow w = u) \ \& \ z \text{ is a friend of } u)$$

and from

$$\forall w(w = y \leftrightarrow w = y) \ \& \ {-z} \text{ is a friend of } y$$

to

$$\exists u(\forall w(w = y \leftrightarrow w = u) \ \& \ {-z} \text{ is a friend of } u)$$

is presumably justified by a principle of existential generalization P_3 which licenses the inference of a sentence of the form: $\exists v_1 \ulcorner (v_1)$ from another sentence of the form $\ulcorner (\alpha)$. Since 'O Cicero = y' is true relative to the assignment of Cicero to 'y,' but '$\exists x$ O Cicero = x' is not true, P_3 is falsified by O. Like P_1, P_3 licenses substitution of terms in the scope of $\ulcorner$ which cannot be justified without ultimately appealing to the corresponding indiscernibility principles. Therefore, like P_1, not only P_3 cannot be defended by the principles of quantification theory alone, but also any reasoning which itself relies on P_3 cannot be used in defense of those indiscernibility principles. That a justification of P_3 requires more than the principles of quantification theory alone may be appreciated by contrasting it with another principle of existential generalization P_4 which licenses the inference of a sentence of the form: $\exists v_2 \lambda v_1 \ulcorner (v_1)]v_2$ from another sentence of the form: $\lambda v_1 \ulcorner (v_1)]\alpha$. Unlike P_3, P_4 does not license substitution of terms in the scope of $\ulcorner$, and unlike P_3, P_4 is not falsified by O.

IV

A less artificial example of a false indiscernibility principle emerges from David Lewis's proposed analysis of modality. Lewis[8] offers the following translation scheme for his operator '$\square$':

DL $\quad \square \phi \alpha_1 ... \alpha_n =_{df} \forall \beta_1 \forall \gamma_1 ... \forall \gamma_n((W\beta_1 \& I\gamma_1\beta_1 \& C\gamma_1\alpha_1 ... \& I\gamma_n\beta_1 \&$
$C\gamma_n\alpha_n) \to \phi\gamma_1...\gamma_n).$

Under the intended interpretation 'W' applies to all and only possible worlds, and 'I' and 'C' represent the relations of being in and being a counterpart of respectively. According to DL, '$\square x = x$' is true relative to an assignment to the variable 'x' just in case (7) is true relative to that assignment; and '$\square x = y$' is true relative to an assignment to 'x' and 'y' just in case (8) is true relative to that assignment.

(7) $\forall w \forall a((Ww \& Iaw \& Cax) \to a = a).$

---

8 David Lewis, 'Counterpart Theory and Quantified Modal Logic' in his *Philosophical Papers* Vol. 1 (Oxford: Oxford University Press 1983), 26-46

(8) $\forall w \forall a \forall b((Ww \ \& \ Iaw \ \& \ Cax \ \& \ Ibw \ \& \ Cby) \rightarrow a = b)$.

According to Lewis, an object may have more than one counterpart in some possible world. Given DL, ' $\Box x = y$ ' is false relative to the assignment of such an object to both 'x' and 'y,' whereas ' $\Box x = x$ ' is true under any assignment. Thus, if there is an object which has more than one counterpart in some possible world, then, given DL, (9) is a false indiscernibility principle.

(9) $\forall x \forall y(x = y \rightarrow (\Box x = x \rightarrow \Box x = y))$.

If (9) is false, then any principle of existential generalization which licenses the inference of ' $\exists y(x = y \ \& \ \Box x = y)$ ' from ' $(x = x \ \& \ \Box x = x)$ ' and any principle of universal instantiation which licenses the inference of ' $-(x = x \ \& \ \Box x = x)$ ' from ' $\forall y-(x = y \ \& \ \Box x = y)$ ' are falsified as well. Moreover, given the assumption that 'x = x' and 'x = y' express the same proposition relative to the assignment of the same object to both 'x' and 'y,' if (9) is false then ' $\Box$ ' does not represent an operation on the propositions expressed by its complement sentences. Kripke[9] has noted some of these features of Lewis' characterization of ' $\Box$.' These points apply, mutatis mutandis, to any sentential operator which gives rise to a false indiscernibility principle. In the case of Lewis's characterization of ' $\Box$,' these points raise doubt that it articulates a notion of metaphysical necessity;[10] but these points do not

---

9 Saul Kripke, *Naming and Necessity* (Cambridge, MA: Harvard University Press 1980), 45

10 Because DL gives rise to false indiscernibility principles, it seems implausible that it defines a notion of metaphysical necessity. According to DL, (i) and (ii) are translated as (i)' and (ii)' respectively.
(i) $\lambda x[\Box x = x]a$.
(i') $\lambda x[\forall w \forall b((Ww \ \& \ Ibw \ \& \ Cbx) \rightarrow b = b]a$.
(ii) $\lambda x \lambda y[\Box x = y]aa$.
(ii') $\lambda x \lambda y[\forall w \forall b \forall c((Ww \ \& \ Ibw \ \& \ Cbx \ \& \ Icw \ \& \ Ccy) \rightarrow b = c]aa$.
Since (i') does not entail (ii'), according to DL, (i) does not entail (ii). But it seems that if ' $\Box$ ' in (i) and (ii) represented metaphysical necessity then (i) and (ii) could

provide evidence that the translation schema DL is formally defective. In particular, the failure of certain principles of existential generalization and universal instantiation on Lewis's account of '□' does not indicate that the quantification in (9) is somehow illicit. These principles presuppose that open sentences which are alphabetic variants of each other have the same truth-value relative to any assignment which uniformly assigns the same objects to the variables which have free occurrences in them. But this is in effect the claim that all indiscernibility principles are true. Therefore the failure of these principles of universal instantiation and existential generalization in a formalism which yields false indiscernibility principles does not indicate that the treatment of quantification in that formalism is defective.

Lewis denies that his characterization of '□' yields a false indiscernibility principle.[11] He would agree that (9) is false, but he would deny that (9) is an indiscernibility principle. His reasons for this claim are not entirely clear to me, but it seems to be his view that (9) is not an indiscernibility principle either because the occurrences of '□' in (9) conceal quantifiers that bind the occurrences of 'x' and 'y' which

---

be paraphrased as (i'') and (ii'') respectively.

(i'') a is necessarily self-identical.
(ii'') a is necessarily identical with a.

However, it is implausible that (i'') does not entail (ii''), and so it seems implausible that □ as interpreted in DL represents metaphysical necessity. This difficulty is independent of the fact that in (i) and (ii) there are occurrences of variables in the scope of □ which are bound by expressions from outside. Suppose that a predicate operator 'nec' was given a counterpart-theoretic semantics along the lines proposed in DL. Then (iii) and (iv) would be translated as (iii') and (iv') respectively.

(iii) nec λx[x = x]a.
(iii') ∀w∀b((Ww & Ibw & Cba) → λx[x = x]b).
(iv) nec λxλy[x = y]aa.
(iv') ∀w∀b∀c((Ww & Ibw & Cba & Icw & Cca) → λxλy[x = y]bc).

Since (iii') does not entail (iv'), according to this proposal, (iii) does not entail (iv). But then, it seems implausible that 'nec' in (iii) and (iv) represents metaphysical necessity.

11 Lewis, 45-6

follow, or because (9) is an abbreviation of (10) which is not an indiscernibility principle.

(10) $\forall x \forall y(x = y \rightarrow (\forall w \forall a((Ww$ & Iaw & $Cax) \rightarrow a = a) \rightarrow$
$\forall w \forall a \forall b((Ww$ & Iaw & Cax & Ibw & $Cby) \rightarrow a = b))$.

In either case, the view is stronger than the thesis that (9) and (10) are synonymous and it is not supported by the translation schema DL alone. Regardless of the plausibility of Lewis's view that (9) is not an indiscernibility principle, his reason for the suggestion that all indiscernibility principles are true seems incorrect. Regarding indiscernibility principles Lewis claims that the schema '$\forall x \forall y(x = y \rightarrow (- x - \leftrightarrow - y -))$' 'says something very uncontroversial indeed, if by "=" we really mean identity: if we have one and the same thing, what's true of it is the same as what's true of it.'[12] Setting aside concerns about whether a schema says anything at all, the claim seems to be false. It is indeed uncontroversial that if we have one and the same thing, what's true of it is the same as what's true of it, but it does not entail that all indiscernibility principles or all instances of the schema above are true. If an indiscernibility principle is false, then there are two open sentences which are alphabetic variants of each other and one of these open sentences is true of some object of which the other open sentence is not true; but it is not the case that if an indiscernibility principle is false then there is an open sentence which is both true and not true of the same object. Unlike Lewis's schema, '$\forall x \forall y \forall z (x = y \rightarrow (z$ is true of $x \rightarrow z$ is true of $y))$' is an indiscernibility principle, and it is presumably true; but it does not entail all instances of Lewis' schema.

---

12 Lewis, 45

V

Some Fregean theories of propositional attitude ascriptions also yield false indiscernibility principles. According to these theories ⌜a believes that φ⌝ (where φ is an extensional open sentence which has free occurrences of a variable α) is true relative to the assignment of an object o to α just in case there is a mode of presentation m of o which is suitably related to a and a believes the Fregean thought which consists of m and the sense of φ relative to a. Since one object may have distinct modes of presentation suitably related to an agent, according to these theories, 'a believes that x ≠ y' may be true relative to the assignment of the same object to 'x' and 'y,' whereas 'a believes that y ≠ y' is false relative to that assignment. But then (11) is an indiscernibility principle which may turn out to be false.

(11) ∀x∀y(x = y → (a believes that x ≠ y → a believes that y ≠ y)).

That (11) may turn out to be false according to these theories of propositional attitude ascriptions is perhaps a good reason to suppose that these theories are false, but it is not a good reason for supposing that these theories are formally defective and that they cannot permit legitimate quantification into propositional attitude constructions.

VI

Reflection on the notion of logical truth also suggests false indiscernibility principles. Though 'logically true' is a predicate of sentences, it seems possible to add to the vocabulary of a language a sentential operator which applies to all and only the logically true sentences of the augmented language, and which permits quantifying in. Suppose that G is the result of augmenting the logical vocabulary of an extensional language with a one-place sentential operator L, and that definition of truth in an interpretation of sentences of G states that

(i) if S is a non-indexical closed sentence of G, and I is an inter-pretation of S, then $\ulcorner LS \urcorner$ is true in I if and only if S is true in all of its interpretations; and

(ii) if S is a non-indexical open sentence of G, and I is an interpre-tation of S, then $\ulcorner LS \urcorner$ is true in I relative to an assignment a if and only if a universal closure of S is true in every interpreta-tion S.

Given these clauses, if 'x = x' and 'x = y' are open sentences of G, then 'L x = x' is true relative to any assignment in any interpretation whereas 'L x = y' is false relative to any assignment in any interpreta-tion. But then (12) is an indiscernibility principle of G which is false in all interpretations.

(2) $\forall x \forall y (x = y \rightarrow (L\, x = x \rightarrow L\, x = y))$.

Kaplan[13] has persuasively argued that two sentences may express the same proposition even though only one of them is logically true. These arguments help to set apart the notions of metaphysical neces-sity and a prioricity from that of logical truth. The characterization of L suggests that these results do not preclude the possibility of quan-tifying into the context 'It is logically true that.'

---

13 David Kaplan, 'Demonstratives' in Joseph Almog, John Perry, and Howard Wettstein, eds., *Themes from Kaplan* (Oxford: Oxford University Press 1989), 481-614

CANADIAN JOURNAL OF PHILOSOPHY
Supplementary Volume 18

The Constitutive A Priori

GRACIELA DE PIERRIS

The modern rationalist tradition initiated by Descartes has as one of its central tenets the independence of the human understanding from the senses. Regardless of the different ways in which independence from experience is understood, there is much common ground among the modern views on the a priori. Yet Kant, culminating this tradition, introduces an entirely new conception of the a priori never before articulated in the history of philosophy. This is the notion of elements in knowledge which are independent of experience but nevertheless closely connected, in a special way, with experience.

Although for Kant the a priori has a privileged position in the structure of knowledge — as it has for other modern rationalist philosophers — one of the most striking, and often neglected, aspect of his conception of the a priori is the great extent to which it is opposed to foundationalism. In particular, Kant's conception strikingly diverges from that of Descartes, who has of course been regarded as providing a rationalist model of an unmitigated foundationalist vision of the structure of justification and knowledge.

Kant believes that knowledge forms a unified body. In this body the propositions in what we might call the *core* of knowledge are a priori, necessary, and thus unrevisable. These core propositions play a distinctively Kantian role in the structure: non-core propositions, in particular empirical propositions, are epistemically related to them in a special way — but not by way of being logically deduced from them. Rather, experience and the whole of knowledge are essentially dependent on the a priori core because without the a priori there would be no experience or knowledge at all. The a priori makes experience possible: it *constitutes* experience.

Kant often uses 'experience' to refer to empirical knowledge (which always contains sensation), or simply to refer to sensation. In addition, he sometimes uses it to include a broad range of notions related to empirical cognition, such as meaningful representation, representation with an objective reference, or representation capable of truth value (that is, representation that does or does not correspond to an object which is independent of our representations). Taking experience in this broad sense, to say that the a priori constitutes experience means not only that the very possibility of empirical knowledge — of sensation becoming an object of knowledge — depends on the a priori, but also that the meaningfulness and objective reference of our knowledge claims depend on the a priori.

Moreover, as we will see below, for Kant the sensory ingredient of experience in turn gives meaning to and legitimizes the a priori. Without the possibility of application to the sensory matter of intuition, the a priori would not amount to knowledge; it would even be devoid of meaning. The constitutive role of the a priori with respect to experience, together with its need for some kind of support from experience, amounts to a reciprocal relation between the a priori and sensory data. The constitutive role of core propositions in the structure of knowledge is foreign to foundationalism, and the reciprocal relation between them and other elements of knowledge is anathema to it.

I wish to address in this paper the broad features of this Kantian conception that make it a unique and revolutionary view. I believe we should not lose sight of the peculiar character of the Kantian notion of the a priori, which I shall call the 'constitutive a priori,' if we seek to understand Kant's system. For this notion is at the heart of what Kant regards as his Copernican revolution in metaphysics. I also consider the Kantian constitutive a priori as crucial for understanding much of twentieth-century philosophy — for example the work of

Carnap and of Wittgenstein. In these philosophers there are also 'fixed' elements among our knowledge claims, such as analytic sentences for Carnap and 'hinge' propositions for Wittgenstein in *On Certainty*. Although these philosophers differ between themselves and with Kant regarding many of the features of these elements — for example for Wittgenstein 'hinge' propositions are neither a priori nor necessary nor unrevisable — they both give to their 'fixed' propositions a Kantian constitutive role in the cognitive enquiry. 'Fixed' propositions in these views are fixed in virtue of their constitutive role, namely making our enquiries possible. The presence of these Kantian alternatives to foundationalism in philosophers as diverse as Carnap and later Wittgenstein shows the far reaching repercussions of the Kantian a priori.[1]

The notion of the constitutive a priori cannot be easily made intelligible in a short presentation, since it is intimately related to many of the most difficult questions of Kant's theoretical philosophy. In order to approach an appreciation, even if a modest one, of the deep transformation that the Kantian constitutive a priori effects in epistemology, I propose to begin by contrasting it with the a priori as conceived by Descartes[2] — who, by giving questions concerning the whole of

---

1   There are of course other more recent philosophers who offer Kantian alternatives to foundationalism — among whom the most prominent is Wilfrid Sellars — although not necessarily by adopting the view that there are fixed elements in the structure of knowledge which play a constitutive role.

2   In this paper, following Kant, I use 'a priori' as a modifier of 'knowledge' or of ingredients of knowledge. Thus in talking about Descartes's a priori I mean Descartes's notion of knowledge (*cognitio* or *scientia*) independent of experience or the intellectual ideas involved in such knowledge. As far as I have been able to determine, Descartes does not use 'a priori' in this Kantian way. Moreover, on the occasion when Descartes uses it to modify 'method of proof,' by the end of the *Second Replies*, he does not mean a method independent of the senses, but rather a method that proceeds, as he puts it, 'from causes to effects.' Descartes is characterizing there — following the medieval and seventeenth century usage of 'a priori' — the analytic method employed in the *Meditations on First Philosophy*. See *Reply to Objections II* in *The Philosophical Works of Descartes*, trans. Elizabeth S. Haldane and G.R.T. Ross (Cambridge: Cambridge University Press

our knowledge and the role of the a priori a leading part in the philosophical enquiry, thereby prepares the ground for Kant. In particular, I propose to draw a contrast between Cartesian rationalist foundationalism and Kant's views. The distinctive features of the Kantian constitutive a priori will become more readily apparent when explained in the context of Kant's opposition to Cartesian or to any other form of foundationalism.

I

The general philosophical approaches of Descartes and Kant have enough in common to allow for an instructive comparison of their views on the structure of knowledge as a whole, and the role of the a priori in this structure. Both philosophers place epistemology at the center of philosophy[3] and give the 'I think' a privileged position in the

---

1967) II, 48. All references to Descartes's works will be from this two volume translation, to be abbreviated as 'HR,' and from *Descartes: Philosophical Letters*, trans. Anthony Kenny (Minneapolis: University of Minnesota Press 1981), to be abbreviated as 'K.' For a reference to Descartes's adoption of the medieval and seventeenth-century usage of 'a priori,' see Alquié's annotation to his edition of the reply in *Descartes, Oeuvres philosophiques*, F. Alquié, ed. (Paris: Garnier 1967), II, 581-5. I owe this last reference to Edwin Curley.

3 That Descartes puts epistemology at the center of philosophy is a widely accepted but not uncontroversial point. Margaret Wilson, for example, in her book *Descartes* (London, Henley, and Boston: Routledge and Kegan Paul 1978) argues that to hold that Descartes accords epistemological questions priority over questions about the nature of reality is misleading. However, by 'epistemological questions or issues' she seems to have in mind mainly Cartesian doubt and the problem of skepticism. She seems to think, in addition, that, because many of Descartes's epistemological views are undeveloped or lack complexity, he does not give priority to epistemology. In this paper I will not assess the intrinsic value, sophistication or complexity of specific epistemological doctrines of Descartes. Nor will I try to answer Wilson on this point. Here I can only assert without argument that regardless of how limited Descartes's epistemological views are, especially in comparison with Kant's, I still believe that Descartes puts epistemology at the center of philosophy — particularly in his most widely read

---

structure of knowledge.[4] Nonetheless, there are fundamental differences between the two philosophers — even with respect to these two very general features of their views.

Descartes's *Meditations* are developed as a search conducted from the point of view of rational human beings with a limited understanding, a search with the goal of arriving at certainties that can ground the most important parts of human knowledge. The Cogito, as the first escape from hyperbolic doubt, is a certainty attained from the human point of view. This prior discovery of the existence of the human mind does not correspond with the priority of beings according to their formal reality[5] — indeed the hierarchy in terms of formal

---

work, the *Meditations*. As it will become clearer below, my conviction is for the most part based on the method followed in the *Meditations*. This is a method conceived in essential dependence of the limitations of human understanding and of the fact of human knowledge.

4 The minimum common ground of adopting the human rational point of view, and of giving a central role to the 'I think' has led to Kantian interpretations of Descartes, such as Martial Gueroult's interpretation of the Cogito in his *Descartes' Philosophy Interpreted According to the Order of Reasons*, trans. Roger Ariew (Minneapolis: University of Minnesota Press 1984), and to Cartesian interpretations of the Kantian transcendental unity of apperception. I reject these interpretations, but I will not offer a full discussion of them here. My main reason for rejecting such interpretations is my conviction that we must understand the two above-mentioned features of Kant's philosophy in connection with Kant's transcendental idealism. This form of idealism is opposed to the transcendental realism of Descartes. It is also opposed to the other side of Descartes's transcendental realism, namely Descartes's empirical psychologism. For English language interpretations of Kant which emphasize the centrality of transcendental idealism in Kant's philosophy, see Graham Bird, *Kant's Theory of Knowledge* (New York: Humanities Press 1962); and Henry Allison, *Kant's Transcendental Idealism* (New Haven and London: Yale University Press 1983).

5 This is the reality *simpliciter* — being or perfection — that entities (including ideas) have, as opposed to the objective reality that only ideas can possess precisely in virtue of being entities that represent something or other. Different entities have different degrees of formal reality: substances have more formal reality than accidents or modes; and the infinite substance has more than finite substances. Ideas can have more or less objective reality depending on the formal

reality is discussed explicitly for the first time in the Third Meditation. In other words, the relationships of dependence among beings according to their metaphysical nature and causal priority is not what guides the unfolding of the *Meditations*, otherwise the *First Meditation* should have been concerned with the nature of the infinite substance: God. The method is dictated by the subjective conditions of thinking, by the conditions of the discovery of truths by *us*, not by the objective relationships of dependence among truths or essences. The Cartesian method in the *Meditations* is not externally imposed on humans by a canon or logic which stands over and above the human mind's processes of connecting its own reasons. The *Meditations* do not follow the order of a pure logic — that is, relationships among concepts or essences that are independent of the facts concerning how human minds can gain access to clear and distinct ideas of the understanding.[6]

---

reality of what they represent. See, for example, *Third Meditation*, HR I, 162, and *Second Replies*, HR II, 56.

6 In my 'Subjective Justification,' *Canadian Journal of Philosophy* **19** (1989) 363-82, I draw the contrast between 'subjective' and 'objective' justification: between psychological-epistemological reasons that a person might possess for believing something and logical reasons that objectively provide grounding for propositions independently of the empirical ways in which believers might establish connections among them. I believe this distinction overlaps in general terms with Descartes's distinction between analytic and synthetic methods. Martial Gueroult, in characterizing the two methods (I, 9), seems to have in mind something very similar to the distinction between subjective and objective justification in my sense. For a recent detailed discussion of the analytic method in the *Meditations*, see Edwin Curley, 'Analysis in the *Meditations*: The Quest for Clear and Distinct Ideas' in *Essays on Descartes' Meditations*, Amelie Oksenberg Rorty, ed. (Berkeley and Los Angeles: University of California Press 1986), 153-76. Curley takes the main distinguishing trait of the analytic method to be its non-deductive character, as opposed to the deductive character of the synthetic method. His description of the non-deductive procedure emphasizes specific ways — such as the introduction of concepts by means of examples, or the 'dialectical method' — by which Descartes attempts to guide any of us, who are attached to the senses and proceed according to common sense, to arrive at the clear and distinct perception of the first principles. Leaving aside the details of Curley's account,

Kant in the *Critique of Pure Reason*[7] also gives epistemology a principal role in his philosophical approach. He, like Descartes, is concerned with the limitations and possibilities of human reason, and his investigation is also conducted from the point of view of rational human minds. This is done in contrast to Leibniz, who departs from the Cartesian procedure of the *Meditations* by comfortably adopting a point of view external to the limited human understanding. Leibniz can be seen as confidently unfolding a metaphysical story that could have been handed down to us by God or could have been written by a non-human logician following the order of reasons of pure logic and of relationships among concepts that are independent of the fact of human knowledge. Nevertheless Kant, contrary to Descartes, and in this respect closer to Leibniz, gives logic — as the discipline that exhibits the forms of judgment and the formal objective relationships of dependence among truths — an extremely important role in his system.

In the Metaphysical Deduction of the *First Critique*, formal Aristotelian logic (which Kant calls 'general logic') offers the clue to the discovery of the a priori concepts of the understanding that are necessary conditions of the possibility of any knowledge. General logic systematizes the forms of judgment, which are independent of the particular character of the objects judged. Since nothing can be an object of experience or of knowledge without being thought, and nothing can be thought without being judged, general logic provides the list of forms of judgment that necessarily underlie any experience and knowledge whatsoever.[8] The prominent position of logic in the construction of Kant's epistemology shows that, in putting epistemol-

---

his understanding of the analytic method does not seem inconsistent with the broad features of my way of presenting the method here.

7 All references to the *Critique of Pure Reason* are from Norman Kemp Smith's translation: *Immanuel Kant's Critique of Pure Reason* (New York: St. Martin's Press 1965), and to the standard numbering of the A (first) or B (second) German editions.

8 See A 50-62/B 74-86; A 67-83/B 92-109.

ogy at the center of philosophy, Kant does not adopt a psychological or empirically subjective point of view — as does Descartes. Another central anti-psychologistic tenet of Kantian epistemology is that the ultimate ground of all judgment and all thought is what Kant calls 'pure or original apperception.' This is a spontaneous act of the understanding — identified with the representation 'I think' — that must be able to accompany all my representations. It is potential consciousness of the act of thinking in abstraction from any contents to which thought might be applied, as opposed to empirical experience of mental states as they succeed each other in time. What Kant calls the 'transcendental unity of apperception' is the unity of self-consciousness in an entirely logical or formal sense. It is formal because it lacks empirical content and does not amount to knowledge of a subject,[9] even though it makes possible the representation of the object of knowledge or experience in general. Transcendental apperception is postulated as a presupposition of experience and knowledge (including experience and knowledge of our own minds or mental states) by philosophical reflection on the possibility of any experience and knowledge. It should be contrasted with empirical apperception, which takes place through introspection or non-philosophical empirical reflection on our individual minds.

The obscurity of the notion of pure apperception is undeniable, and this is not the place to attempt to clarify it, but this much is clear in the doctrine: pure apperception is self-consciousness as the a priori condition of the possibility of any particular act of thinking, and so it is certainly different from the empirical self-consciousness of a given individual thinker considered by Descartes.[10] According to Kant, Descartes never arrives at the conception of the transcendental unity

---

9 Kant says: 'Certainly, the representation "I am," which expresses the consciousness that can accompany all thought, immediately includes in itself the existence of a subject; but it does not so include any knowledge of that subject, and therefore also no empirical knowledge, that is, no experience of it' (B 277).

10 See A 106-8, and B 131-40 (sections 16-18 of the Transcendental Deduction of the Pure Concepts of the Understanding in the B edition).

of apperception, since he either attends solely to empirical self-consciousness or erroneously turns this empirical self-consciousness into a metaphysical entity, the soul (which, for Kant, can only be an idea of reason unknowable to us).[11] Moreover, Kant criticizes Descartes most explicitly in the Refutation of Idealism for taking the existence of the empirical self as an absolutely certain premise while at the same time calling into question the existence of the physical world. Kant here interprets Descartes as confusing transcendental self-consciousness with a determinate awareness of one's own mental states succeeding one another in time. The former is a condition of all rational thinking and thereby a condition of any knowledge whatsoever (including our knowledge of the existence of the external world). The latter amounts merely to empirical knowledge of a particular empirically existing subject. This confusion leads Descartes illegitimately to attribute the certainty of transcendental self-consciousness to empirical self-consciousness.[12]

---

11 See The Paralogisms of Pure Reason: A 341-8/B 399-406; A 349-405; B 407-32. For a very original and thorough discussion of Kant's philosophy of mind, see Karl Ameriks, Kant's Theory of Mind: An Analysis of the Paralogisms of Pure Reason (Oxford: Clarendon Press 1982). For another helpful, although much briefer, English language commentary on this topic, see Henry Allison, ch. 13. I am not suggesting that either of these Kant scholars would agree with the sentences preceding this note. For an exposition from a Descartes scholar who seems to disagree with the contrast I am making between Descartes and Kant on the transcendental self, see Martial Gueroult, I, ch. 3-4. In these chapters Gueroult gives a Kantian-transcendental interpretation of the Cartesian Cogito.

12 This part of the Critique is Kant's answer to skepticism regarding the possibility of knowledge of things in space. Descartes's 'problematic idealism' denies that we can have immediate experience and thus certainty with respect to the existence of objects outside our minds. For Kant we have immediate knowledge of objects in space, since space is an a priori intuition that makes it possible that there be an object of knowledge for us in the first place. Kant's solution to the problem raised by 'problematic idealism' involves turning the Cartesian argument of the First and Second Meditations against Descartes by establishing a necessary connection between empirical self-consciousness — Descartes's Cogito — and immediate experience of objects in space (see B 274-9).

Thus, although both Descartes and Kant adopt the standpoint of the rational human mind, for Kant, unlike Descartes, there is a level of self-consciousness which is an a priori logical condition that makes possible the rational activities of any empirical human mind but is not identified with any such mind. Furthermore, Descartes and Kant also disagree regarding what is cognitively possible for the empirical human mind. Descartes can be seen, from a Kantian point of view, as endowing the finite empirical individual human self with something akin to the intellectual intuition that, according to Kant, only God can possess. Of course clear and distinct perception in Descartes does not create its object the way God's intellectual intuition does for Kant.[13] Moreover, Cartesian clear and distinct perception can be activated only fleetingly and after disciplined effort, due to the fragility of human memory and the power of the prejudice in favor of the senses. Finally, for Kant, God's intellectual intuition is an immediate but also a *non-conceptual* grasp of the object of knowledge, whereas, on the contrary, in Descartes, clear and distinct perception with the mind's eye is a state of the understanding. Nevertheless, there are the following three parallels between clear and distinct perception in Descartes and God's intellectual intuition in Kant.

First, Cartesian clear and distinct perception amounts to a single comprehension of essences that does not involve a step by step procedure or mediation, but is instead akin to visual instantaneous intake of a given visual field involving immediate relation to an object or singular content. For Kant, on the contrary, our understanding, unlike God's, is discursive.[14] This means that our understanding operates by means of (a priori or empirical) general concepts, which are not in immediate relation to an object or singular content, but rather to other representations (be they concepts or

---

13 See, e.g., B 72, and B 139. This clarification was prompted by the comments of an anonymous referee.

14 For a discussion of the discursive character of human understanding in contrast to the intuitive character of God's intellect, see Kant's *Critique of Judgment*, sec. 77.

intuitions).[15] Concepts are characterized as predicates of possible judgments, and Kantian judgments involve highly complex unification of diverse concepts and intuitions.[16] The act of judgment, to which all acts of the understanding can be reduced, is neither single, nor simple, nor instantaneous.[17]

Second, although Cartesian clear and distinct perception is unaided by anything foreign to the intellect, it is also unaided by intellectual inferential processes. Indeed, Descartes subordinates the logical inferential processes of proving truths as understood by contemporary formal logic to clear and distinct perception. For example, in Rule XI of the *Rules for the Direction of the Mind* (HR I, 33-5), Descartes regards it as a problem that memory is usually unable to bring to the present singular act of intuition of a conclusion all the diverse mental acts

---

15 In order for an a priori concept to acquire or to be applied to a content (to have an object), a mediating a priori intuitional third element is needed. See the First *Critique*, chapter on The Schematism of the Pure Concepts of Understanding, A 173/B 176 ff.

16 In the Metaphysical Deduction Kant says: 'Thus in the judgment, "all bodies are divisible," the concept of the divisible applies to various other concepts, but is here applied in particular to the concept of body, and this concept again to certain appearances that present themselves to us. These objects, therefore, are mediately represented through the concept of divisibility. Accordingly, all judgments are functions of unity among our representations, instead of an immediate representation, a *higher* representation, which comprises the immediate representation and various others, is used in knowing the object, and thereby much possible knowledge is collected into one' (A 69/B 93-4).

17 Kantian 'judgments' would roughly correspond — without the complexities associated with Kant's doctrine of judgment — to Cartesian ideas when understood as propositions. But 'judgment' in Kant can also be understood as the act of judging, and thus it can also correspond to Cartesian perception of ideas. What Descartes calls 'judgment' is the act of assenting to or dissenting from, affirming or denying, ideas apprehended by the understanding, and does not belong to the faculty of understanding but to the faculty of choice or free will. (See *Fourth Meditation*, HR I, 171-9.) Therefore, whereas clear and distinct perception belongs to the understanding, apprehension of ideas (propositions) *as true* must be an act of the will. For difficulties associated with these doctrines see the works cited below in note 20.

involved in the steps of the proof leading to this conclusion. He offers the solution of running over all the steps of the proof repeatedly in his mind until he can pass so quickly from the first to the last step that practically no step is left to the memory. The assumption here is that the understanding of a proof, and thus its success as a vehicle for attaining truth, requires the presentation of the whole proof at once before the mind's eye.[18]

For Kant, God's intellectual intuition, precisely because it is non-conceptual, does not involve or need logic. But the human intellectual process essentially involves the a priori concepts of the understanding which are inextricably connected with the logical functions of judgment. A priori or empirical concepts are predicates of possible judgments, and a priori concepts in particular are derived from the logical forms of judgment exhibited in formal logic. These forms in turn play distinctive roles in inferential (syllogistic) processes.

Third, contrary to the Cartesian picture of achieving intellectual immediate knowledge entirely without the aid of non-intellectual contents, Kant believes that we humans, unlike God, cannot find in our own minds a *content* for our intellections — there are no innate ideas for Kant.[19] Nor can we find in our own minds the *content* of our

---

18 For Descartes's hostility towards logic, see Edwin Curley, *Descartes Against the Skeptics* (Cambridge, MA: Harvard University Press 1978), 25-34. For the same topic, and a discussion of the contrast between Descartes and Leibniz regarding their differing conceptions of proof, see Ian Hacking, 'Proof and Eternal Truths: Descartes and Leibniz,' in *Descartes: Philosophy, Mathematics and Physics*, Stephen Gaukroger, ed. (Sussex: The Harvester Press 1980), 169-80. Hacking argues, among other points, that the Cartesian independence of truth from proof is illustrated by Descartes's doctrine that the eternal truths depend on God's will. For Leibniz and for us, as Hacking rightly points out, if a complete set of Euclidean axioms is true, then necessarily the Pythagorean theorem is true too. But for Descartes, God is at liberty to create a Euclidean but non-Pythagorean universe.

19 In my 'Kant and Innatism,' *Pacific Philosophical Quarterly* 68 (1987) 285-305, I discuss the connection between Kant's stand against innatism and his transcendental and anti-psychologistic views. There I argue for the view that to make a priori knowledge rest on innate ideas amounts in the end to psychologism.

intuitions. Such a content can only come from outside the mind, in virtue of our being sensibly affected by objects. Only God, according to Kant, gives himself the content of his knowledge by creating it and is thereby able to apprehend with his intellect such a content at once without mediation. Only God has a non-conceptual, non-mediated, intellectual grasp of the object of knowledge. Descartes does not, as I suggested above, possess the highly developed notions of concept and of judgment deployed by Kant, and his use of the notions of idea and of perception of ideas is ambiguous,[20] but he would agree in general terms with Kant's view of God's understanding. For he would agree that God is not constrained to applying concepts to intuitions in order to have knowledge. The disagreement between Descartes and Kant concerns the *human* intellect.

I emphasized above that for Descartes we do not create for ourselves the contents of our understanding. But, for Descartes, this is precisely because God puts them there as innate ideas. Therefore, we also do not need to be affected by matter to understand the fundamental features of the physical world. In the Cartesian view, we have direct access to an inner content sufficient by itself for building the basic parts of the sciences — including the basic parts of physics — and for understanding our experience of the external world. Through this inner content we can also have knowledge of the existence of God, and of causal relations between God and us, even though God and the corresponding causal relations are beyond the bounds of what we can experience. For Kant, on the contrary, in order to have any knowledge whatsoever, and, in particular, in order to have empirical knowledge of the physical world, we need to be affected by the external world.

---

20 Some illuminating discussions of the difficulties of Descartes's views on 'ideas,' thoughts, consciousness, perception with the mind's eye, judgment, and so on, are, for instance, Edwin Curley, 'Descartes, Spinoza, and the Ethics of Belief' in *Spinoza, Essays in Interpretation*, M. Mandelbaum and E. Freeman, eds. (La Salle, IL: Open Court 1975), 159-89; Anthony Kenny, *Descartes: A Study of his Philosophy* (New York: Random House 1968), ch. 5; Margaret Wilson, ch. 4.

The Cartesian self-sufficiency of the contents of the understanding in relation to experience has a complementary side which Kant rejects as well. This aspect furthers the disagreement between the two philosophers concerning what is cognitively possible for the empirical human mind. The issue concerns how the truth (or the possibility of truth) of our knowledge claims based on the understanding can be guaranteed or established.

For Descartes, when we are working within the context of a science, such as geometry, we are not concerned with giving philosophical foundations to our knowledge, and we can regard clear and distinct ideas of the understanding as a guarantee of truth. Thus Descartes can be interpreted as holding that at a certain level of the intellectual enquiry we can establish, by inspecting our minds alone, that the necessary and sufficient conditions for truth have been satisfied. However, at another level, namely in the context of the philosophical reflection generated by hyperbolic doubt, a justification based on clear and distinct ideas does not by itself secure the truth of the ideas. There is no ultimate philosophical or metaphysical guarantee based on our clear and distinct ideas alone that, for example, the physical world does have the essential feature — extension — that our intellect attributes to it. In the *Meditations* the metaphysical guarantee is attained only when Descartes gives a proof of the existence of a veracious God. Therefore, from the point of view of the meditator who searches for ultimate philosophical conditions of truth, clear and distinct ideas of the understanding are a necessary but insufficient condition of truth. Since clear and distinct ideas must be certified by the existence of a non-deceiving being who is superior and external to human minds, the ultimate philosophical condition for the correspondence between the intellectual representations of human minds and the reality knowable to them is independent of and external to human minds.[21]

---

21 I am aware that my interpretation of Descartes here is insufficiently developed and *prima facie* controversial; however, this is not the place to defend it. The issues involved are directly relevant to the topic of the Cartesian Circle. All of the

For Kant, however, the a priori conditions of the possibility of our experience and knowledge are at the same time conditions constitutive of the possibility of the very reality with which our knowledge claims are concerned. This is one of the central tenets of Kant's transcendental idealism. The reality[22] that, in Descartes, our clear and distinct ideas are supposed to match is a reality wholly independent of the human mind; precisely because it is so independent a veracious God is needed to secure the possibility of a match. For Kant this Cartesian reality transcends the realm of the object of knowledge; it is entirely unknowable to us. It is a reality that, from the philosophical point of view of the critical reflection on the conditions of the possibility of human knowledge, is acknowledged to be independent from the features common to minds with a discursive understanding and a mode of intuition according to space and time. Cartesian reality is a reality as it is in itself independently of the a priori conditions that make it into an object for us.

Kant holds, contrary to this Cartesian view (a type of view that Kant labels 'transcendental realism') that the reality with which our knowledge is concerned is phenomenal reality, reality as it appears to us. A priori conditions contributed by the mind provide structure to some-

---

secondary sources on Descartes mentioned in this paper have interesting albeit different interpretations of Descartes's solution to the problem of the Circle.

22 Reality for Descartes should not be equated with existence. Thus in the *Fifth Meditation*, Descartes says: 'I discover in myself an infinitude of ideas of certain things which cannot be esteemed as pure negations, although they may possibly have no existence outside of my thought, and which are not framed by me, although it is within my power either to think or not to think them, but which possess natures which are true and immutable. For example, when I imagine a triangle, although there may nowhere in the world be such a figure outside my thought, or ever have been, there is nevertheless in this figure a certain determinate nature, form, or essence, which is immutable and eternal, which I have not invented, and which in no wise depends on my mind, as appears from the fact that diverse properties of that triangle can be demonstrated...' (HR I, 179-80). The proof of the existence of God in this *Meditation* depends on the possibility of this and related distinctions.

thing independent of the mind — to something unknowable by us if not subject to these conditions. Kant seeks to reveal, from the philosophical standpoint, that our knowledge claims can match a reality independent of the mind only if such reality, whatever it is, conforms in the first place to the a priori conditions of our knowledge. Anything that can be a candidate for making our knowledge claims true or false must be so articulated by the mind. It follows that the Kantian philosophical conditions of the possibility of assigning truth-values to our knowledge claims are entirely dependent on and internal to features common to all human minds.[23] Yet, this is not to say that we can establish the truth or the possibility of truth of our knowledge claims simply by inspecting the contents of our minds.

II

For Descartes there is knowledge grounded in pure thinking, in the intellect alone. This knowledge is not only independent from the senses with respect to its grounding, it is also acquired independently of experience. The ideas of the understanding, according to Descartes, are not formed by abstraction from what we acquire through the senses. The understanding is thus independent of sensation both with respect to the origin and with respect to the justification of its ideas. In place of abstraction from sensation Descartes postulates that the human mind is innately furnished by God with the ideas needed for understanding whatever a finite mind is constrained to understand. Therefore, despite the fact that ideas of the understanding are absolutely independent of experience, we can have a priori knowledge of the physical world. Although there is an important relation between the ideas of the intellect and empirical observations in the actual

---

23 Notice that here, when talking about Kant's doctrines, unlike when I describe Descartes's views, I speak of the 'possibility' of truth, rather than of truth *simpliciter*. The reason for this qualification will become clearer below.

development of Descartes's physics,[24] such observations do not affect the truth or the justification of the ideas of the understanding; they only supplement intellectual ideas in the course of physical investigation.

Kant, in the Introduction to the *Critique*, claims that although all knowledge begins with [*anfangen mit*] experience, there is knowledge — a priori knowledge — that arises [*entspringen aus*] absolutely independently of experience (B 1). Therefore the independence of the a priori in Kant is not to be interpreted as an independence with respect to origin—namely, as an independence in terms of not being abstracted from sensation. The independence of the a priori in Kant must be viewed as referring to the grounds or justification of knowledge.[25]

For Kant a priori knowledge includes the knowledge of logic, of space and time (mathematics), and the knowledge of the laws of the understanding that involve the categories. The latter in turn ground the a priori part of Newtonian physics. All this knowledge is absolutely independent of sensation in so far as the knowledge claims of which it consists are grounded entirely independently of sensation. No particular empirical propositions enter directly into their justification. Thus Kant is in agreement in this respect with the traditional conception of the a priori.[26] However, the Kantian independence of

---

24 Gerd Buchdahl, for example, appealing to the *Principles*, among other texts, points out that physical assumptions enter crucially into Descartes's scientific method, and that according to Descartes we are free to frame any physical assumptions provided that their deduced consequences agree with observations. See G. Buchdahl, *Metaphysics and the Philosophy of Science* (Oxford: Basil Blackwell 1969), 79-154.

25 I argue for this point in my 'Kant and Innatism,' of which this present paper can be regarded as a development and qualification. In particular I here attempt further to clarify Kant's claim that a priori knowledge arises absolutely independently of experience.

26 Empiricists, such as Hume, share with Kant and Descartes the general characterization of a priori knowledge as knowledge justified or grounded independently of sensations (impressions for Hume). The notion of justification or grounding, as opposed to origin or formation of an idea, must be what Hume

the a priori from sensation is not, in another sense, absolute. For there is a reciprocal relation between the a priori and sensation established by the Copernican revolution.

There is a positive and a negative claim involved in Kant's conception of his Copernican revolution, a positive and a negative claim with respect to the relationship between a priori knowledge and sensation. The two claims together amount to a claim of reciprocity between a priori knowledge and sensation.

The positive claim of the Copernican revolution can be taken as directed against both empiricism and rationalism:

> There are only two possible ways in which synthetic representations and their objects can establish connection, obtain necessary relation to one another, and, as it were, meet one another. Either the object alone must make the representation possible, or the representation alone must make the object possible.... In the latter case, representation in itself does not produce its object in so far as *existence* is concerned, for we are not here speaking of its causality by means of the will. None the less the representation is *a priori* determinant of the object, if it be the case that only through the representation is it possible to *know* anything *as an object*. (A 92/B 124-5)[27]

has in mind when he draws the distinction between reasoning on the basis of 'relations of ideas' alone, and on the basis of 'matters of fact.' (See D. Hume, *Enquiry Concerning Human Understanding* (Oxford: Oxford University Press 1975) sec. IV, part I.) Otherwise he could not hold consistently both this distinction and his basic tenet that all ideas are ultimately originated in impressions. Hume can also be interpreted as sharing with Descartes the view that a priori knowledge ('relations of ideas') is *entirely* independent of sensation, as opposed to the view that there is a reciprocal relation as the one discussed here. This unlikely alliance between Descartes and Hume and other empiricists is due to the fact that all of them are pre-Kantian. Of course empiricists do not share with Descartes the view that ideas of the understanding are independent of sensation with respect to their origin, and do not share the rationalist claim that we can have a priori knowledge of the physical world. The empiricist attack on the latter consists in an attack on innate ideas; therefore, it does not affect Kant's views.

27 The Copernican revolution is announced in the Preface to the second edition of the *Critique* at B xvi, which explicitly links the Copernican revolution with the explanation of a priori knowledge. Other brief presentations of the main point of the Copernican revolution are, for example, at A 114, A 128-9, and B 166-7.

This positive claim goes against empiricism and simultaneously transforms, in a radical way, the traditional rationalist claim that there is no knowledge of the physical world without the a priori. The Kantian view is that the object of knowledge itself is the product of a determination by the faculty of understanding together with the faculty of intuition of something independent of the mind. The a priori elements in knowledge for Kant consist of the a priori forms of intuition (space and time), the a priori concepts or categories of the understanding (substance, causality, community, and so on), and the principles of the understanding corresponding to the categories (such as the causal principle). These a priori elements are not only conditions of the possibility of knowledge of the physical world but also conditions of the physical world itself as an object of knowledge. Whatever is given in sensation is nothing to us — it does not become experience — if it is not formed and synthesized by space, time and the categories, if it does not conform to the a priori ingredients of experience. Experience is a possible object of knowledge in the first place precisely because it has built into it the determinations imposed by the a priori. This positive claim of the Copernican revolution is the claim that the a priori *constitutes* experience or the object of knowledge.

The negative claim of the Copernican revolution is directed exclusively against rationalism. This is the claim that only experience (containing sensation) can give content to the a priori and can legitimize it as knowledge:

Sensible intuition is either pure intuition (space and time) or empirical intuition of that which is immediately represented, through sensation, as actual in space and time. Through the determination of pure intuition we can acquire *a priori* knowledge of objects, as in mathematics, but only in regard to their form, as appearances; whether there can be things which must be intuited in this form, is still left undecided. Mathematical concepts are not, therefore, by themselves knowledge, except on the supposition that there are things which allow of being presented to us only in accordance with the form of that pure sensible intuition. Now *things in space and time* are given only in so far as they are perceptions (that is, representations accompanied by sensation) — therefore only through empirical representation. Consequently, the pure concepts of the understanding, even when they are applied to *a priori* intuitions, as in mathematics, yield knowledge only in so far as these intuitions — and therefore indirectly by their means the pure concepts also — can be applied to empirical intuition. Even, therefore, with the aid of [pure] intuition, the categories do not afford us any knowledge of things; they do so only through their possible application to *empirical intuition*. In other words, they serve only for the possibility of *empirical knowledge*; and such knowledge is what we entitle experience. Our conclusion is therefore this: the categories, as yielding knowledge of *things*, have no kind of application, save only in regard to things which may be objects of possible experience. (B 147-8)[28]

Against his rationalist predecessors,[29] Kant argues in the *Critique* that the demonstration by pure thought of, for example, the existence and attributes of God cannot amount to knowledge. Descartes's use of the causal principle in arguing for the existence of God is illegitimate since we can know about causal relations only in so far as they concern entities in space and time. The category of causality can have a meaning beyond its logical use only if, as a condition of a possible experience, it relates to appearances, that is, only if it relates to things as they appear to us in space and time. In general, the a priori concepts of the understanding do not provide us with knowledge unless they are applied to spatio-temporal things — to contents given according to the forms of human intuition. In other words, in order to achieve knowledge, understanding needs to relate to a priori intuition, and the latter needs to be given a content, i.e., the matter of intuition (sensation).

---

28 For other passages that make the same point, see for example the beginning of the chapter on Phenomena and Noumena at B 298/A 239 ff., or the Schematism at B 178/A 139, B 185/A 146, or at B 186/A 147. In these passages Kant is explicit not only about the fact that the a priori does not amount to knowledge if it is not applicable to empirical intuition, but also about the fact that it lacks meaning or content if it is not so applicable.

29 The negative claim against traditional rationalism has in turn a double aspect as it applies to philosophy and to non-philosophical knowledge. Speculative a priori metaphysics which seeks to know an unknowable realm should be replaced by an a priori metaphysics that concerns itself with the conditions of knowledge of appearance, of things as we experience them. In addition, non-philosophical a priori knowledge, such as mathematics, amounts strictly speaking to knowledge only if it is applicable to experience.

Anything of which we cannot have any sensible experience we cannot know. We cannot know things as they are in themselves independently of the a priori features imposed on them by our faculties of understanding and intuition. What is known — the object of knowledge — is not the nature of things independently of these two faculties. Reason is the faculty of thinking, not of knowing, entities, such as God, which can never be given in sensation. A priori knowledge of the understanding does not give us knowledge of the ideas of reason — of God, freedom, and immortality — since they concern a subject matter entirely beyond the bounds of sense.

The a priori intuitional ingredients of knowledge, space and time, which according to the positive claim of the Copernican revolution have a pivotal role in turning sensation into a knowable object for us,[30] are also affected by the negative claim of the revolution. In the Aesthetic Kant argues that since space and time are a priori, they do not represent a reality completely independent of our minds. Consequently space and time cannot give us knowledge of things as they are in themselves, namely, of things as they are independently of the ways in which human minds are necessarily constrained to experience them. Space and time give us knowledge of appearances, but not of what lies beyond the limits of human experience. Moreover the knowledge they can give us is not strictly speaking knowledge if it is not applicable to sensation. Thus geometry, the study of space, is not to be regarded as fully amounting to knowledge until it is taken in

---

30 One central aspect of Kant's revolution of the a priori is the introduction — in addition to the a priori concepts of the understanding — of necessary a priori ingredients of experience that are intuitional. Understanding and intuition are two separate faculties, and to the extent that each provides separately a priori necessary elements of knowledge they are in a certain sense independent. Yet the pure a priori concepts of the understanding and the pure a priori forms of intuition are ultimately not independent from each other in knowledge, since the categories must be schematized — subsumed under space and time — in order for the principles of the understanding associated with them to be applicable to an empirical content, and thus to amount to knowledge.

conjunction with physics. The latter includes a posteriori data and hence sensation.

The two sides of the Copernican revolution are nicely put together in the following text:

> Thus no one can acquire insight into the proposition that everything which happens has its cause, merely from the concepts involved. It is not, therefore, a dogma, although from another point of view, namely, from that of the sole field of its possible employment, that is, experience, it can be proved with complete apodeictic certainty. But though it needs proof, it should be entitled a *principle*, not a *theorem*, because it has the peculiar character that it makes possible the very experience which is its own ground of proof, and that in this experience it must always itself be presupposed. (A 737/B 765)

This formulation of the synthesis of the positive and negative sides of the revolution adds a new wrinkle: the applicability to sensation demanded of the a priori concepts and principles of the understanding (in this case the causal principle) has to be proved. As I will explain in the following section, the required proof establishes the legitimacy of the concepts and principles of the understanding and appeals in a certain sense to experience — without, however, thereby robbing the concepts and principles of the understanding of their a priori status.

It follows from the Copernican revolution that the traditional conception of the a priori is on firm ground only with respect to our knowledge of formal logic and other cases of (a priori) *analytic* knowledge. For Kant, to show the possibility of *synthetic* a priori judgments is to show that it is possible to have a priori knowledge of something other than the workings of the understanding as a faculty independent of intuition. It is also to show that this knowledge is directly grounded on resources internal to our human faculties (our mode of intuiting — space and time — and the categories). According to Kant, in the picture operating in the traditional view (for example, in Descartes) it is impossible to give a satisfactory explanation of how we can have a priori knowledge of the physical world, since the physical world on that view is entirely independent of our minds. The only explanation of such a knowledge available to Descartes is that we have innate ideas about the physical world — for instance the innate idea that the essence of matter is extension, and the innate ideas of geometry — and that these ideas are right because they have been implanted in our minds by a veracious God.

From a Copernican point of view this conception fails for at least two reasons. First, the Cartesian explanation of a priori knowledge of the physical world in terms of innate ideas assumes that we can know the physical world without experiencing this world. Consequently the Cartesian explanation does not acknowledge that we cannot know anything that lies beyond the limits of experience. Complementarily it does not require that the a priori be legitimized by its applicability to experience. The negative claim involved in the Copernican revolution is thereby contradicted. Second, the traditional conception of a priori knowledge does not arrive at the entirely novel and paradoxical Kantian insight involved in the positive claim of the Copernican revolution: namely, that a priori knowledge itself makes sensation into experience thus into a possible object of knowledge. According to Kant, after this revolution we can satisfactorily explain both that we must know the physical world by experiencing it, and that we can have a priori knowledge of the physical world. This is because sensation — whose possible presence delimits possible knowledge — must conform to a priori knowledge in order to be knowable at all.

III

I will now use the Kantian and Cartesian views discussed so far to explain Kant's opposition to foundationalism. Approaching the constitutive a priori from the standpoint of a contemporary epistemological concern will improve our understanding of the distinctive features of the Kantian a priori.

The label 'foundationalism' is used in contemporary epistemology for a variety of views. The common conception shared by different versions can be explained as follows: every proposition that we are justified in claiming to know is either itself self-justifying (self-supporting) — that is, it does not derive its justification or support from other propositions — or it is justified (supported) by some other propositions that are in turn either self-justifying or justified by self-justifying propositions. Hence the self-justifying propositions comprise the foundation of the totality of our knowledge claims, and the non-foundational propositions depend (immediately or mediately) for their justification on the foundational ones. The whole body of knowledge claims forms a structure in which knowledge claims are like building blocks ordered by non-symmetrical dependency relations. Some propositions depend for their support on the self-supporting ones and nothing else; they in turn play the role of supporting others which depend directly on them, and thus only indirectly on the self-supporting ones; and so on. These relations form a chain of dependency in only one direction: the supported depend on the supporting propositions but not vice versa.[31] In rationalist foundationalism the self-justifying propositions are a priori, and the type of inferential relation that establishes the dependency between foundational propositions and the rest is deduction. Contemporary versions of foundationalism are principally empiricist versions. For the most part their self-supporting propositions are not a priori, and the inferential relations of dependency among propositions are non-deductive (such as evidential relations).[32]

Among Descartes's works the *Rules* fits most neatly with the central elements of rationalist foundationalism. According to this work we must reject merely probable knowledge and trust only indubitable knowledge. The goal of certainty in knowledge concerns all the sciences taken together as a single endeavor since all sciences are interconnected. Yet certainty has so far been achieved only by arithmetic and geometry; therefore, the other sciences must imitate them. The first principles of the mathematical sciences are known with certainty by intuition, which is produced by the 'light of

---

31 See for instance Ernest Sosa, 'The Raft and the Pyramid: Coherence versus Foundations in the Theory of Knowledge' in *Midwest Studies in Philosophy V: Studies in Epistemology*, Peter A. French, et al., eds. (Minneapolis: University of Minnesota Press 1980), 4-5.

32 Roderick Chisholm can be regarded as the contemporary English language paradigm of empiricist foundationalism. See, for example, his *Theory of Knowledge* (Englewood Cliffs, NJ: Prentice-Hall 1977).

reason' alone. The rest of the propositions are consequences derived from the first principles by rational deduction. The intuitive apprehension of the propositions that are absolutely simple allow us to proceed to the knowledge of all others by simple intuitive steps.[33] The simple truths or principles known by intuition are thus, in contemporary terminology, self-justifying or self-supporting and constitute the foundation of all knowledge.

In later writings, such as the *Discourse on Method*, the *Meditations*, and the *Principles of Philosophy*, Descartes raises the possibility of philosophical doubt regarding the simple intuitive propositions of the mathematical sciences. He finds the solution to this kind of doubt again in a priori knowledge, although this time in metaphysical certainties. A priori metaphysical knowledge of the existence of the self and of God is proposed as the grounding of all knowledge. Metaphysics provides the roots for the tree of all the sciences.[34] Nonetheless, the structure of our knowledge, in the early as well as in the later writings, is conceived as having an a priori foundation which does not epistemologically depend on anything else and from which the basic knowledge of other sciences necessarily follows by means of deduction. This is the picture that has led contemporary epistemologists to regard Descartes as the paradigm of traditional foundationalism. Although this view of Descartes needs qualification, it is on the whole right — at least for the relationship between

---

33 See *Rules* I-VI, HR I, 1-19. The emphasis on the simplicity of the foundational truths is a peculiarity of Descartes, not to be found in most other foundationalist views. Gueroult places a great deal of importance on the simple character of the nature of the Cogito in the *Meditations*. See Gueroult, I, ch. 3. The simplicity of foundational truths should be contrasted with the complexity of Kant's judgments discussed above.

34 Thus in a letter to Mersenne of 28 January 1641, Descartes says that the six Meditations contain all the foundations of his Physics, K, 94; in the introduction to the French translation of the *Principles* he says that: 'philosophy as a whole is like a tree whose roots are metaphysics, whose trunk is physics, and whose branches, which issue from this trunk, are all the other sciences' (HR I, 211).

the basic truths of metaphysics and the basic parts of the rest of knowledge.[35]

Three aspects of the Cartesian foundationalist conception can be illuminatingly contrasted with the Kantian view. The first concerns the difference between the character of our a priori knowledge of the base or foundation of knowledge for Descartes and the character of our a priori knowledge of the core of Kant's structure. The second concerns the epistemological independence of the elements in the foundation for Descartes and in the core for Kant. The third concerns the type of logical relationship between the foundation in Descartes or the core in Kant, respectively, and the rest of our knowledge claims. An essential feature of this third point of divergence involves the question of whether, once we have established the right connections between the grounding elements of knowledge (foundation or core) and our other knowledge claims, truth or only the possibility of truth has been established. The Kantian views on these three points are intimately tied with one another; indeed, they are simply different aspects of a single view: the constitutive a priori and the Copernican revolution in metaphysics.

For Descartes, as has been stressed repeatedly above, our a priori knowledge of the foundation consists in the perception by the understanding of clear and distinct ideas. The truths that we so perceive are said (for example, in the *Meditations* and in the *Principles*) to be known by the 'natural light.'[36] In the geometrical (synthetic) exposition of the *Meditations* at the end of the *Second Replies* they are said to be 'intelligible *per se*,' 'evident,' or 'self-evident.' Some of the propositions called 'axioms' are supposed to be immediately evident or self-evident,

---

35 Clearly, for scientific method this picture amounts to an oversimplification. As I pointed out above, Gerd Buchdahl and other commentators point to the empirical elements in Descartes's derivation of physics. Furthermore, the tension in Descartes's conception of his scientific method between the use of the hypothetical-deductive method and deduction can undermine the certainty of science. See G. Buchdahl, 118-55.

36 In the Third Meditation at HR I, 160-5; in Principle XI at HR I, 223; and so on.

whereas for other axioms meditation is needed in order for them to become evident.[37] I take it that the minimal feature shared by Cartesian foundational propositions is their evidence or self-evidence; and I interpret this to consist in the fact that if these propositions are understood, then necessarily they are true and believed to be true (leaving aside the question of the possibility of raising a metaphysical doubt about some of them before the proof of the existence of a veracious God).[38] In the *Rules* the examples of foundational self-evident propositions are mathematical, while in the *Meditations* and the *Principles* they are metaphysical; but both the mathematical and the philosophical propositions share this central feature — evidence or self-evidence — which makes them candidates for the role of being foundational.

Kant is very explicit about his disagreement with any such conception of the character of our a priori knowledge of the core principles which for him are conditions of the possibility of all knowledge. Among

---

37 'I bid them carefully rehearse those propositions, intelligible *per se*, which they find they possess, e.g., *that the same thing cannot at the same time both be and not be; that nothing cannot be the efficient cause of anything*, and so forth; and thus employ in its purity, and in freedom from the interference of the senses, that clarity of understanding that nature has implanted in them, but which sensuous objects are wont to disturb and obscure. For by this means the truth of the following Axioms will easily become evident to them' (HR II, 54); 'Among other things they must reflect that while possible existence indeed attaches to the ideas of all other natures, in the case of the idea of God that existence is not possible but wholly necessary. For from this alone and without any train of reasoning they will learn that God exists, and it will be not less self evident to them than the fact that number two is even and number three odd, and similar truths' (HR II, 55). For an interesting discussion of Descartes's use of these notions, see Anthony Kenny, ch. 8.

38 Compare my use of 'evident' with Bernard Williams's use of this word and others such as 'self-verifying,' 'incorrigible,' 'pragmatically self-defeating' and so on, in B. Williams, *Descartes: The Project of Pure Enquiry* (New York: Viking Penguin 1978), 72-88. In this work Williams gives the following definition: 'that a proposition is *evident* (with respect to A) means that if it is true, then A believes it' (77). I am using 'evident' in a more standard way.

these are philosophical principles — the principles of the understanding — whose specific epistemological character is derived again from the discursive nature of our understanding. In the chapter of the *Critique* entitled 'The Discipline of Pure Reason in its Dogmatic Employment,' Kant draws a sharp contrast between philosophical and mathematical knowledge. He says that *'philosophical* knowledge is the *knowledge gained by reason from concepts*; mathematical knowledge is the knowledge gained by reason from the *construction* of concepts' (A 713/B 741). Philosophy is concerned exclusively with universal concepts, whereas mathematics cannot achieve anything with concepts alone but concerns itself with construction in pure intuition (A 715-16/B 743-4). Intuition here is not, of course, intellectual intuition *à la* Descartes, but intuition as used by the geometer when producing demonstrations via the construction of geometrical entities.[39]

The difference between philosophy and mathematics does not arise because philosophy is conceived by Kant as consisting of analytic propositions produced by the mere analysis of concepts. On the contrary, philosophy as a reflection on the conditions of the possibility of any experience consists of synthetic a priori propositions.[40] The only intuition given a priori is the form of intuition — space and time — and mathematics is the a priori science that studies this form. But in philosophy no intuition is given a priori due to the discursive nature of the philosophical endeavor. In other words, philosophy deals with a priori concepts (such as the concepts of reality, substance, force, and so on) which concern the possibility of empirical knowledge — of *sensible* experience.[41]

---

39 For an explanation of the notion of construction in pure intuition and of its central role in Kant's conception of geometry, see Michael Friedman, 'Kant's Theory of Geometry,' *The Philosophical Review* **44** (1985) 455-506.

40 Thus Kant says: 'There is indeed a transcendental synthesis [framed] from concepts alone, a synthesis with which the philosopher is alone competent to deal; but it relates only to a thing in general, as defining the conditions under which the perception of it can belong to possible experience' (A 719/B 747).

41 'A transcendental proposition is therefore synthetic knowledge through reason,

The mathematical method has the advantage that it can realize its concepts in a priori intuition. But philosophy cannot attain knowledge of the natural world through its a priori discursive concepts alone, because it is unable to intuit a priori and thus confirm the reality of such a world. The success of the mathematical method can, however, give rise to the illegitimate expectation that it can be applied in philosophy; and this — typically rationalist — illusion therefore neglects the differences between the two disciplines (A 724-5/B 752-3). The definitions, axioms, and demonstrations so essential to mathematics cannot be achieved or imitated by the philosopher (A 726-7/B 754-5 ff.). Since the philosophical synthetic principles are derived from a priori concepts rather than from a priori intuition, they cannot be immediately certain; and it follows, for Kant, that there are no axioms in philosophy. There is no knowledge of the philosophical synthetic principles that is immediately and directly obtained from the concepts occurring in them. These principles can be regarded as certain only after a proof of their validity has been given — that is, after a transcendental deduction or philosophical legitimation showing that the categories involved in them are applicable to objects of *empirical* intuition. From the fact that the philosophical principles at the core of knowledge require a transcendental proof, it follows that they are not evident.[42]

---

in accordance with mere concepts; and it is discursive, in that while it is what alone makes possible any synthetic unity of empirical knowledge, it yet gives us no intuition *a priori*' (A 722/B 750). Here Kant means by 'transcendental proposition' a proposition of philosophy.

42 'Now one concept cannot be combined with another synthetically and also at the same time immediately, since, to be able to pass beyond either concept, a third something is required to mediate our knowledge. Accordingly, since philosophy is simply what reason knows by means of concepts, no principle deserving the name of an axiom is to be found in it.... But a synthetic principle derived from concepts alone can never be immediately certain, for instance, the proposition that everything which happens has a cause. Here I must look round for a third something, namely, the condition of time-determination in an experience; I cannot obtain knowledge of such a principle directly and immediately

The second difference between Kant's conception of a priori principles and Cartesian foundationalism relies on the very same Kantian point on which the lack of evidence of the principles rests: the need for a transcendental deduction of the categories associated with the philosophical principles at the core of knowledge. This need shows that they are not, to put it in a terminology used by some contemporary foundationalists, self-justifying or self-supporting. In particular, it has the peculiarity of making the principles *dependent* on experience for their legitimation. The objective reality of the categories and principles is established when it is shown that they do apply to human experience in general because they are a priori features necessary to any possible experience with a spatio-temporal structure, and thus necessary to any actual human experience.

Kant sometimes puts the point of the dependency of the a priori on sensory experience, as I mentioned above, by saying that the sensory ingredient of experience gives meaning and content to the a priori elements of knowledge. In particular, without their application to the sensory matter of intuition, the categories would not only be devoid of objective reality and truth, but also of meaning. Pre-Copernican rationalist attempts to apply the concepts of the understanding, such as substance and causality, beyond logic to what we cannot experience, make the use of these concepts illegitimate and deprive them of meaning or content.

Kant shows the truth of his Copernican view by proving the possibility of synthetic a priori knowledge. Synthetic a priori judgments, such as those of mathematics, the transcendental principles of the understanding, and the basic laws of natural science, make our expe-

---

from the concepts alone. Discursive principles are therefore quite different from intuitive principles, that is, from axioms; and always require a deduction. Axioms, on the other hand, require no such deduction, and for the same reason are evident — a claim which the philosophical principles can never advance, however great their certainty. Consequently, the synthetic propositions of pure, transcendental reason are, one and all, infinitely removed from being as evident ... as the proposition that *twice two make four'* (A 732-3/B 760-1).

rience, and knowledge of it, possible. Unlike analytic judgments (for example, logic) they extend our knowledge beyond the concepts contained in them since they essentially concern experience. Nevertheless, they are still a priori since they concern only the possibility of human experience. Their truth is not directly grounded on particular, actual experiences — the subject matter of synthetic a posteriori judgments — but on all the sensory representations and only those that our minds can constitute as knowledge. In other words, in order to show that synthetic a priori judgments are true, we need only to appeal to the universal structural features of any possible experience we can have. Synthetic a priori judgments need to be confirmed only by the necessary traits of any of our experiences, no matter the sequences of sensations that confirm or disconfirm synthetic a posteriori judgments.[43]

Hence, there is no inconsistency in Kant between the a priori character of the categories and principles, on the one hand, and their dependency on experience for their meaning and objective reality, on the other. For in the unfolding of the transcendental deduction of the categories there is no appeal to any actual synthetic a posteriori judgment, but only to possible experience in general. The proof of legitimacy consists in an argument for the claim that the core principles are exhibited in any possible experience that we can have. This proof thereby includes actual experience — intuitional empirical contents, and these contents are thus shown to share with any other contingent content that we might possibly experience the ineliminable and indispensable structural features so legitimized.

To sum up: Kantian core propositions are not self-supporting because they are in need of proof. The proof legitimizes the a priori by showing its applicability to possible experience — and the proof therefore essentially involves the negative claim of the Copernican

---

43 In the *Critique*, in the section on the Postulates of Empirical Thought, Kant gives as the first postulate: '1. That which agrees with the formal conditions of experience, that is, with the conditions of intuition and of concepts, is *possible*' (A 218/B 265).

revolution. But the proof consists in showing that the a priori makes possible (constitutes) its own ground of proof — the proof therefore essentially involves the positive claim of the Copernican revolution as well.[44]

Foundational propositions in Descartes's system, on the other hand, do not have the constitutive role assigned to Kantian core propositions by the positive claim of the Copernican revolution. More importantly in the context of the present discussion, Cartesian foundational propositions are not in need of any further support, deduction, proof, or legitimation — least of all from experience. Nor do they need to borrow a content or meaning from experience. They do not depend in these respects on experience even if understood as the possibility of experience in general. For, as the negative claim of the Copernican revolution reminds us, Cartesian foundational propositions purport to extend our knowledge to a realm beyond the limits of possible experience — an unknowable realm, according to Kant. For example the causal principle is illegitimately applied to non-spatio-temporal beings. Traditional rationalism is thus oblivious to constraints imposed by possible experience. Consequently, foundational propositions are taken by the traditional rationalist to be completely independent of experience: both from particular experiences and from experience conceived as a possibility.

---

44 As I suggested earlier, there is a strong claim involved in the proof: not only are the categories (and a priori intuitions) necessary conditions for us to experience (represent) things the way we do, but they are necessary conditions for there being an objective world distinct from our contingent ways of representing it. The stronger claim, or more specifically our *knowledge* that the stronger claim is true, is the only one suitable for an answer to skepticism. Barry Stroud in his 'Transcendental Arguments,' reprinted in *Kant on Pure Reason*, Ralph Walker, ed. (Oxford: Oxford University Press 1982) 117-31, makes a similar point regarding the strength required of transcendental arguments if they are to succeed in answering the skeptic. Stroud argues that recent attempts to use transcendental arguments to answer skepticism rely on the verification principle. Although he does not say it explicitly, he seems to suggest that Kant's argument also relies on the verification principle. I believe Kant's argument does not need to rely on such a principle, but this is not the place to argue for this view.

Finally, with respect to the type of relationship between Cartesian foundational propositions and the rest of the body of knowledge, the Cartesian relationship is one of deductive implication between the truth of the foundational premises and the truth of specific knowledge claims. As we saw above, Descartes gives a secondary role to purely logical proofs and suggests that deduction must be ultimately certified by intuition. Moreover, Descartes's central philosophical work, the *Meditations*, does not follow the synthetic (geometrical/deductive) method, but the analytic method. Yet the analytic method is only the human method of discovery — the method of beings limited by a finite understanding, by the prejudices of common sense, by the grip of sensory ideas, and so on. It is the meditator's method for the discovery of those indubitable truths that, once in place, serve as a foundation from which the central parts of the body of knowledge, such as the basic parts of physics, follow deductively.[45]

The Kantian view of the relationship between core propositions and the rest of our knowledge follows from the points already made about the positive claim of the Copernican revolution. Although Kant uses the word 'deduction' to refer to his proof of the objective reality of the categories, he does not mean by it what formal logicians do. He uses the term rather in the juridical sense of his time.[46] If Kant did use it in the logician's sense, what logical implication would he take himself as showing? One interpretation might be that the objective reality of the categories is implied by observable features of our actual experience. Thereby the categories would be necessary conditions, in the

---

45 For details on how the *Meditations* might relate to the foundations of Cartesian physics, see E. Curley, ch. 8; for the role of God in the derivation of the laws of motion, see M. Gueroult, 'The Metaphysics and Physics of Force in Descartes,' in Stephen Gaukroger, ed., 196-229.

46 Dieter Henrich has shown this in 'Kant's Notion of a Deduction and the Methodological Background of the First *Critique*,' in *Kant's Transcendental Deductions: The Three 'Critiques' and the 'Opus Postumum'*, Eckart Förster, ed. (Stanford: Stanford University Press 1989), 29-46. This legal notion of a deduction refers to a justification of a claimed right and concerns only acquired rights — as opposed to innate rights.

logical sense, of the facts we experience, of the actual truth of experiential claims. But this would amount to deriving the categories directly from empirical facts — from the truth of synthetic a posteriori judgments — and would consequently void the a priori character of the categories. It would also mean that the principles associated with the categories are not necessary truths. On this interpretation, contrary to what Kant claims, the proof would be empirical, a type of derivation that according to Kant is only suitable for empirical concepts.[47]

The interpretation of the relationship between the a priori and the rest of our knowledge in terms of deduction in the logician's sense would mean either that the truth of empirical propositions logically implies the truth of core propositions, or that the truth of core propositions logically implies the truth of empirical propositions. The first alternative is eliminated on the basis of the above explicit rejection of

---

47   See section 13 of the Transcendental Deduction (A 84-92/B 116-24). The following paragraph from that section makes the point under discussion very explicit: 'Let us take, for instance, the concept of cause, which signifies a special kind of synthesis, whereby upon something, A, there is posited something quite different, B, according to a rule. It is not manifest *a priori* why appearances should contain anything of this kind (experiences cannot be cited in its proof, for what has to be established is the objective validity of a concept that is *a priori*); and it is therefore *a priori* doubtful whether such a concept be not perhaps altogether empty, and have no object anywhere among appearances.... Appearances might very well be so constituted that the understanding should not find them to be in accordance with the conditions of its unity.... If we thought to escape these toilsome enquiries by saying that experience continually presents examples of such regularity among appearances and so affords abundant opportunity of abstracting the concept of cause, and at the same time of verifying the objective validity of such a concept, we should be overlooking the fact that the concept of cause can never arise in this manner. It must either be grounded completely *a priori* in the understanding, or must be entirely given up as a mere phantom of the brain. For this concept makes strict demand that something, A, should be such that something else, B, follows from it *necessarily and in accordance with an absolutely universal rule*. Appearances do indeed present cases from which a rule can be obtained according to which something usually happens, but they never prove the sequence to be necessary' (A 90-1/B 122-4).

it by Kant. The second alternative neglects a central aspect of Kant's conception: the categories, and in general the a priori in knowledge, are necessary conditions of the possibility and intelligibility of any human experience, not of the actual contingent truth of particular empirical experiences or knowledge claims. If there is to be any meaningful human experience at all, if our representations are not to be chaotic but are to have an objective counterpart, if the manifold of sensation is to have the required unity for it to belong to a unified experience, if we can truly or falsely predicate something of it — then the a priori must be a feature common to all our representations and their objects. Therefore, if there is an 'if-then' in this direction, it cannot be a deductive implication between the a priori and the truth of particular empirical knowledge claims. The a priori is rather a necessary condition of our empirical knowledge claims being meaningful, having an object, belonging to a unified experience, or having a truth value at all.[48] This is as much as a transcendental argument can prove. The Kantian procedure therefore has no resemblance with Cartesian deduction.

The difference in procedure is the difference between logical deduction of the truth of that which the premises ground and a Kantian transcendental proof. In the foundationalist enterprise the independent truth of the a priori premises of the deduction establish the actual truth of the derived (a priori or empirical) conclusions. The Kantian transcendental argument is an argument that shows the

---

48 Gordon Brittan has very clearly captured this point in his adaptation of the semantic notion of presupposition to the discussion of the anti-reductionism in Kant's philosophy of science. To distinguish presupposition from implication, Brittan defines the former as: 'A *presupposes* B if and only if (a) if A is true, then B is true, (b) if (not-A) is true, then B is true.' Thus, for instance, unlike the case of logical deduction, the analogue of *modus tollens* for presupposition does not hold. See G. Brittan, *Kant's Theory of Science* (Princeton: Princeton University Press 1978), ch. 1. Brittan criticizes, and successfully shows to be wanting, other alternative views of 'necessary condition' (not discussed here) that preserve the deductive interpretation of the link between the categories and principles, and the rest of knowledge.

relationship between the a priori and experience by showing the constitutive role of the former with respect to the latter. However, this constitutivity concerns only, as we have seen, the possibility of experience. Thus in a successful Kantian transcendental argument only the *possibility* of meaning, objective reference, knowledge, and truth is established. Moreover, the a priori, which is the source of such a possibility (i.e., which makes possible meaning, objective reference, knowledge, and truth), is itself legitimized by the proof.

The central features of the Cartesian foundational role of the a priori are inherited by Spinoza and Leibniz. Kant, in providing rationalism with an empiricist twist, distances himself from this tradition and starts a far-reaching revolution in the conception of the structure of knowledge as a whole. The effects of this Copernican turn are still present in our century. Without a priori intuition, a contemporary philosopher such as Carnap gives formal logic — the syntax of language — the constitutive role Kant gives to space, time, and the categories. Without a priori necessary presuppositions, and while rejecting the conception of a unified single body of knowledge, a very different contemporary philosopher such as Wittgenstein acknowledges the need for fixed, although revisable, constitutive points in the ongoing piecemeal process of building and rebuilding our knowledge claims. The deep influence of the Kantian constitutive a priori is still with us; but a fuller discussion of this point shall be left for another occasion.

CANADIAN JOURNAL OF PHILOSOPHY
Supplementary Volume 18

Kant's A Priori Methods For Recognizing Necessary Truths

J.A. BROOK

In the second edition, Kant summarized the question behind the *Critique of Pure Reason* this way: 'How are *a priori* synthetic judgments possible?' (B19)[1] We can easily understand his interest in synthetic judgments; he thought that analytic ones could not tell us anything new (A5-6=B9). There are only two ways to get judgments that are analytic: by drawing out what is contained in our concepts and by combining the resulting propositions inferentially into arguments. Neither could ever tell us anything not already 'thought in [the concepts we have used], though confusedly' (A7=B10-11), and even if either could, it could not give us anything against which to test it for truth or falsity. 'In the *mere concept* of a thing no mark of its existence is to be found' (A225=B272; cf. Bxvii-xviii). In the search for knowledge, analytic judgments get us nowhere. That is why analysis is useless for establishing propositions of traditional metaphysics

---

1 References to the *Critique of Pure Reason* will be given in the text using the standard 'A' and 'B' notation. 'A' refers to the pagination of the first edition (1781) and 'B' to that of the second edition (1787). (Of the numerous editions of the *Critique*, Kant prepared only these two himself.) I will use Norman Kemp Smith's 1927 translation, *Immanuel Kant's Critique of Pure Reason* (London: MacMillan 1963), sometimes with minor changes. Except in one part of the paper noted later, a reference only to one edition means that the passage in question does not appear in the other one.

about God, freedom, and immortality, as Kant argues in the Dialectic. Few would disagree with this verdict on analytic judgments, or criticize a preference for synthetic ones. But why was he so interested in those synthetic judgments that are a priori? As we will soon see, the answer to this question quickly leads us to Kant's interest in necessary truth, and to some peculiarities in what he offers us, in both his theory of necessity and this theory of the a priori.

I think the most immediate answer to our question is that, as Kant saw it, both the kinds of synthetic judgment that most interested him are a priori, the judgments that make up mathematics and physics and those that would have to make up metaphysics if it contains knowledge at all. The former are a priori because the propositions they express are necessarily and universally true, not contingently true or true of only part of a domain. Except for the ones Kant rescues, the latter do not contain real knowledge, but if they did, this knowledge would have to be obtained a priori. We have no sensible awareness of what these propositions describe, neither God, freedom (uncaused choices) and immortality, nor the things Kant rescues.

In addition to tying the two sides of his project together in this way, Kant might have had other reasons to be especially interested in the a priori, though here we can only speculate. In his time, philosophers (and not just philosophers) were interested in what the mind could do unaided by sensible observation. Hume had recently launched a stinging attack on the very possibility of the mind coming to know anything new in any way other than by sensible observation. And, of course, theology, morality, and psychology were conducted almost entirely by non-empirical analysis, the latter in the form of rational psychology.[2]

---

2 Kant's attack on rational psychology in the chapter on the paralogism is, to my mind, the most successful discussion in the whole of the *Critique of Pure Reason*. Kant's attempt to 'deny knowledge' in various domains 'in order to make room for faith' (Bxxx) was at the heart of his reasons for writing the *Critique of Pure Reason*, though this has sometimes been overlooked.

By 'a priori,' Kant means 'known independently of experience' (B2), where by 'experience' Kant means and from now on I will mean 'sensible awareness.' (At least that is what he meant here. He used 'a priori' in other ways, too, a point to which we will return.) By 'independently of experience,' Kant means that some aspect of our belief in a judgment is based on something other than what we observe or could observe, and yet is not based on inference either. As we will see later, the 'something other' is a certain exercise of our cognitive or conceptual imagination.

I Privileging Necessity

If the above partly explains why Kant started with a priori synthetic knowledge, it was still a peculiar place to start. Why should it matter whether a judgment is believed or known a priori or not? Surely what matters is whether it is true and we are justified in believing it — whether it is knowledge. Kant, however, had a more restricted view of what counts as knowledge, or, perhaps a better way to view it: he placed stringent conditions on justification. I think this puts us on the trail of his deepest reason for privileging a priori knowledge. For Kant, we do not have genuine knowledge about something until we know not just its contingent features but things about it that are necessarily so (here we do not need to worry about what kind of necessity he might have had in mind). But all knowledge is expressed in judgments, propositions, etc., and we can know that a judgment, proposition, etc., is necessarily true only by a priori means. 'Experience teaches us that a thing is so and so, but not that it cannot be otherwise' (B3). Thus only propositions, judgments, etc., known a priori, at least in part, could contain genuine knowledge. And that is why Kant emphasized synthetic judgments that are a priori. What mattered about a judgment being a priori is that this reflected its necessity.

In addition, Kant thought it evident that we have such knowledge. As was true of most philosophers in his time, Kant took mathematics to be the exemplar of knowledge, and it seemed obvious to him that the propositions of mathematics are necessarily true (cf. B4-5, B17,

B20-1; we will return to these passages).[3] Kant had in mind mainly arithmetic and Euclidean geometry, though later he included algebra (A717=B745ff.) and must have held the same view of calculus and analytic geometry. It seemed similarly evident to him that the propositions of physics (Newtonian physics) have the same necessity. Thus it seemed evident to him that we already have knowledge that consists of necessary truth. Since all knowledge that goes further than merely spelling out what is already built into concepts is also synthetic, and, as Kant thought, not only physics but also mathematics goes further than that, he also saw these two bodies of knowledge as synthetic. He then takes as his task to show how these types of synthetic a priori knowledge are possible and where similar knowledge is not possible (in metaphysics). Indeed, carrying out this two-sided task was the single broad goal of the first *Critique* (B19).[4]

The synthetic, necessary, and therefore a priori knowledge that Kant had in mind is knowledge of general propositions, propositions which say something about all members of a class or kind. Even the best possible empirical support for a general proposition, Kant thought, would never ensure that it is universally true (B3-4). Presumably his thought was that if a proposition is not necessary, it is not guaranteed to be true of all members of the class or kind it is about, only of those members so far observed; it is thus vulnerable to refutation. When a proposition is necessarily true, this limitation is overcome. Thus, it is superior to a contingent one; unlike the latter, the former is not merely approximative, limited to as much of the world as we have observed or to merely inductive generalizations, rules of thumb. For us to *know* (and not just believe) that a general proposition is true, we must know that it is necessarily true. It describes what will

---

3 This of course was the general view at the time. Descartes took geometry as his exemplar of certain knowledge. As a very different example, we might recall that in 1763 the Berlin Academy proposed as a topic, 'Are the Metaphysical Sciences Amenable to the Same Certainty as the Mathematical?'

4 This is how Patricia Kitcher sees Kant's central task, too (*Kant's Transcendental Psychology* [New York: Oxford University Press 1990], 15).

always be the case in our world as we observe it, indeed not just in our world but in any world, and with guaranteed accuracy, complete invulnerability to refutation. That is to say, it yields certainty. (If so, it is also proof against some important forms of skepticism. However, skepticism did not become a concern for Kant until the second edition, as a result, it is believed, of misunderstandings of the first edition broadcast by Garve and Feder in their famous review.[5]) Kant was clearly uneasy about privileging the necessary, or perhaps about his lack of arguments for doing so ('reason ... is so insistent upon this kind of knowledge,' he says (A2-3), seeming to imply, '... but I am not sure why'). But he seems never to have questioned it. In fact, merely *being* necessary is not enough; to have the superior sort of knowledge of something, we must also *know* that the propositions describing it are necessary. Otherwise, even if *the proposition* contains superior knowledge, we do not. To know that a general proposition contains knowledge, then, two conditions must obtain: (1) the properties it ascribes to the object or state of affairs it describes must have 'true universality and strict necessity' (A2, B2), and (2) we must know that they do (A2 and B2 imply this, too).

In addition to the arguments I have just reconstructed, doubtless other considerations pushed Kant in the direction of believing that genuine knowledge must consist of necessary and universal truths. Perhaps the most important additional one was his long pre-critical romance with rationalism. Indeed, until recently most philosophers have believed that necessary truths have special epistemic virtues.

---

5 Paul Guyer says that Feder was the villain. Apparently the passages that upset Kant were mostly added by Feder to Garve's original draft (*Kant and the Claims of Knowledge* [New York: Cambridge University Press 1987], 434).

II The Focus On A Prioricity Rather Than Necessity

Whatever his reasons, Kant's decision to start with a priori judgments and their possibility disguised important differences between the two kinds of a priori judgment mentioned earlier. What struck him about mathematics and science was not so much that we know a feature of the judgments contained in them a priori so much as that these judgments are necessarily true. At B17, for example, he considers the judgments, 'that in all changes of the material world the quantity of matter remains unchanged; and that in all communication of motion, action and reaction must always be equal,' and says, 'both propositions, it is evident, are ... necessary ....' The connection to the a priori is that to gain the knowledge that these judgments are *necessarily* true, we have to use a priori means (cf. B3 again). By contrast, what struck him about metaphysics was that we do not have sensible access to the various objects of its inquiries. Thus, if we are aware of them at all, it must be by a priori means. However, not only are these judgments not necessarily true, they are not true at all, not as far as mere mortals can know, at any rate. (Perhaps Kant thought that if they were true, then they would be necessarily true, but I will not investigate that strange, Kripkean modal construction.) So whereas the a priori-related feature of metaphysical judgments is our lack of sensible access to their objects, the a priori-related feature of mathematics and science is that the propositions that make them up are necessarily true.

Rather than focusing on this necessity, however, Kant chose to focus on the a prioricity of our knowledge of it. One result of this is that his views on both necessity and the relationship of necessity to a prioricity are seriously underdeveloped. For him, necessity is the prior notion, and he uses it to construct a criterion, in fact the only criterion he offers in the Introduction, of a prioricity — 'if we have a proposition which in being thought is thought as *necessary*, it is an *a priori* judgment ...' (B3). (Since necessary judgments are also universal, universality is an equally good criterion, one moreover that no inductive judgment can ever satisfy [B4].) However, first, necessity is not a terribly good criterion because it does not apply in any straightforward way to metaphysical judgments, if it applies to them at all; and second, and far more importantly, Kant does not tell us how we manage to recognize the necessity of judgments or discriminate the necessarily true from the merely true. On B4, he says 'it is easy to show that there actually are in human knowledge judgments which are necessary and in the strictest sense universal,' but he makes no attempt to do so, not in the Introduction at any rate.

Why did Kant think that the judgments of mathematics and at least some of the judgments of physics are necessarily true? He simply thought that this is evident. Recall the remark from B17 quoted just above. Or consider the footnote to B21, where he says that 'we have only ... to consider the propositions at the beginning [i.e., at the foundation] of (empirical) physics ... in order to be soon convinced that they constitute a *physica pura*, or *rationalis* ...' (B21), that is to say, a body whose 'beginning' propositions at least are necessarily true. For a somewhat more complicated example, consider Kant's response to Hume on causality. Kant represents Hume as urging that 'an a priori proposition' with respect to the connection of an effect with its cause 'is entirely impossible' (B19-20), and responds as follows:

> If he [Hume] had envisaged [the] problem in all its universality, he would never have been guilty of this statement, so destructive of all pure philosophy. For he would then have recognized that, according to his own argument, pure mathematics, *as certainly containing a priori synthetic propositions*, would also not be possible; and from such an assertion his good sense would have saved him. (B20, my emphasis)

One wonders what Quine would say about that! The important point, however, is that Hume did not attack the a prioricity of causal propositions, not directly at least; he attacked their necessity. To be sure, as one of his arguments he did urge that we could never know the truth of such propositions a priori. But he made this point to show that these propositions are not necessarily true, not because it is intrinsically important.[6] And when Kant says in response that mathematics at least

---

6 Hume uses the denial of a priori knowledge argument in the *Enquiry Concerning Human Understanding* (1748), Charles W. Hendel, ed. (Indianapolis: Library of the Liberal Arts 1955), 42. In *A Treatise on Human Nature* (1736), L.A. Selby-Bigge,

is certainly a priori, his basis for saying this, I think, was his certainty that its judgments are necessarily true.

In short, in the Introduction at least, Kant seems to have simply taken it for granted that the judgments of mathematics and science are necessary, and then used this concept of necessity to anchor his notion of the a priori.[7] Like cognitive science two hundred years later, Kant tended to take the credentials of knowledge-claims at face value and concentrate instead on the conditions under which we make them, how we could be aware of their various features, and how they hang together. He then focused his attention on the consequent claim that necessity could only be recognized a priori. How is it possible to make or recognize the connection between subject and predicate in such judgments a priori and recognize that it is necessary a priori (A9=B13)? (Moreover, Kant did not even stick with this topic, as we will see.)

We are suddenly faced with a host of questions. Why was Kant so sure that the propositions of mathematics and at least the 'beginning' propositions of physics are necessarily true? Did he have something better than his sense of the evident to back him up, something to justify his boast that 'it is easy to show that there ... are in human knowledge judgments which are necessary and in the strictest sense universal' (B4)? What kind of necessity did he have in mind? It is not at all clear why Kant was certain that the truths of mathematics and physics are necessary, or what he thought would lend support to this certainty.

Something else is far from clear, too. If only an a priori cognitive capacity could construct or recognize the necessity of a necessary truth, what is this capacity like? What lets us *construct and recognize*

---

ed. (Oxford: Clarendon Press 1888) he does not refer to a prioricity in the relevant section at all (cf. 78-84).

7 Kant made the same assumption about the necessity of the propositions of mathematics and physics in *Prolegomena to Any Future Metaphysics* (1783), revision of Carus trans. by Lewis White Beck (Indianapolis: Library of Liberal Arts 1950).

necessary truths? In the case of mathematics, Kant's answer to this question is clearer, in general terms at least, than how he would have responded to the questions about necessity. We come to recognize the necessity of a mathematical judgment by constructing an instance of the state of affairs it describes in something called *pure intuition*. Notice that this argument has nothing to do with necessary conditions of experience, Kant's most characteristic way of approaching the a priori. We will examine the significance of that later. Maybe in clarifying how Kant thought we can recognize mathematical truths a priori, we can also find something to help us resolve our puzzle about other kinds of necessary truth and about how he could be so sure that certain truths were necessary. Before we embark on these explorations, however, we must first make some distinctions explicit that have only been implicit so far.

III The Scope of the A Priori: Capacities and Propositions, Origin and Way of Knowing

As will be clear from the above, Kant's theory of the a priori has two fundamental parts: one to do with judgments (propositions, principles, etc.), and one to do with cognitive capacities. Note that this distinction, fundamental to his whole epistemology and theory of mind, has nothing directly to do with the division of a priori judgments and propositions into analytic ones and synthetic ones. Both sides of this latter division are found within the judgment part of the division I am discussing. Unlike contemporary philosophers, who usually restrict the term 'a priori' to propositions (their modal status or epistemic grounding: Kripke for example),[8] Kant also applied the term to certain capacities, the cognitive capacities we use to gain knowledge.

---

8 Saul Kripke, 'Naming and Necessity,' in G. Harman and D. Davidson, eds., *Semantics of Natural Languages* (Dordrecht: D. Reidel 1972)

A priori cognitive capacities do (at least) two very different jobs in Kant. One is the job of ordering sensible input into judgmentally unified representations. The other is the job of proving necessary propositions and recognizing their necessity. Kant's views on the former task are well known; the capacities used in it include the forms of intuition — the capacity to form representations of space and time and to locate things spatially and temporally — and the forms of judgment — the capacity to make judgments using the concepts and inference-patterns of Aristotelian logic, mainly in the specific form of the categories. I will focus, however, on the less-studied task of using the capacities to recognize and prove necessity.

A priori propositions also come in two kinds. There are those that do no more than spell out what is contained in a subject-term. These are the analytic a priori. And there are those that connect the subject-term to a predicate not contained within it, yet where no sensible awareness can determine either the soundness of the connection (metaphysics) or its necessity (mathematics and physics). These are the synthetic a priori.

A priori cognitive capacities and a priori propositions connect in various ways. Perhaps the most important is that a capacity to use a priori propositions, principles, etc., is a major component of the capacity to make judgments. That Kant thought that synthetic a priori propositions, principles, etc., play a big role in our judgment making is well known. However, he also thought that analytic a priori propositions, principles, etc., play an important role. Our capacity to judge is structured by the forms of judgment. These forms of judgment are themselves a priori, not acquired from experience. In order to use them, the concepts and principles of inference that make them up must be spelled out, in the categories and the inference-principles derived from the categories. The propositions that spell out these concepts and forms of judgment, that describe the marks [*merkmalen*] of each concept or form that is 'thought in [it]' (A8), 'breaking it up into those constituent concepts that have always been thought in it, though confusedly' (A7=B11), will be analytic. All this points up something important: certain analytic propositions, namely those 'breaking up' a priori concepts and forms of judgment, play a far larger role in Kant's picture of cognition, and also in Kant's picture of the mind, than is often noticed.[9]

As well as two different things that can be a priori, there are two different ways in which something can be a priori. It can be *knowable* independently of experience or its *origins* can be in something other than experience. Kitcher has coined the useful terms a priori$_o$ (for 'a priori origins') and a priori$_k$ (for 'known a priori') to capture this distinction (15). Given the literal meaning of 'a priori,' those two ought to exhaust the meanings of the term. Some commentators, Kitcher included, think Kant used the term in a third sense, too, as a rough synonym for 'necessary,' as in 'necessary and universal' truths. Kitcher has coined an additional term for this sense. She calls it a priori$_1$

---

9 Two secondary issues arise in connection with this discussion of the analytic a priori. The first is that we should acknowledge that Kant accepted that we have and use analytic propositions linking concepts derived from experience, too (B3). I do not need to consider this kind of analytic proposition here. The second concerns his view of the relationship between analyticity and definition.

It would be natural to think that when Kant talks about 'breaking [a concept] up into those constituent concepts that have always been thought in it, though confusedly' (A7=B11), he is talking about defining the concept. However, in the only section of the first *Critique* devoted explicitly and single-mindedly to definition, Kant raises very Putnam-like objections to the very possibility of defining concepts:

... an empirical concept cannot be defined at all, but only made explicit [perhaps something like being explicated in Carnap's sense]. For since we find in it only a few characteristics of a certain species of sensible object, it is never certain that we are not using the word, in denoting one and the same object, sometimes so as to stand for more, and sometimes so as to stand for fewer characteristics (1. *Definitions*, A727=B755-A733=B760).

Kant then illustrates the problem, as did Putnam two hundred years later, by the example of gold.

The relation of this skepticism about definition, which comes very late in the *Critique*, to Kant's ready acceptance of analyticity in the Introduction, deserves more exploration than I can give it here. Unlike our contemporaries, Kant did not base analyticity upon definitions (cf. L.W. Beck, 'Kant's Theory of Definition' [*Studies in The Philosophy of Kant* (Indianapolis: Bobbs-Merrill 1963), 61-73], and D.P. Dryer, *Kant's Solution for Verification in Metaphysics* [London: George Allen & Unwin 1966], 324).

(for 'logically a priori'). Some contemporary philosophers certainly use the term 'a priori' in this sense, Putnam for example.[10] I am not sure, however, that Kant did. Even when he referred to propositions that he took to be necessary as a priori propositions, as in 'synthetic a priori propositions,' he calls them a priori, I think, *because* they are necessary, not as an *alternative term for* necessity. Kant was clearly able to distinguish necessity and a prioricity in the Introduction. I see little reason to think that he suddenly lost this ability later. Indeed, he speaks specifically of necessity throughout the work (cf. A93=B126, A104, A106 and B219f. for just a few of the available examples) and explicitly separates necessity and a prioricity at A93=B126, B219 and other places. In short, I think he used the term 'a priori' in only the two ways Kitcher captures in her terms 'a priori$_k$' and 'a priori$_o$.' (He does explicate the notion(s) in a variety of ways, however; for one curious one, cf. A148=B188).

Let us now connect this distinction between the two ways of being a priori, being knowable non-sensibly and originating non-sensibly, to the distinction between the two kinds of thing that can be a priori, propositions, etc., and capacities. The two distinctions go together, but not in perfect tandem. What makes capacities a priori is their origin. Thus they are a priori$_o$. We could not acquire them from experience because we must already have them to have experience (sense-dependent, judgmentally unified experience at any rate). Moreover, since the forms of intuition and the forms of judgment are not propositions but *means of acquiring* knowledge, they do not have modal status and therefore the question of the knowability of their status, a priori$_k$ or otherwise, does not even arise. Not being *objects* of knowledge, they are neither necessary nor contingent. The a priori capacities can be *described* in propositions, of course, and these propositions

---

10 See, for example, his 'There is at least One A Priori Truth,' reprinted in *Philosophical Papers, Vol. 3: Realism and Reason* (Cambridge: Cambridge University Press 1983). The truth he has in mind is *not every statement is both true and false*. He means that this statement is necessary truth, and could not be false, not that we know its truth independent of experience (though he might believe that, too).

would then be either necessary or contingent and therefore either a priori$_k$ or a posteriori. But the forms of intuitions and the forms of judgment themselves do not have modality. The situation is a little more complicated with respect to a priori propositions, principles, etc. They can be a priori in both ways, both a priori$_k$ and a priori$_o$. For Kant, the propositions, principles, etc., required for experience are clearly a priori$_k$; they express necessary truths and we can know this only a priori$_k$. However, they are also a priori$_o$. Because they are required for experience, they could not be acquired from it. Nevertheless, when Kant calls a proposition, principle, or judgment a priori, he generally means that it is a priori$_k$, and when he calls a cognitive capacity a priori, he almost always means that it is a priori$_o$.

IV A Slide in Kant's Articulation of the Problem

We left two issues hanging. One concerned Kant's basis for his certainty that mathematics and physics contain necessary truth, the other how he thought we could recognize such necessity a priori, that is to say, by what we can now call a priori$_k$ means. Let us begin with how Kant himself sets up these issues in the Introduction. He begins with analytic propositions, which he defines as those 'in which the connection of the predicate with the subject is thought though identity,' and glosses 'though identity' as:

> [the predicate] adding nothing to the concept of the subject, but merely breaking it up into those constitutive concepts which all along have been thought in it, though confusedly.... (A7=B10-11)

Synthetic propositions are all the rest, where the understanding must rely on 'something else (X) ... if it is to know that a predicate, not contained in [the concept of the subject], nevertheless belongs to it' (A8). Kant offers the following example of the two processes of gaining knowledge:

> By ... analysis I can apprehend the concept of body through the marks [*merkmale*] of extension, impenetrability, figure, etc., all of which are thought in this concept. To extend my knowledge, I then look back to the experience from which I have

derived this concept of body, and find that weight is always connected with the above marks [*merkmalen*]. Experience is thus the X which lies outside the concept A, and on which rests the possibility of the synthesis of the predicate "weight" (B) with the concept (A). (A8)[11]

He then turns to the question of what this X could be in the case of a synthetic a priori (i.e., synthetic necessary) proposition, and says,

It cannot be experience, because [the concepts in a synthetic a priori proposition are connected], not only with greater universality, but also with the character of necessity, and therefore completely a priori and on the basis of mere concepts. (A9=B13)

In the first edition, he then says,

A certain mystery lies here concealed; and only upon its solution can the advance into the limitless field of the knowledge yielded by pure understanding be made sure and trustworthy. What we must do is to discover ... the ground of the possibility of a priori synthetic judgments, [etc.] (A10)

— and stops!

Kant's treatment of analytic propositions is not without its problems.[12] What interests me here, however, is how little he says about what allows us to connect a predicate to a subject in such a way that

---

11 Kemp Smith translates '*merkmale*' and '*merkmalen*' as 'characters.' I think that term misses both the simplicity and the special technical sense of '*merkmal*,' a term whose literal means is 'mark,' 'sign,' 'indication,' etc., but which often means something like 'differentiating feature' (*differentiae*) in Kant's work. (What exactly the term means, however, is controversial.)

12 Henry Allison gives a good account of them (*Kant's Transcendental Idealism* [New Haven, CT: Yale University Press 1983], ch. 4) and they have been explored by many other commentators. Because Jonathan Bennett argues that, in the end, so-called synthetic a priori propositions are really just unobviously analytic ones, he in particular devotes a lot of attention to the problems in Kant's account of analyticity (*Kant's Analytic* [Cambridge: Cambridge University Press 1966], ch. 1 and 3). Kitcher makes some interesting remarks about the resemblances between Kant's remarks on analytic connections and Quine's attack on the very idea (27).

the result is both synthetic and necessary. He tells us that it 'cannot be experience,' and that it is 'on the basis of mere concepts' (cf. the quotation from A9=B13 just above), but that is all. Neither claim is very helpful, and the second one also contradicts his characterization on A8 of syntheticity and risks reducing synthetic necessity to a form of analyticity. In the second edition, Kant provided some additional material. He deleted the final remark just quoted, and added two new sections. Though they contain a full summary of the approach to mathematics, natural science (physics), and metaphysics as bodies of synthetic a priori propositions laid out in the *Prolegomena*, written in the meantime, they too say little about how propositions can be both synthetic and a priori (necessary) or what kind of X could allow us to recognize a priori$_k$ that a synthetic proposition is necessary.

The new material of the second edition does do something else, however. It helps us spot something going wrong. In the transition from the just-quoted passages of the first edition to the new sections of the second, Kant is making a slide from one topic to another one, presumably without noticing it. The new topic then occupies not just the new sections written for the second edition but most of the rest of the book. The topic he starts with is necessity and a prioricity. In the new material, he then introduces the question: 'How are a priori synthetic judgments possible?' (B19)[13] So far so good. However, this question is ambiguous. It could mean:

1. How is it possible for these judgments to be necessary, and/or to be a priori$_k$?

or it could mean:

2. How is it possible for us to *make* such judgments, *have* the propositions that result?

---

13 That Kant had this question in mind in the first edition, too, is indicated by way we end up with a parallel question if we change the equivalent part of the deleted first-edition passage into a question: 'What ... is ... the ground of the possibility of a priori synthetic judgments[?]' (A10)

Kant now slides from the first question to the second — and does not touch the first again in the entire Doctrine of Elements, i.e., for four-fifths of the book.

Kant's answer to 2 is, roughly, that it is *possible* for us to make these judgments and have these propositions because it is *necessary* that we make and have them if we are to have experience (of certain kinds). This argument-strategy then becomes the central strategy of the whole Doctrine of Elements, both the Analytic and the Dialectic: i.e., for the next four-fifths of the book. I will refer to it as *the central strategy*. It is very important to see why it does not address the question in interpretation 1, Kant's official topic in the Introduction, but only the one in 2. Before I attempt this task, however, I want to clarify the ambiguity itself.

To help us see how 1 is different from 2, consider a passage where Patricia Kitcher gets caught by the same ambiguity. She is attempting to reconstruct the central strategy:

> Kant's general argumentative strategy can be framed in terms of the three senses of "a priori" [presented earlier]. He will justify our ability to know certain a priori$_1$ [i.e., necessary] propositions, by showing through an a priori$_k$ argument, that these propositions contain elements that are a priori$_o$. (18)

Leave aside the question of the merits of this reconstruction for the moment and instead ask, what does Kitcher think Kant wants the argument to do? Does he want it to justify our conviction that certain propositions are *necessary* and/or a priori$_k$ (1 above)? Or does he want it to 'justify our ability' to *have and use* such propositions (2 above)? Once again, the ambiguity lies in the question. Kitcher's 'justify our ability to know certain a priori propositions' perfectly reproduces the ambiguity in Kant's 'How are a priori synthetic judgments possible?' (B19) The strategy Kitcher describes could not even touch the first question, it would seem. That a proposition contains elements that are a priori$_o$ does nothing to show that it is necessary or that this necessity is knowable a priori$_k$. The central strategy is an a priori$_k$ argument, so the whole argument that certain propositions and principles are required for experience and therefore are a priori$_o$ is an a priori$_k$ argument. But from that it does not follow that there is anything a priori$_k$ in our *knowledge* of these propositions and principles themselves.

Indeed, in the Introduction, Kant argued in precisely the opposite direction: *from* necessity *to a prioricity!*[14] These last observations introduce our next topic: the relation of the central strategy to necessity and a prioricity.

V Necessity and the Central Strategy

The central strategy argues that propositions and principles of mathematics and physics, some of them at least, are a priori by arguing that, because we must use these principles and propositions to have experience, we could not acquire them from experience. This is an a priori$_k$ argument for an a priori$_o$ conclusion. Many people take this strategy to be Kant's main or even only way of arguing for the necessity of certain propositions and principles. That, however, is not how Kant himself presents it. In the remarks introducing the Transcendental Deduction chapter, he presents it as a way of *justifying our application* of these propositions and principles to objects of sensible experience (A85=B117). We are *justified* in applying them because we *must* apply them; using them is a necessary condition of having experience (or experience of certain sorts). Thus it is at least not obvious that either (a) Kant's central project or (b) the central strategy he uses to pursue it have anything much to do with the necessity ascribed to propositions and principles in the Introduction.

Some might want to object that Kant was *not* concerned with any necessity other than being a necessary condition, even in the Introduction. Kitcher might be an example. '[Kant] employs an unusual sense of "necessity." Something is necessary if it is true in all worlds we could experience constituted as we are' (23-4). If something must be the case

---

14 One commentator who gets the direction of Kant's argument right is William Harper ('Kant on the A Priori and Material Necessity,' in Robert E. Butts, ed., *Kant's Philosophy of Physical Science* [Dordrecht: D. Reidel 1986] 239-72). Though he does not make the point explicitly, the whole structure of his paper presents Kant as arguing *from* necessity *to a prioricity*.

in all worlds we could experience, that is necessity enough. If this objection is sound, most of what I say in this paper is misguided. But is it sound? Arguments of the central strategy have the form:

> 3. Necessarily (If experience, then S is P [or we must judge that S is P, or whatever]).

It would seem on the face of it that 3 is very different from 4:

> 4. Necessarily (If experience, then *necessarily* [S is P] [or we must judge that *necessarily* (S is P), or whatever]),

though the semantics of the difference have been the object of some debate. It would seem, on the one hand, that the central strategy can only generate arguments having the form of 3, but, on the other, that in the Introduction Kant views the propositions of mathematics and physics as having the form of the consequent of 4, as being necessarily and universally the case in themselves. What they describe 'must necessarily be so' (A1) and 'cannot be otherwise' (B3). If it would take an argument of the form of 4 to demonstrate this necessity, not one of the form of 3, arguments of the central strategy do not touch the question of why the propositions of mathematics and physics are necessary in themselves, or how they are a priori$_k$ knowable.

Now it will be objected that I am begging the question against Kitcher. If she is right, the necessity of A1 and B3 *just is* whatever necessity arguments of the form of 3 show propositions and principles, and also the forms of intuition, to have. By arguments of this form, we can infer that a proposition or principle obtains, or a form of intuition applies, in all worlds that we could experience. Is it so clear that Kant wanted any stronger necessity than this? It is hard to be certain, but it is reasonably clear that he did. Kant had in mind propositions and principles describing what *cannot* be otherwise. But all arguments of the form of 3 support is the idea that if the events or states of affairs in question were to be otherwise, they could not be *experienced* by us. That is a very different thing from saying that they *could not* be otherwise, *must necessarily* be as they are (A1 and B3). In short, as well as being necessary for experience, Kant had in mind that the propositions and principles of mathematics and physics are themselves necessary and universal. Clearly he continued to subscribe to the same view of their necessity throughout, as the Second Analogy and the Postulates of Empirical Thought make clear. Indeed, Kant's discussion of the third Postulate makes reference to both ways of being necessary.[15]

Among Kant commentators who have seen that he had more than necessity relative to experience in mind, Dryer, Harper, and perhaps Allison come to mind.[16] Harper points out that in the Postulates Kant even distinguishes between something like formal or logical necessity (in connection with possibility, the first Postulate) and material or causal necessity (third Postulate) (A218-34=B265-87), 245-8. At least by implication, Allison also has Kant advocating necessity other than necessary conditions, because he sees that the necessity of mathematical propositions is what Kant had in mind when he talked about the necessity of mathematics and physics (80). Dryer, however, makes the most important point.

Dryer begins by pointing out that for Kant the necessity of mathematics and physics is no weaker than the necessity of an analytic proposition. He then observes that with all three, the necessity consists in the fact that we see that the concept of the one is 'inseparable' from the concept of the other. I think that Dryer is on to something, but I would put it this way. The necessity consists not in the impossibility of *experiencing* something without something else, but in the fact that we can find no way to *think* of the one without the other.[17] When an alternative to a pattern of events E or a state of affairs SA cannot be *conceived*, we have grounds for holding that E or SA *could not* be

---

15 A further complication is that Kant also had a notion of *necessary existence*. Indeed it is in terms of this notion that he first explicates the schematized form of category of necessity, strangely enough (A145=B184), even though he explicates the category itself in other terms, in the second edition at least (B111).

16 In a criticism that has attained some notoriety, P.F. Strawson charges that Kant's argument for the necessity of causal propositions (the Second Analogy) runs the two together (*The Bounds of Sense* [London: Methuen 1967], Part Two: III).

17 99ff. and many other references to necessity. Both Dryer's distinction and my recasting of it smack of psychologism — a problem for another paper.

otherwise (this, of course, is not the only way to support a claim of necessity). Merely being necessary for experience provides nothing comparable. Or to put the point another way, the proposition 'If we have experience, then E (SA) obtains' may have more than the necessity of a necessary condition; we may not be able to conceive of ourselves having experience without E or SA obtaining. But from this it does not follow that E or SA are themselves necessary.

If so, the central strategy can provide no argument at all that propositions and principles are themselves necessary or for the claim that this necessity is knowable only a $priori_k$, their centrality in the overall structure of the *Critique* notwithstanding. Though themselves a $priori_k$, as I have said, these arguments only show that the things they are about are a $priori_o$. Contrary to Kitcher, 'an a $priori_k$ argument that propositions contain elements that are a $priori_o$' has no power to show that such propositions are necessarily true (her a $priori_l$). For all that such an argument could show, a proposition that we require in order to have experience (a $priori_o$) could even be contingent. From another direction, notice that arguments of the central strategy establish the same necessity for the forms of intuition, space and time, as they do for any proposition or principle. However, it does not even make sense to consider whether the forms of intuition 'must necessarily be so' (A1) or not; they are not even propositional. Put yet one more way, if the argument of the Transcendental Deduction is right, a $priori_o$ elements will be a part of every proposition, and so of contingent ones as much as necessary ones. That a proposition is a $priori_o$ or has a $priori_o$ elements tells us nothing about its modal status or how we know that status.

VI A Better Strategy

It is far from clear that Kant ever thought through the relation of the central strategy to propositional necessity far enough to see all this. Indeed, he may even have believed at times that the central strategy could justify his conviction that what the propositions of mathematics and physics describe 'necessarily must be' as they are (A1). It is hard to say. However, he did have a second strategy, and it may have been his considered one. To approach it, recall the one passage in the Introduction that does seem to be directly relevant to establishing the necessity of propositions and how we recognize this necessity a priori$_k$. I have in mind the discussion of construction in mathematics on B15-16. Whatever we may think of this discussion, it does at least delineate a strategy. The strategy is to form an image of what a proposition describes and then construct a procedure for demonstrating it.[18] To work, we must do this in pure, not empirical intuition — the non-empirical, a priori$_o$ intuition of space (geometry) and time (arithmetic) that we all have (A713=B741), and the faculty we use to do this is productive imagination (though Kant does not formally introduce the term until A118 and first gives it this role only on A157=B196, The Highest Principle of All Synthetic Judgments; A165=B205 does so more clearly.) Here we do have a strategy with prima facie potential to demonstrate that the propositions of mathematics at least are necessary, without appeal to sensible experience or analysis of concepts. At any rate, it has more potential than the central strategy. Unfortunately, Kant offers nothing similar at this stage for the propositions of physics.

Indeed, he does not even tell us how the strategy is supposed to work. *How* could constructing geometric figures, patterns of successive units, proof procedures, etc., in pure intuition, whatever that is, allow us to recognize that mathematical propositions are necessary? Perhaps the reason for this is that Kant introduced the strategy not to show that mathematics is necessary or a priori$_k$ knowable, but to show that it is synthetic. Whatever, he does not mention the strategy again in the whole Doctrine of Elements, except for a few allusions on

---

18 In an important paper on what Kant really had in mind by construction in geometry, Friedman convincingly argues that the important thing we construct in pure intuition is not an image, an imagined instance, of the object of a mathematical proposition but a procedure for demonstrating it: a sequence of Euclidean constructions, or a sequence of calculations, that is to say, symbolic manipulations ('Kant's Theory of Geometry,' *The Philosophical Review* **94** [1985] 455-506).

occasions when he finds himself talking about mathematics (A162=B203ff.; A221-4=B268-72; A240=B299). There is also an interesting remark on A157=B196, in The Highest Principle of All Synthetic Judgments:

> Although we know a priori in synthetic judgments a great deal regarding space in general and the figures which productive imagination describes in it [an allusion to the method of construction?] ... yet even this knowledge would be nothing but a playing with a mere figment of the brain, were it not that space has to be regarded as a condition of the appearances which constitute the material for outer experience [an application of the central strategy].

'Mere figment' may be dramatic license; what is important about this passage is that Kant is distinguishing something, something to do with the internal structure of spatial relationships, from the central strategy, their application to 'appearances.'

Kant also says nothing more about the faculty that allows us to recognize propositional necessity a priori$_k$. Even if the central strategy could prove that some propositions are necessary, what would allow us to *recognize* this feature of them? Yet, because it was vital to Kant that he show that the propositions of mathematics and at least some propositions of physics are necessarily true, he just had to show they are knowable a priori$_k$, at least in part. Given the difficulties facing the central strategy in this regard, it would be remarkable if he had nothing else to offer.

Sure enough, if we look far enough, we do find something else. The issues we are examining are fundamentally methodological: how do we do the things that we do? Thus, we might expect to find them addressed in the often-neglected last part of the book, The Transcendental Doctrine of Method, and that is what we find.[19] The first of the

---

19 D.P. Dryer is one commentator who does not neglect these sections of the Doctrine of Method (see esp. ch. 7). My view of Kant's theory of a priori$_k$ proof owes a lot to his work, though I disagree with him on a fundamental point, as we will see. Among recent English-speaking commentators, Patricia Kitcher makes some references to these passages (14-17), as does Michael Friedman, in an important article on the method of construction. There is also a brief but

two chapters of this part of the book is called The Discipline of Pure Reason. In the first Section of this chapter, The Discipline of Pure Reason in its Dogmatic Employment, and the fourth, The Discipline of Pure Reason in respect of its Proofs, Kant lays out just the account that we have been seeking. He tells us how we can know that propositions are necessary, he tells us how we can recognize their necessity a priori$_k$, and, indeed, he tells us how to do the former by doing the latter. The account is far from pellucid, but at least it is there. The basic idea is that exploring our conception of 'an object [of experience] in general' (A788=B816) can do the same job for necessary truths about objects of experience as constructions in pure intuition do for geometry and arithmetic (or that 'symbolic constructions' do for algebra).

Moreover, this technique is of more than historical interest. If we remove the idea that it is exploring propositions describing what 'could not be otherwise,' as I think we should do anyway, and view it as a method for exploring very general constraints on relations and systems in the imagination, it becomes something very like a method at the heart of contemporary cognitive science, the method of exploring the general constraints on systems with thought-experiments. Cognitive science is exploring constraints on systems able to perform cognitive tasks whereas Kant is exploring constraints on the propositions we can construct in mathematics

---

interesting footnote on the method of construction in Ted B. Humphrey, 'The Historical and Conceptual Relations between Kant's Metaphysics of Space and Philosophy of Geometry,' *Journal of the History of Philosophy* **11** (1973) 483-512 and L.W. Beck discusses various parts of the *Methodenlehre* in a number of works. As a rule, however, it is hardly mentioned; Strawson, Bennett, Allison, and Guyer are among the well known examples.

An exception to this general rule is found in students of Kant's philosophy of mathematics. They tend to pay a lot of attention to the remarks in the *Methodenlehre* about construction in geometry at least, and, to a lesser extent, those about what Kant calls 'symbolic construction' in algebra; cf. M. Thompson, 'Singular Terms and Intuitions in Kant's Epistemology,' *Review of Metaphysics* **26** (1972-73) 314-43; C. Parsons, 'Infinity and Kant's Conception of the "Possibility of Experience"' and 'Kant's Philosophy of Arithmetic,' both collected in *Mathematics in Philosophy* (Ithaca, NY: Cornell 1983); and Friedman.

and physics, but otherwise the parallel is close. Indeed, Kant himself explored constraints on cognitive systems using the same method in other places, the subjective part of the Transcendental Deduction being the most notable example. Here is what Kant has to say about the technique.

VII How to Discover A Priori that A Synthetic Proposition is Necessary

Few philosophers have ever tried to maintain that any knowledge, let alone the most important kind of knowledge, is both synthetic and necessary. Until recently, most philosophers accepted that some propositions are necessarily true. Both Kant's immediate rationalist predecessors and virtually all post-Humean empiricists have also maintained, however, that such propositions are analytic. Since 1950, on the other hand, many philosophers have come to believe that much of what was called analytic truth is really synthetic. But these philosophers also maintain that such truths are neither necessary nor knowable a priori$_k$. A great deal has been written on these issues in the last few decades. All I will try to show here is how Kant thought we could recognize propositions that avoid this fork, propositions that are necessary yet still synthetic.

Kant begins his discussion in the Discipline of Pure Reason by reminding us that the propositions of geometry and arithmetic, though synthetic and a priori, can be demonstrated, as he puts it a bit later, 'intuitively through the construction of the[ir] concept' in pure intuition (B748).[20] (Throughout this part of the *Critique*, when Kant speaks of concepts he seems to mean propositions, or representations that are expressed in statements and so have propositional structure, not concepts in a strict sense. I will speak of propositions.) To construct

---

20 Since the pages are exactly the same except for the page-numbers in the two editions in the Method, I will cite only the page numbers in B from now on.

here 'means to exhibit a priori the intuition which corresponds to the concept' (B742). So we demonstrate that a mathematical proposition is necessarily true and recognize its necessity by constructing a non-empirical instance of the state of affairs it describes, complete with the spatial and/or temporal positions and relations such a state of affairs would display. We can do this empirically (though then we would never get necessity), but when we do it non-empirically, we do it 'by imagination alone' (B741), that is to say, by the 'middle' of the three faculties of sensibility, imagination and understanding that we require to represent (intentional [A104]) objects (cf. Transcendental Deduction, A101, A118, A120).[21] To construct and explore the spatial and temporal features of such an instance by imagination alone, we must have a non-empirical ('pure') representation of space and time in what Kant calls pure intuition.

Generally, Kant gives few examples. However, he does give some examples of this process. Recall the one in the Introduction. How do we determine that $7 + 5 = 12$, he asks? (B15) 'I may analyze my concept of such a possible sum as long as I please,' he says,

> still I shall never find the 12 in it. Instead, we have to go outside these concepts and call in the aid of the intuition which corresponds to one of them, our five fingers, for instance ... adding to the concept of 7, unit by unit, the five given in intuition. (B15)

The example he now takes up is the triangle, and 'what relation the sum of its angles bears to a right angle' (B744). He makes the important point that we could never determine this relationship by examining our concept of a triangle. Then he describes how a geometrician would proceed, by the method of construction familiar from high school. Similarly with any fundamental proposition of geometry: to see that 'shortest distance between two points' and 'straight line' together

---

21 The most interesting study of the role of the imagination in Kant's model in general is Wayne Waxman's *Kant's Model of the Mind* (Oxford: Oxford University Press 1991). Waxman argues that for Kant the imagination plays a large role, not just in the sort of imaginative exercise I am exploring, but also in ordinary sensible representation. Dryer emphasizes the role it plays, too.

make up a necessary proposition, we must imagine drawing a straight line. We then see that only such a line could mark out the shortest distance between two points. That is to say, we see that any other way of constructing a line will produce one that is longer. Next making the claim that algebra also uses a process of construction, but out of symbols rather than lines and circles (a claim that some might find less convincing), Kant concludes that what gives mathematics its decisive superiority over the philosophers' examination of concepts is this method of construction (B749).

This story about construction and its relation to demonstration, which I have sketched in only the broadest outline, is fairly well known; in note 19 I cited a sample of the authors who have explored it. Kant clearly has nothing but respect for construction as a method of demonstration. He urges that there is no more need for a critique of reason in this employment than in its purely empirical employment (B739). Here what interests me is not this story but what Kant contrasts it with. By comparison to mathematics, the employment of reason in philosophy is unreliable and prone to delusions of grandeur; and constructions are not available to help us out (a point to which I will return). Nevertheless, Kant thinks that he can sketch a method that is just as good. His discussion has two parts. One is found in Section 1 of the chapter we are discussing, the other in Section IV. In Section 1, Kant tells us what an adequate method of proof in philosophy cannot be like; 'meditat[ing] on concepts' gets nowhere, yet it is impossible to *construct* a priori instances of the concepts that interest us. In Section IV, he tells us about the only way that will work. Even though Kant does not say so explicitly, if the method he describes there works, given the propositions in philosophy credited to it, it will also have provided the justification Kant sought in the Introduction for our conviction (or at any rate, his conviction) that, like mathematics, the fundamental propositions of physics also contain necessary and universal truths.[22]

---

22 That Kant does not make this point explicitly is remarkable. Yet he never distinguishes physics from philosophy nor treats the former separately any-where in the chapter. We come to realize that if his method justifies the state-

This method has received little independent attention, perhaps because it looks a lot like the central strategy and perhaps because Kant develops it in even less detail than he develops the method of construction. However, not only is the method not just a repetition of the central strategy, it goes beyond the latter in one crucial respect. As a result, Kant claims for it what cannot be claimed for the central strategy: the capacity both to prove[23] that certain propositions are necessarily true a priori$_k$ and to let us recognize this necessity a priori$_k$.

Why are imagined constructions not available for the synthetic propositions of philosophy and physics? These are propositions about causes and what the other categories describe (B752). Only quantities allow of being constructed; we can obtain knowledge of qualities 'only through concepts' (B743). The reason is that we have no pure intuition of what quality concepts name: 'the only intuition that is given a priori is that of the forms of appearance, space and time' (B748). Thus, we can 'cannot represent [such a concept] in intuition ... except in an example supplied by experience' (B743). (By contrast, both Dryer and Allison suppose that proving the necessity of scientific and philosophical propositions requires the representation of imagined objects in pure intuition, just as in

---

ments in philosophy that Kant credits to it, it also justifies his conviction that some of the propositions of physics are also necessary and universal only from the examples he uses. I have in mind in particular the example of causality that figures so centrally in the definitive statement of the method in Section IV (B816), but the way he discusses the other categories in Section I points in the same direction (B752). I should note, if only to say that I will not discuss, the complicated question of the relation of a priori$_k$ and a posteriori pursuits in physics. That Kant clearly recognized the central role of the latter comes through more clearly in the *Prolegomena* and *The Metaphysical Foundations of Natural Science* than in the first *Critique*. Very roughly, I think a posteriori investigations give us grounds for thinking that propositions of physics are true, while a priori$_k$ investigations establish that what they assert could not be otherwise.

23 'Prove' (*beweise*) is the word Kant uses (B811ff.). Though the method cannot *demonstrate* the propositions of philosophy, neither construction nor demonstration being available in philosophy (B754-5), it can *prove* them. I will leave the sorting out of this distinction to another occasion.

mathematics.)[24] As becomes clear a bit later, what Kant means is that qualitative concepts are a device for synthesizing other, empirical intuitions, and do not come equipped with an intuition of themselves (B747). This is not exactly a transparent distinction. I think Kant means that simply by having for example the concept of a triangle, we can imagine what a triangle would look like (for Kant, this would require constructing an image of a triangle (A120)), but from the concept of a cause alone, we cannot imagine what a cause would look like. For that, we also need to become aware of real events that are related to one another.

If we cannot proceed by way of construction, then how can we proceed to prove that the propositions of metaphysics and physics

---

24 Dryer, ch. 7; Allison, 78-80. Thus there had to be something wrong with both accounts. I will not inquire into what. To be fair, Dryer does recognize that Kant says what I just quoted him as saying (285). He just thinks Kant did not mean quite what he says there. In favor of both commentators, I should also acknowledge that, in later works, Kant himself says on occasion that pure intuition is required to prove synthetic a priori propositions (e.g., *What Real Progress Has Metaphysics Made in Germany Since the Time of Leibniz and Wolff?* Ted Humphrey, ed. and trans. [New York: Abaris Books 1983], Ak. XX, 266, quoted by Allison on 78, and the passages quoted by Dryer on 284-5.) However, there is some question as to whether the works in question are a reliable indication of Kant's views. They are certainly completely inconsistent with the view expressed in the first *Critique*. It should additionally be noted that this issue may be smaller than it looks. Virtually anyone looking at what Kant says about the object in general would arrive at the view that it is some kind of singular representation, therefore something like a representation in pure intuition. I return to this issue briefly below.

It seems to be a little unclear when *What Real Progress ...* was written. Humphrey suggests 1793 as the probable date; a competition on the same topic was being held by the physics class (!) of the Academy of Berlin (see the translator's introduction, 13). De Vleeschauwer says that Kant mailed three manuscripts subsequently edited into this work to a friend in 1800, apparently viewing them as ready for publication. See *The Development of Kant's Thought* (1939), trans. A.R.C. Duncan (London: Thomas Nelson and Sons 1962). Whatever, it is a late work (Kant died in 1804, just short of his 80th birthday), not even published during Kant's lifetime, and it is flatly inconsistent with the first *Critique* on the point in question.

are necessary and recognize their necessity, both a priori$_k$? In Section I, Kant offers a highly original idea, though he puts it obscurely. The propositions and concepts in question are devices for synthesizing empirical intuitions, and they come complete with constraints on how they can be used. If we want to examine these constraints for necessity, the only way to do so, Kant suggests, is to examine the most general concept of the objects to which we apply them, 'the concept of a *thing* in general' (B748) or, as he puts it later, 'an object in general' (B816). Now ask, how are necessity and this object related? It is vital to get this clear. Is Kant just asking — the central strategy again — what the conditions for experiencing an object in general are? I think not. I think he is urging that exactly the reverse relationship is the important one. By studying what a thing in general must be like, we can explain the constraints on our a priori$_o$ propositions and concepts. So let us form a representation of an object in general and find out what such an object must be like. And that is all we find in Section I. (Why is this notion not a representation in pure intuition? A good question. The answer may again be that from its concept alone, we could not imagine what such a thing would look like.)

Or rather, that is *almost* all we find in Section I. After an interesting discussion of why philosophy does not have available to it definitions, axioms or demonstrations (the foundations of physics, too?), Kant concludes the section as follows:

> pure reason does, indeed, establish secure principles, not however from concepts alone, but always only indirectly through relation of these concepts to something altogether contingent, namely, *possible experience*. (B765)

This assertion immediately gives rise to a question. Was the earlier reference to a thing in general really introducing something new, or is Kant simply reintroducing the central strategy, confusing the a priori$_o$ and necessary conditions of experience with the a priori$_k$ and necessary truth? We do not get a full answer to these questions until Section IV. However, Kant brings up the object in general again in the very next sentence: 'When such experience (that is, *something as object of possible experiences*) is presupposed, these principles are indeed apodeictically certain [true necessarily]' (my emphasis). That is, Kant is again separating the idea of an *object* of possible experience out for specific attention,

243

precisely *distinguishing it from* the *conditions* of possible experience. He seems to think he can get something out of the former that he cannot get out of the latter. It is time to turn to Section IV.

The first paragraph of that section once more raises the question whether Kant is doing anything more than reintroducing the central strategy. It also once again distinguishes between the conditions of experience and of an object of experience:

> The proof proceeds by showing that experience itself, and therefore the object of experience, would be impossible without such a connection. (B811)

Kant will soon reverse this inference, back to the direction we just saw in B765.

The passage in which he gives his definitive statement of the method of proof in metaphysics begins on B815 with the curious claim that there can be only one proof for each transcendental proposition (by 'transcendental' here, he seems to mean not only necessary for experience but also necessarily true). The reason seems to be that all such proofs 'can contain nothing more than the determination of an object in general' (B816) and we only have a concept of one object in general. To show how such a proof might go, Kant takes as his example the principle of universal causality, the principle that necessarily every event has a cause. In the Transcendental Analytic, he says,

> we derived the principle that everything which happens has a cause, from the condition under which alone a concept of happening in general is objectively possible — namely, by showing that the determination of an event in time, and therefore the event as belonging to experience, would be impossible save as standing under such a dynamical rule. (B816)

I do not know what Kant is referring to in the Analytic. Certainly he did nothing like what he sketches here in the proof of the Second Analogy, which is about the relation of causality to our ability to experience events, not to fixing events themselves in time. Perhaps Kant thinks he did more there than he did, did more than apply the central strategy when that is all he did. At any rate, notice two things. First, Kant distinguishes between conditions of *being* an event, and conditions of it belonging to experience. This shadows the earlier distinction between conditions of *being* an object and conditions of *experiencing* an object. Second, Kant returns the direction of the inference to the order of B765. We again establish that something could belong to experience (satisfies the conditions of experience) by showing that it could be.

In these distinctions we can find, at last, the method of proof we have been looking for. Granting that a state of affairs SA being necessary for us *to experience* an object O or event E does not show that this or any link between SA and O or E 'could not be otherwise' (cf. B3), the same limitation would not seem to apply if SA is necessary for O or E to *exist*. Here a statement of the form,

5. If O [or E], then SA,

would indeed state something that 'must necessarily be so' (A1). Put in terms of the distinction we developed out of Dryer earlier, here SA being true of O is not just a condition of us *experiencing* O, it is a condition of us *conceiving of* O. In the present example, 'the *determination* of an event in time' (my emphasis), not just 'the event ... belonging to experience,' would be impossible if the event were not caused. If, however, we cannot fix a time for an event, then not only can we not conceive of *experiencing* the event, we cannot conceive of the event even *existing*. (For present purposes, I do not need to examine whether Kant's argument is sound.)

Kant drew a distinction between conditions of *experience* and conditions of being a possible *object* of experience and cognate distinctions repeatedly in the Discipline chapter. It seems to me likely that he did so precisely because examining the latter opens the way to arguments like the one just sketched, but examining the former does not. That is to say, examining the conditions of being an object or an event has a potential to establish that certain features of objects 'must necessarily be so' (A1), but examining the conditions of experiencing the event or object does not.[25] Thus we

---

25 It is over this distinction that Dryer and I part company. Dryer does not give the kind of weight I give to the distinction between conditions of having experience and conditions of being an object (ch. 7). He also thinks that one can somehow establish that propositions are necessarily true by finding out that having and

at last have the method of proof that Kant set out in the Introduction to seek but from which he soon got diverted (for the next nearly 800 pages) by switching to the question of how we can *have* propositions that are synthetic but a priori. Contrary to what Kant implies in the passage from B816 quoted just above, I have not found any place in the Analytic where he used anything like this method, and he certainly did not discuss it earlier. He mentioned the method of construction a few times, as we noted earlier, but never this method of examining an object in general.

The interesting question now becomes this. How, that is, by the use of what capacity, do we recognize that a proposition like the causal principle is necessary? What plays the role in this sort of proof that construction in pure intuition plays in mathematical demonstration? Here Kant offers us even less than he offered concerning construction. He says a little. Such proofs are conceptual yet ostensive (*ostensiv*), ostensive yet non-intuitional. That is to say, though based on concepts and specifically the concept of an object in general, not intuitions, such proofs are ostensive, not just *acroamatic* (B763) — sentential — and *apagogical* — syllogistic (B817-8). But that is not much. 'Ostensive' — what does that mean? (Kant uses the term in only one other place in the whole *Critique*, as part of a claim that the concept of a highest intelligence does not refer to anything that exists [A671=B699].)

Here I think we have to allow that there is a lacunae in Kant's system, one that Kant seems not to have noticed. The problem begins with pure intuition. Kant wants to restrict pure intuition to representations of the spatial and temporal. When we explore the concept of an object in general, we are exploring its qualities and

---

using them is a necessary condition of experiencing. Thus he does not see that the direction of proof in the method of proof in philosophy of the Discipline chapter is *from* the conditions of being an object *to* the conditions of experiencing an object, not the reverse. That is to say, he does not see the method of proof Kant describes in this chapter as anything more than a repetition of the central strategy.

relations, not the structure of its shape or its iterative (for Kant, temporal) properties. Thus we cannot be exploring the object in general in pure intuition. Kant had some reasons for wanting to restrict pure intuition, but he did not need to restrict it this severely. His criteria of empirical reality do not need the restriction and would continue to block the ontological extravaganzas of his predecessors without it. Moreover, restricting pure intuition this tightly creates some real problems for him. Aside from the specific problem of accounting for our awareness of the necessity of necessary truths, perhaps the most intense problem it creates for him is that there is suddenly no place for productive imagination to operate with respect to such truths. Yet if forming a notion of an object in general is not an exercise of the imagination, it is hard to see what it could be. It is not an exercise of reproductive imagination, which is the process of carting previously-experienced representations up into the present, so that leaves only productive imagination. Kant has a problem. Indeed, Kant should have seen that he had a problem even within the boundaries of mathematics. Suppose his account in terms of pure intuition works for demonstration in geometry and arithmetic. How could it provide an account of calculation in algebra, or calculus, or analytic geometry, all of which use what he himself calls *symbolic* construction?

In my view, Kant could go either of two ways. He could free the image-building activity of productive imagination, the activity of forming imagined instances of concepts and propositions, from its servitude to pure intuition. Or he could expand pure intuition to include more than imagined spatial and temporal phenomena. We could do the former at less cost to Kant's overall system than the latter. Since Kant himself gives us little to help us build such an account, we have to invent it for ourselves. Go back to the idea that proof in philosophy is ostensive. Here I think Kant means the following. To prove the causal principle, we use not only our concept of causality (which would get us nowhere by itself) but also a representation of an object in general. That is why this kind of proof 'combines with the conviction of its truth insight into the sources of its truth' (B817). This representation is a 'singular representation,' a representation of a single instance of an object stripped of all its contingent features.[26] Since the object need not be represented as having spatial or perhaps even as having temporal features, the representation of it could be said not to be a representation in pure intuition, in the strict sense of the term. However, in other respects, the representation would be like one in pure intuition.[27]

Now the meaning of Kant's allusions to ostension becomes clear. Reference to this imagined object would be a kind of ostension. Opening up the notion of productive imagination as we have, we might now call it ostension in the productive imagination![28] If we adopt the above suggestion, proof in philosophy would be as ostensive as in geometry and more ostensive than in algebra (at B745, Kant explicitly contrasts geometry as ostensive with algebra as symbolic). That seems right. If so, Kant's claim that such proofs are proofs obtained 'from concepts' (B752) might have to be modified, but this claim might have to be modified anyway. Even without our additions, it is difficult to see how we could reconcile this claim with the claim that such proofs are ostensive. Anyway, how could a form of proof that is not analysis of concepts and must involve more than discursive reasoning be purely conceptual?

The sort of activity we are discussing is close to unique. It is not conceptual analysis, yet it is not empirical either. It is research in the imagination. It is easy to see why Kant thought of it as a priori$_k$, yet aimed at synthetic propositions. Clearly, it does not aim to generate analytic truths. Yet it is also a priori$_k$, independent of experience, not a posteriori. One of Kant's most important ideas is that in order to experience, we must have time-fixing, space-fixing,

---

26 *Lectures on Logic*, §1, Ak. IX, 91. As Allison points out (80), we need a representation of an instance of some sort to prove synthetic propositions, and this sort of singular representation does not suffer from the limitations of inductive generalization.

27 That is why I said earlier that the issue between Dryer and Allison and me on the issue of pure intuition may be smaller than it looks.

28 The lack of enthusiasm Wittgensteinians might feel for this latter idea can easily be imagined.

and conceptual capacities available to us. Whatever order or divisions there may be in things in the world, the perturbations of the sensitive surfaces of our body (retinas, ear drums, finger tips), which are the basis of sensible representation, do not come pre-ordered, certainly not with the order of the world. Thus, we need abilities that are independent of that order if we are to recognize it, abilities that 'our own faculty of knowledge supplies from itself (sensible impressions serving merely as the occasion)' (B3).[29] As Kant put it in a letter to Beck late in his life, 'We must *synthesize* if we are to recognize anything as *synthesized* (even space and time).'[30] Curiously enough, we can use these capacities to explore the structure of imagined objects just as well as empirically-encountered ones. Indeed, Kant thinks that investigating imagined objects has an advantage over real ones; it can determine whether the objects' properties and relationships must be as they are. Thus, such explorations are the a priori$_k$ method Kant recommends for investigating whether synthetic propositions are necessary.

VIII Links to Current Work

As will be clear by now, I conceive of Kant's notion of proof in philosophy as very much like our contemporary notion of a thought-experiment. However undeveloped it might be, in one respect Kant's notion takes us further than most contemporary discussions. If proof in philosophy is an exercise of productive imagination, generating

---

29 Kitcher provides a fine account of this strain of a priori$_0$ constructivism in Kant's thought (ch. 3 and 4, particularly 72, 77, and 80). As she also notes, it allows us to answer the charge that Kant's whole doctrine of synthesis is built upon an archaic, atomistic theory of sensible stimulation. Her kind of account also captures a lot of what is living in transcendental idealism. In recent cognitive science, the general idea behind it has really taken off, indeed in a number of different directions and under a number of different names.

30 Letter of July 1, 1797 (Ak. XI, 514)

and exploring a representation of an object in general, the next question is: using such a representation, how could we generate a proof? If our account of this form of proof above needed an analogue of representing lines and figures in pure intuition, I think it now needs an analogue of the activity of construction. Notice that to prove the causal principle, we imagine what we would have to know to do something. Specifically, we imagine ourselves fixing an event in time; then we explore what we would have to know to do so. This feature of the method gives it an efficacy that no exploration of the content of a concept could ever have. If we are imagining the *doing* of something, we are imagining ourselves *working through a causal process*: what we need to do it and where the absence of something would stop us from doing it. As a result, the findings of this sort of thought-experiment have a clarity and a certainty that, for example, neither analysis of a concept nor trying to spot the essential properties of an imagined object could ever have.[31] Compare the thought-experiment we give to undergraduates of trying to imagine a leaf in Siberia suddenly turning blue for no cause. This experiment is notoriously inconclusive. What makes it so, I think, is that we have no idea what the underlying mechanism might be like.[32]

Though the explorations in the imagination that we now call thought-experiments are the heart and soul of both cognitive science and a lot of contemporary philosophy, we know little about how the mind is able to do them. Dennett has made a start with his exploration of intentional objects and of the idea of a 'notional

---

31 The view I am developing here would fit very naturally with Friedman's view that the job of construction in mathematics is to invent and work through a demonstration or calculation in the imagination (496ff.). The virtues of causal-mechanism explanations have been explored recently by Wesley Salmon in *Scientific Explanation and the Causal Structure of the World* (Princeton: Princeton University Press 1984) and Richard Miller in *Fact and Method: Explanation, Confirmation, and Reality in the Natural and Social Sciences* (Princeton: Princeton University Press 1987).

32 Asking for a mechanism comes pretty close to begging the question in this case, but I will let that difficulty pass.

world,' but the topic is radically under-examined.[33] (His notional world strikes me as very much like Kant's intuition with a population of representations added.) Indeed, imagination and therefore thought-experiments play a role in all science. Even if science starts from observables, as soon as it postulates unobservables to explain the observed, it leaves the realm of the experienced actual and enters the realm of the imagination.

If Kant was on to a method that has continued, in one form or another, to play a large role in philosophy and science, it does not follow, of course, that it could do what he thought it could do. Can demonstrations in the imagination establish that propositions are necessarily true? This is a big question and one that has been hotly debated the last two decades. On the one hand, people like Kripke have argued with great vigor that it can.[34] On the other hand, people like Dennett and the Churchlands argue that thought-experiments yield results no different in modal status from 'real' experiments, and, moreover, suffer the additional liability of not being under the discipline of reality. Though my sympathies are with the latter view, I will not try to adjudicate that dispute here. Just describing the dispute allows us to do one useful thing. It allows us to distinguish between research into a special kind of truth, and a special kind of research. Whether or not Kant was researching a special kind of necessary truth, I would submit that he most certainly laid out the rudiments of a special kind of research.

In fact, the important question concerning the propositions he claimed to be true necessarily and universally is not whether they are necessary but whether they are true. Indeed, it is hard to see any good reason why Kant himself insisted that the propositions in question are necessary. If these propositions turn out to be just contingent statements of abstract and high-level constraints on what objects or objects

---

33 Intentional objects in 'Two Aspects of Mental Images,' in *Brainstorms* (Montgomery, VT: Bradford Books 1978), notional worlds in 'Beyond Belief,' in *The Intentional Stance* (Cambridge, MA: Bradford Books/MIT Press 1987).

34 'Naming and Necessity'

of certain kinds could be like, why should this matter to him? Kant himself, of course, had a strong predilection for necessary truths. If we can find no good reason for this predilection, however, that in itself would make him significantly more accessible and palatable to contemporary theorists.

CANADIAN JOURNAL OF PHILOSOPHY
Supplementary Volume 18

EPR As A Priori Science

JAMES ROBERT BROWN

Contemporary empiricism is closely allied with naturalism. Not only do empiricists hold that all our knowledge is based upon sensory experience, but they also tend to offer some sort of causal account of how this experience comes about.[1] The causal ingredient in knowledge seems very plausible — after all, my knowing that there is a tea cup on my desk is based on sense impressions which are caused by the cup itself. Photons come from the cup to my eye; a signal is then sent down the optic nerve into the visual part of the brain, and so on. And without that causal process, I likely wouldn't have the knowledge that I do have.

It would seem not unfair, then, to characterize contemporary empiricism as holding to following: *knowledge of X is based on sensory experience for which there is an underlying physical causal connection between the knower and X; there are no other sources of knowledge.*

It might seem that *causal empiricism* (as I shall call it) is more restrictive than earlier forms of empiricism. I suppose it is, in that

---

1 A representative example can be found in the volume edited by Hilary Kornblith, *Naturalizing Epistemology* (Cambridge, MA: MIT Press 1985).

knowledge requires a causal connection in addition to sensory experience. But the causal ingredient is a very natural complement to the older empiricism and fits in very well with other views that are all the rage, such as causal theories of reference, causal decision theory, etc.

Such a doctrine would seem to do complete justice to a very wide range of cases. As well as mundane cup-on-the-table-in-front-of-me examples, causal empiricism easily handles the unobservable. We know about electrons, for instance, because we have appropriate sense experience of white streaks in cloud chambers and because that very experience is causally connected via the white streaks to electrons themselves. (Being electrically charged, electrons ionize the water molecules in the cloud chamber which in turn emit light in the visible part of the spectrum, etc.)

Similarly, we can know about the future. This morning's cloud formations caused a sensation in me that leads me to believe (at noon) that it will rain later tonight. Those very cloud formations this morning are the cause of tonight's rain. So not only do I have the relevant sensory experience, but I am also causally connected to the future rain — not directly connected, of course, but indirectly connected via this morning's clouds. (These clouds are said to be 'the common cause' of both the rain and my belief that it will rain.)

A caution about the causal connection is required. The thesis is only that such a connection must exist in order for there to be knowledge. Knowing what the appropriate connection might be is certainly not required. Our ancestors, for instance, knew about cups on tables long before they knew about photons.

With this account of contemporary empiricism in mind, we can formulate an appropriate characterization of a priori knowledge: *knowledge of X is a priori if and only if it is knowledge which is independent of any causally based sense-experience.*

Causal empiricists, given this definition, will say that a priori knowledge is impossible. Indeed, a characterization like this, stressing the causal aspect, seems to be in the back of the minds of some empiricists when they attack mathematical platonism. Platonists believe that there is an independent realm of mathematical objects existing outside of space and time, and that mathematicians can 'grasp' or somehow or other 'perceive' them. The most popular empiricist attack on platonism uses the causal ingredient and argues as follows: since mathematical objects are abstract entities outside of space and time, there can be no causal connection between them and us; therefore, even if they did exist, they would be unknowable, in principle.[2] We shall soon see whether this argument is effective.

A couple of important points should be noted. First, a priori knowledge doesn't mean *certain* knowledge. What is acquired a priori could be given up due to later evidential considerations; there is no contradiction in taking the a priori to be fallible. (Nor, by the way, need the a priori, which is an epistemological notion, have anything to do with necessity, which is metaphysical.) Second (and this is related to the first point), 'knowledge' is perhaps not quite the right term to use here. After all, if we allow that a priori beliefs rightly can be given up, then we better not suggest they have to be true; perhaps 'justified belief' would be better than 'knowledge.' I will, however, continue to use 'knowledge,' but it should be understood in this looser sense.

In the balance of this paper I plan, first, to provide an example of a piece of knowledge which cannot fit the causal empiricism mould.[3] The example will be drawn from quantum mechanics, the EPR-Bell result. And even though it is well known, it will be essential to go through it in detail to see why it is so relevant to the issue at hand. After this is done, I will offer some speculations and dogmatic pronouncements which will result in the conclusion that we can indeed have very significant a priori knowledge of the physical world.

---

2 See, for example, P. Benacerraf, 'Mathematical Truth,' reprinted in Benacerraf and Putnam, eds., *Philosophy of Mathematics*, 2nd ed. (Cambridge: Cambridge University Press 1983); and H. Field, *Science Without Numbers* (Oxford: Blackwell 1980).

3 An earlier version of the argument to follow was first briefly given in my 'π in the sky' in A. Irvine, ed., *Physicalism in Mathematics* (Dordrecht: Kluwer 1989) and repeated in my book, *The Laboratory of the Mind: Thought Experiments in the Natural Sciences* (London & New York: Routledge 1991). I have changed my view on some key aspects of the argument, and in some respects I present the whole in greater detail here.

James Robert Brown

I EPR and the Bell Results

The makers of QM understood their formalism in a rather straight-forward, classical way.[4] Erwin Schrödinger, for example, thought of the $|\psi\rangle$ in his equation as representing a physical entity, say, an electron which he conceived as a wave, more or less spread out in space.

Max Born proposed that $||\psi\rangle|^2$ should be understood as the probability density for the location of an electron. On his view the electron is a particle; the state vector $|\psi\rangle$ just tells us the probability amplitude of its being located at various places. The waves of so-called wave-particle duality are probability waves — they are a reflection of our ignorance, not of the physical world itself which is made of localized particles existing independently of us.

We can think of Schrödinger's view as an ontological interpretation of QM, since $|\psi\rangle$ is about the world, and Born's as an epistemological interpretation, since $|\psi\rangle$ is about our knowledge of the world. Since neither of these philosophically straightforward interpretations works, the attractiveness of the anti-realist Copenhagen approach becomes somewhat inevitable.

The Copenhagen interpretation is mainly the product of Niels Bohr, though there are numerous variations. Bohr thought the wave and particle aspects of any physical system are equally real; $|\psi\rangle$ has both ontological and epistemological ingredients. As Heisenberg put it, 'This probability function represents a mixture of two things, partly a fact and partly our knowledge of a fact.'[5] A state of superposition, on this view, is not a mere state of ignorance — *reality itself is indeterminate*. An electron, for example, does not have a position or a momentum until a position or a momentum measurement is made; the very act of measuring makes the magnitude measured. In classical physics

---

4 For a thorough account of early interpretations of QM (as well as present-day ones) see M. Jammer, *The Philosophy of Quantum Mechanics* (New York: Wylie 1974).

5 W. Heisenberg, *Physics and Philosophy* (New York: Harper and Row 1958), 45

(as standardly understood), observations *discover* reality, but in QM, according to Bohr and Heisenberg, they somehow or other *create* the world (or at least the micro-world).

This view is reflected in the mathematical formalism of quantum mechanics. Measurement outcomes — ways the world could be — correspond to the basis vectors (eigenvectors) $|a_1\rangle$, $|a_2\rangle$ ... of a so-called Hilbert space, a possibly infinite dimensional vector space. (More strictly, an 'observable,' which is a property such as momentum, will have a complete set of eigenvectors and eigenvalues associated with it, whereas 'position' which is an incompatible property, will be associated with a different, incompatible set.) But the state of the system $|\psi\rangle$ need not correspond to any one of these base states; instead, it might be a superposition of several of them.

In a nutshell, realists are tempted to say reality is one way or another and that superpositions merely reflect our ignorance. Anti-realists deny this; they hold that the micro-world is indeterminate until measurement puts the world into one of the base states.

The anti-realism of the Copenhagen interpretation was met head-on by the beautiful thought experiment dreamed up by Einstein,

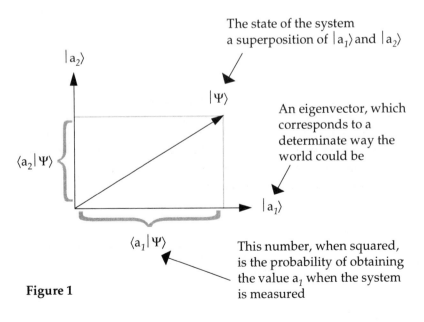

The state of the system a superposition of $|a_1\rangle$ and $|a_2\rangle$

An eigenvector, which corresponds to a determinate way the world could be

This number, when squared, is the probability of obtaining the value a_1 when the system is measured

Figure 1

257

Podolsky, and Rosen, now commonly known as EPR.[6] The argument proceeds by first characterizing some key notions.

Completeness: A theory is complete if and only if every element of reality has a counterpart in the theory. Thus, if an electron, for example, has both a position and a momentum, but the theory assigns a value only to one and not the other, then that theory is incomplete.

Criterion of Reality: If, without disturbing the system, we can predict with probability one the value of a physical magnitude, then there is an element of reality corresponding to the magnitude. The qualification 'without disturbing the system' is central. The Copenhagen interpretation holds that measurements do disturb the system, so ascribing an independent reality to any magnitude cannot be based on a (direct and possibly disturbing) measurement.

Locality: Two events which are space-like separated (i.e., outside each other's light cones) have no causal influence on one another. They are independent events. This follows from special relativity which holds that nothing, including causal connections, travels faster than light.

The more perspicuous Bohm version of the EPR argument starts with a system, such as an energetic particle, which decays into a pair of photons; these travel in opposite directions along the z axis. Ignoring all but polarization, each photon, call them L and R (for left and right), is associated with its own two-dimensional Hilbert space. The polarization or spin eigenstates will be along any pair of orthogonal axes, say, x and y, or x' and y'. In any given direction a measurement (which only yields eigenvalues) will result in either +1 for the spin up state

---

6 A. Einstein, B. Podolsky, and N. Rosen, 'Can Quantum Mechanical Description of Reality Be Considered Complete?' *Physical Review* (1935)

or -1 for the spin down state. We can represent these as $|+\rangle_L$ and $|-\rangle_L$, respectively, for the L photon, and $|+\rangle_R$ and $|-\rangle_R$ for R.

The spin of the system is zero to start with and this must be conserved in the process. Thus, if L has spin magnitude of +1 in the x direction then R must have -1 in the same direction to keep the total equal to zero. A composite system such as this, in the so-called singlet state, is represented by the equation

$$|\psi\rangle_{LR} = 1/\sqrt{2} \, (\, |+\rangle_L \otimes |-\rangle_R + |-\rangle_L \otimes |+\rangle_R)$$

If we measure the spin of the L photon we then know the state of R since the measurement of $|\psi\rangle_{LR}$ immediately puts the whole system into one or other of the two eigenstates. Suppose our measurement resulted in L being polarized in the x direction (i.e., has spin up in the x direction). This means the state of the whole system is $|+\rangle_L \otimes |-\rangle_R$, from which it follows that the remote photon is in state $|-\rangle_R$, i.e., it has spin down in the x direction. (Choosing the x direction is wholly arbitrary; any other direction could have been measured.) While it might be conceded that the measurement on L may have 'disturbed' it (i.e., created rather than discovered the measurement result), the same cannot be said of R which should be unaffected by our actions. We (at the left wing of the apparatus) are able to predict with complete

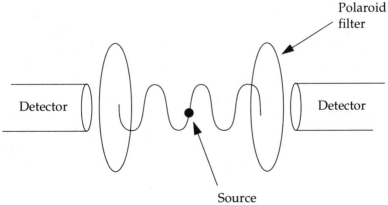

Figure 2

Polaroid filter

Detector

Detector

Source

certainty the outcome of the measurement on the R photon, and since (by the locality principle) we could not have influenced it in any way with a measurement of L, it follows (by the criterion of reality) that the R magnitude exists independently of measurement. Since this is not reflected in $|\psi\rangle$, it follows (by the criterion of completeness) that QM does not completely describe the whole of reality. EPR then concludes that the theory must be supplemented with local hidden variables in order to give a full description. A local hidden variable is nothing but a factor in the source that is causally responsible for the outcomes at L and R; it's the common cause.

Let us now look at this argument through the eyes of causal empiricism. In the case of the spin state of the near photon, L, our knowledge is based on observation, on direct sensory experience. Our knowing that L has spin up is relatively unproblematic and can be fully accounted for in terms of causal empiricism. But we also immediately know that the remote photon, R, has spin down. How is this knowledge possible? We cannot have any sort of direct observation of R, since it is outside of our light cone. However, if (and this a crucial *if*) there is something at the source which is causally responsible both for the spin state of L and for the spin state of R, then we can be causally connected to R via this common cause in the past of both L and R. Thus, our knowledge of R would be analogous to our knowledge of the future. Put another way, since we do have knowledge of R, there must be something in the common past of L and R which causally grounds our knowledge.

Compelling though EPR is, it can't be right. This is the upshot of several related findings known collectively as the Bell results. Bell's original derivation of an inequality which bears his name was rather complicated, but versions are now so simple that it would be a shame to pass it by. I'll begin with a simple derivation of a Bell-type inequality, then briefly describe its experimental refutation.

Let us start by considering an EPR-type set-up. Unlike EPR, however, we will consider measurements of spin in different directions, say, along **a** and **a**' for the L photon and **b** and **b**' for R. There are four possible pairs of measurements that could be made:

(**a**, **b**), (**a**', **b**), (**a**, **b**'), (**a**', **b**') (where (**a**, **b**) means the L photon is measured for spin along the **a** axis and R along the **b** axis). A spin up result of a measurement has value +1, and spin down -1. Now define a correlation function, $c(x, y)$ as follows:

If a = 1 and b = 1, then $c(\mathbf{a}, \mathbf{b}) = 1 \times 1 = 1$;
if a = 1 and b = -1, then $c(\mathbf{a}, \mathbf{b}) = 1 \times -1 = -1$;
and so on for **a′**, **b′**, etc. (where a = 1 means that the result of measuring the L photon in the **a** direction is +1, etc. Note that **a** is the direction of measurement and a is the result.)

We imagine running the experiment many times. After N tests, with a_i being the ith result, we have the generalized correlation function defined as

$$c(\mathbf{a}, \mathbf{b}) = 1/N \; \Sigma_i a_i b_i.$$

We will now make two key assumptions.

Realism: Each photon has all of its properties all of the time; in particular, each has a spin up or spin down magnitude in every direction whether there is a spin measurement made in that direction or not.

This assumption is embedded in the mathematics as follows. Let a_i (or a'_i, b_i, b'_i, respectively) be the result of the ith measurement, if made in the **a** (or **a′**, **b**, **b′**, respectively) direction. The value is either +1 or -1 and this value exists whether the measurement is made or not. In particular, if photon L is measured in the **a** direction then it cannot be measured in the **a′** direction; nevertheless, even though we can't know what it is, we still assume that it has one value or the other. This is the core of realism — measurements do not create, they discover what is independently there.

Locality: The results of measurement on one side of the apparatus do not depend on what is happening at the other side. The outcome of a spin measurement on photon L is independent of the *direction* in which R is measured (i.e., the orientation of the apparatus), and is even independent of whether R is measured at all.

Formally, the locality assumption is captured by having the value a_i be independent of the values b_i and b'_i. So if a measurement of L in the **a** direction would result in +1 if R were measured in the **b** direction, it would still be +1 if R were measured in the **b'** direction instead.

Now consider the following expression:

$$a_i b_i + a_i b'_i + a'_i b_i - a'_i b'_i$$

Rearranging terms we have

$$a_i(b_i + b'_i) + a'_i(b_i - b'_i)$$

Since the a terms equal +1 or -1, and since one of the terms in parentheses equals 0 while the other equals either +2 or -2, the value of the whole expression is

+2 or -2

Taking the absolute value, we have

$$\left|\, a_i b_i + a_i b'_i + a'_i b_i - a'_i b'_i \,\right| = 2$$

This holds for the ith measurement result. The generalization for N measurements is therefore

$$\left|\, 1/N \sum_i a_i b_i + a_i b'_i + a'_i b_i - a'_i b'_i \,\right| \leq 2$$

In terms of the correlation function we have

$$\left|\, c(\mathbf{a}, \mathbf{b}) + c(\mathbf{a}, \mathbf{b'}) + c(\mathbf{a'}, \mathbf{b}) - c(\mathbf{a'}, \mathbf{b'}) \,\right| \leq 2$$

This is a simple form of Bell's inequality. It means that when spin measurements are done for arbitrary directions **a** and **a'** on the L photons and **b** and **b'** on the R photons, we can expect that degree of correlation.

It is important to stress that the inequality is derived by a simple combinatorial argument based on two commonsense assumptions: realism and locality. After many tests the correlation between the L and R photons, taken a pair at a time, must satisfy this inequality — if the assumptions of realism and locality both hold.

QM, however, makes a different prediction. An experimental test pitting QM against Local Realism (as it is often called) is thus possible. (Amazingly, a metaphysical theory has empirical consequences.)

To get specific QM predictions we need to specify directions in which the spin measurements are to be made. Let **a** = **b**, otherwise the orientations of **a** and **b** can be arbitrary; furthermore, let **a'** be -45 degrees and **b'** be +45 degrees from the common **a**/**b** direction.

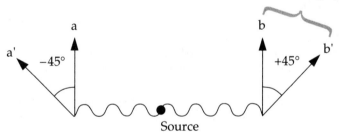

Different orientations of the measuring apparatus

Figure 3

According to QM the correlation functions have the following values:

$c(\mathbf{a}, \mathbf{b}) = -cos\ 0 = -1$
$c(\mathbf{a}, \mathbf{b'}) = -cos\ 45 = -1/\sqrt{2}$
$c(\mathbf{a'}, \mathbf{b}) = -cos = -1/\sqrt{2}$
$c(\mathbf{a'}, \mathbf{b'}) = -cos\ 90 = 0$

What this means is that if (in the first of the four cases), L is measured in the **a** direction and has, say spin up, then R measured in the **b** (= **a**) direction will not have spin up. They are perfectly negatively correlated. In the fourth case when L and R are measured at right angles to each other the results of measurement are completely uncorrelated. The other two cases yield results in between.

We now substitute these values, derived from QM for these same angles, into the Bell inequality:

$$\left| -1 - 1/\sqrt{2} - 1/\sqrt{} - 0 \right| = 1 + 2/\sqrt{2} > 2$$

Thus, at these angles, QM and Local Realism diverge in their predictions, making an empirical test possible of what previously was thought to be pure speculative metaphysics. There have been several tests of the inequality and in almost every one QM has made the right predictions, Local Realism the wrong ones. Of all these tests, the ones carried out by Aspect et al.[7] have been the most sophisticated.

The crucial feature of the Aspect experiment is the presence of very fast optical switches which direct L photons to either **a** or **a'** and R photons to either **b** or **b'** measurements. They each pick a direction randomly, while the photons are in flight. The reason this is consid-

---

7   A. Aspect, et al., 'Experimental Tests of Realistic Theories via Bell's Theorem,' *Physical Review Letters* **47** (1981) 460-3; 'Experimental Realization of Einstein-Podolsky-Ryan *Gedankenexperiment*: A New Violation of Bell's Inequalities,' *Physical Review Letters* **49** (1982); 'Experimental Test of Bell's Inequalities Using Time-Varying Analyzers,' *Physical Review Letters* **49** (1982)

ered important is that in earlier experiments the setting of the distant measuring device was fixed long before the measurement, thus allowing the possibility of a subliminal signal between the distant wings of the apparatus and hence, the possibility that they could 'communicate' with one another. Of course, that may seem bizarre, but the QM world is so weird that it is always nice to have one more possibility ruled out, however farfetched it may seem to common sense.

II The Upshot

Here's the moral for causal empiricism: *it won't work*. Our knowledge of the measurement result at the far wing of the apparatus cannot be based upon any sort of causal connection with that outcome. First, it cannot be directly connected, since that would violate special relativity; and second, it cannot be indirectly connected via a common cause in the past either, since that would amount to local hidden variables, the very thing ruled out by the Bell results. Consequently, we have knowledge of some part of the physical world which is not the result of any physically causal sensory process.

At this point readers may object and voice the obvious reply which comes to mind: our knowledge of the remote outcome is due to a theory-based calculation that we can easily make. We have directly measured, say, spin up on our side, and we know the theory, i.e., total spin is conserved; so we conclude that the remote outcome must be spin down. We do this sort of inferring all the time, as for instance when we know two things from experience which serve as premises ('It is raining,' and 'If it is raining then the ground is wet') and we deduce a third from these premises ('The ground is wet'). We needn't inspect the ground directly to know this, yet we still know it from experience. Isn't our knowledge of the remote outcome in the EPR set up is like that?

Alas, it is not. Consider the conditional sentence, 'If it is raining then the ground is wet.' It is really a kind of generalization, a mini-law of nature; so let's call it our theory. (It's analogous to the quantum mechanical theory about spin conservation which allows us to draw the inference about the remote outcome.) But what is the relation of my belief in this theory to particular bits of rained upon wet ground? That is, what is my relation to the theory's instances? If my (presumably true) belief in the theory is appropriately *causally connected to each and every instance* of wet ground (perhaps they are linked via the Big Bang), then causal empiricism is saved (at least in the wet ground case). But this makes the wet ground example completely unlike the EPR case, since there is no such causal connection in the latter. My belief in spin conservation is not causally connected to the physically remote spinning photon — not even via the Big Bang.) On the other hand, if my belief in the rain-makes-the-ground-wet theory is not causally connected — some how or other — to all the particular wet grounds, then the two cases are similar, but causal empiricism is equally wrong in both. (Generalizations have always been problematic for causal theories of knowledge.)

Ignoring 'my belief in the theory' and instead focusing on the theory itself, we can raise similar problems. First, if a theory is an abstract entity, then it can only be in causal contact with the remote photon in some sense of 'causal contact' that no normal empiricist would allow. And second, if the theory is my token of the theory (i.e., the physical textbook I carry to my wing of the measuring apparatus and use when making calculations), then by the Bell results the theory is definitely not in causal contact with the remote photon. (Contrast this with the fact that I come into causal contact with Moses just by looking at the printed word 'Moses' in my copy of the Old Testament, since there is a causal chain leading from Moses to the printing of his name.)

At this point one might say that at best the argument shows that the *causal* ingredient in causal empiricism is wrong, not that we have a priori knowledge. Perhaps we have been too rigid in characterizing knowledge; a priori knowledge could come about by violating either the sense-experience condition or the causal condition. Maybe we should abandon the latter. After all, the causal theory is a rather recent addition to the empiricist outlook; it's not at all a part of the tradition handed down from Locke, Berkeley, Hume, Mill, and the positivists, and so can easily be jettisoned.

However, it's not so easy to concede this point. Traditional empiricists only claimed knowledge of sense-data, while typical contemporary empiricists want knowledge of the world. The causal ingredient seems a necessary and plausible link between sense-experience and the world that we try to get a grip on. Moreover, Gettier-type counter-examples to the traditional analysis of knowledge have been met by including a causal ingredient: the knower must not only have true justified belief, but must be causally connected to the object of knowledge, as well.[8] To abandon the causal component in contemporary empiricism is to allow a large class of problems back into the fold. A different route is preferable, one with a significant liberalization of the notion of cause.

The causes in the causal theory of knowledge have always been thought of as efficient causes of a completely physical sort. (Photons come from the tea cup, interact with the rods and cones in the eye, etc.) Let us expand the causal theory of knowledge to include the causal powers of abstract objects. Thus, we will suppose there are abstract objects — numbers, values, properties, laws of nature — and that these things causally interact with us, though not in any sort of physical way.[9] Following Gödel,[10] we can say that (in some special cases) we 'perceive' these independently existing abstract objects just as surely as we perceive tea cups. This sort of perception — often called intuition — has much in common with ordinary experience; but since it does not involve the ordinary physical senses, any knowledge deriving from it is justly called a priori. Let us so baptize them: if knowledge is based on sensory experience involving a physical causal

---

8 For a spectrum of views on this issue see G. Pappas and M. Swain, eds., *Knowledge and Justified Belief* (Ithaca, NY: Cornell University Press 1978).

9 It's tempting to appeal to Aristotle's notion of a formal cause — but I will resist, since it is not at all clear how an Aristotelian form could cause a knower to know that some particular has the relevant property which it does have in virtue of the formal cause.

10 K. Gödel, 'Russell's Mathematical Logic' and 'What Is Cantor's Continuum Problem?' reprinted in Benacerraf and Putnam, eds., *Philosophy of Mathematics*, 2nd ed. (Cambridge, MA: Cambridge University Press 1983)

connection, then it is a posteriori; if it involves an abstract causal connection, by-passing the physical senses, then it is a priori.

But we still want to understand how it is possible to know the remote measurement result in an EPR-type experiment. Given that there is no physical causal connection from the remote spin state to ourselves at one wing of the apparatus, how do we come to know about the result at the other wing? Is this a priori knowledge or not?

At this point I want (somewhat dogmatically) to adopt a realist view of the laws of nature. A law is not a Humean regularity; nor is it the best overall systematization of the occurrent facts of the world, as the Ramsey-Lewis account would have it. Rather, a law of nature is a relation among properties. It relates universals to one another and is an abstract entity in its own right. This is the view recently championed by David Armstrong, Fred Dretske, and especially Michael Tooley (who holds the most platonic version, which I find very attractive).[11] With this account of laws in mind, my suggestion is simply this: first, the distant correlations of an EPR setup are caused — though not physically caused — by a law of nature, and second, our knowledge of the remote measurement results is caused — but again, not physically — by the very same law.

Simple though the suggestion is, it is somewhat difficult to appreciate, much less accept. Far from thinking that correlations are *caused* by laws of nature, the natural temptation is to think that correlations *are* laws of nature. This is because we are so heavily imbued with the Humean supervenience outlook: laws are summary descriptions of events; there is nothing to a law of nature over and above the physical happenings themselves. But there are countless reasons for abandoning such a view and adopting a realist outlook. When we do, all sorts of problems are solved, including the ones with which I am here concerned.

---

11 D. Armstrong, *What is a Law of Nature?* (Cambridge, MA: Cambridge University Press 1983), F. Dretske, 'Laws of Nature,' *Philosophy of Science* **44** (1977), and M. Tooley, 'The Nature of Laws,' *Canadian Journal of Philosophy* **7** (1977)

The upshot for a priori knowledge should now be clear: *we have some*. And not only do we have a priori knowledge, but we have a priori knowledge of the physical world. Empiricists have traditionally tried to trivialize the a priori, making it turn, for instance, on linguistic usage.[12] And those who looked more fondly on the a priori usually confined their sympathetic accounts to mathematics; a priori knowledge of the physical world has not really had serious champions since the seventeenth century. But we can see that in the EPR example, this is exactly what we have.

When we measure the near photon we come to know its spin direction in a way which is entirely amenable to standard empiricist principles; but our knowledge of the spin of the remote photon must be a priori. We are causally connected to the remote photon only via a law of nature; that law is an abstract entity, outside of space and time, and so, our normal physical senses are not involved. Our knowledge of the remote spin state is non-sensory; and since it is via the abstract entity, it must be a priori. In this way we have a priori knowledge of the physical world.

I realize that the forgoing argument is not entirely perspicuous. It may be helpful to come at it in a slightly different way, this time contrasting the knowledge of the remote spin with out knowledge of the future — both being outside our past lightcones. We know that future bananas, at a certain stage in their ripening, will be yellow. Clearly, we are not in direct causal contact with those future bananas, since the future does not cause the present. (Similarly, we are not in direct causal contact with the photon at the remote wing of the EPR apparatus, since it's outside of our light cone.) We do have direct experience of some yellow bananas. (Similarly, we have direct experience of the spin of the near photon.)

The bananas that we do see are descended from earlier bananas, and so are causally connected to the 'first' bananas. Those 'Adam and Eve' bananas are causally connected, not only to the ones we see, but

---

12 A.J. Ayer, for example, does this in his famous chapter on the a priori in *Language, Truth, and Logic* (London: Penguin 1971).

to all bananas, including those in our future. In this roundabout way we are causally connected to all future bananas. Thus, we are physically causally connected to the objects of our knowledge, and our knowledge of the color of next year's banana crop is, therefore, a posteriori knowledge and can be accounted for fully by causal empiricism.

But here the analogy breaks down. By the Bell results, there is nothing in the source that is anything like the Adam and Eve bananas. Anything like a self-replicating DNA molecule which is causally connected to its descendants would be a local hidden variable, which we know to be impossible. There is, nevertheless, I claim, a causal connection between us and the distant photons, but the connection is not in any sense physical; it is an abstract law of nature. It is this law which causally connects us to the remote photon's spin. And because this connection is via the abstract realm, not involving the physical senses, our knowledge of that remote spin state is, therefore, a priori.

III Thought Experiments

EPR may seem an isolated, bizarre example; and knowing the spin of a distant photon is pretty boring stuff, anyway. But the wonderful thing about the EPR example is that it opens a door. It makes thinkable what hasn't been thinkable since the hey day of rationalism — we can learn significant things about nature a priori. I'll conclude with my favorite thought experiment, Galileo's wonderful argument in the *Discoursi* to show that all bodies, regardless of their weight, fall at the same speed.[13] It may well be a genuine example of significant physics done a priori.

The thought experiment begins by noting Aristotle's view that heavier bodies fall faster than light ones (H > L). We are then asked to

---

13 Galileo, *Discourse on Two New Sciences*, trans. S. Drake (Madison, WI: University of Wisconsin Press 1974), 66f.

imagine that a heavy cannon ball is attached to a light musket ball. What would happen if they were released together?

Reasoning in the Aristotelian manner leads to an absurd conclusion. First, the light ball will slow up the heavy one (acting as a kind of drag), so the speed of the combined system would be slower than the speed of the heavy ball falling alone (H > H+L). On the other hand, the combined system is heavier than the heavy ball alone, so it should fall faster (H+L > H). We now have the absurd consequence that the heavy ball is both faster and slower than the even heavier combined system. Thus, the Aristotelian theory of falling bodies is destroyed.

But the question remains, 'Which falls faster?' The right answer is now plain as day. The paradox is resolved by making them equal; they all fall at the same speed (H = L = H+L).

Though the reasoning in Galileo's thought experiment is fallible, it is not a piece of standard empiricist, a posteriori knowledge. Rather, we are justified in calling this a case of a priori physics. Very briefly, here's why: first, there have been no new empirical data. I suppose this is almost true by definition; being a *thought* experiment rules out new empirical input. Second, Galileo's new theory is not logically deduced from old data; nor is it any kind of logical truth.[14]

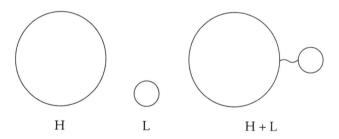

H   L   H + L

Figure 4

---

14 For a detailed defense of the a priori character of this thought experiment, and for a discussion of thought experiments in general, see my *The Laboratory of the Mind: Thought Experiments in the Natural Sciences* (London: Routledge 1991).

271

How does it work? Again, my speculation must be brief. Mathematical platonists hold that we can perceive mathematical objects. I suggest that something similar is going on here. Thought experiments, such as Galileo's, help us to 'see' the relevant law of nature. Remember, a law of nature is an abstract object, similar to a mathematical entity. The causal connection we have to such entities is not a physical one. Nor are the ordinary physical senses involved. Yet the thought experiment has led us to a very significant fact about the world. Given our characterization of a priori knowledge, Galileo's thought experiment gives us a paradigm example of it.

The discussion of Galileo must remain tantalizingly brief. (See my *Laboratory of the Mind* for a fuller discussion.) But backed up by the EPR example which shows the possibility, the Galileo example suggests that a priori physics can actually give us wonderful results, just as Plato and the finest minds of the seventeenth century believed.[15]

---

15 The editors, B. Hunter and P. Hanson and one of their readers, provided me with extensive useful comments, for which I am very grateful; I wish to thank SSHRC for its generous support.

CANADIAN JOURNAL OF PHILOSOPHY
Supplementary Volume 18

Gaps, Gluts, and Paradox[1]

A.D. IRVINE

I Two Paradoxes

Consider the following sentence schema:

This sentence entails that ϕ.

Call a sentence which is obtained from this schema by the substitution of an arbitrary, contingent sentence, s, for ϕ, the sentence CS (for 'Curry's Sentence'). Thus,

(CS) This sentence entails that s.

Now ask the following question: Is CS true?

1 Early drafts of this paper were read at the Department of Philosophy at Simon Fraser University and at the 1992 Annual Congress of the Canadian Philosophical Association in Charlottetown. I would like to thank Peter Apostoli, Bryson Brown, Philip Hanson, Ed Mares, Tom Patton, Dick Robinson, Steven Savitt and an anonymous referee for their many helpful comments prior to publication, and David Stove for giving me the idea to write this paper.

One sentence classically entails a second if and only if it is impossible for both the first to be true and the second to be false. Thus 'Xanthippe is a mother' entails 'Xanthippe is female' if and only if it is impossible for both 'Xanthippe is a mother' to be true and 'Xanthippe is female' to be false. CS makes a claim about a purported entailment. Thus, CS is true if and only if it is impossible for both the sentence it mentions as entailing a second to be true and the sentence it mentions as being entailed by the first to be false. In other words, CS is true if and only if it is impossible for both CS to be true and s to be false. In yet other words, CS is false if and only if it is possible for both CS to be true and s to be false.

Is CS true or false? In other words, is it possible (or impossible) for both CS to be true and s to be false? The following argument shows CS to be true: Entailment is, by definition, truth-preserving. In other words, what is entailed by a true sentence must also be true. Now, because of what CS says, if CS were true, then s would be entailed by CS. It follows that in every case in which CS is true, s will be true as well. Thus, it is impossible for both CS to be true and s to be false. In other words, CS is true.

Of course, as mentioned, what is entailed by a true sentence is also true. In this case s is entailed by CS. So, since CS is true and s is entailed by CS, s must also be true. Yet s is a completely arbitrary, contingent sentence. This is Curry's paradox.

In Curry's original formulation, material implication was used rather than classical entailment.[2] Thus the paradox is closely related (if not identical) to what is sometimes also called 'Löb's Paradox,' a paradox based upon the sentence schema

If this sentence is true, then ϕ.

---

2 The paradox originally appeared in Haskell B. Curry, 'The Inconsistency of Certain Formal Logics,' *Journal of Symbolic Logic* 7 (1942), 115-17. It is not difficult to see that the paradox can be formed using other connectives or relations (e.g. relevant entailment), in addition to both material implication and classical entailment.

By substituting an arbitrary, contingent sentence, s, for ϕ we obtain

If this sentence is true, then s,

which, in turn, is classically equivalent to

(C) This sentence is false $\lor$ s.

C, however, cannot be false (for if it were, its first disjunct must be both false and true). Yet, if C is true it follows that s must be true (since at least one disjunct must be true, and its first disjunct cannot be true). So since C is true, s.

When stated this way, Curry's paradox is also closely related to the traditional Epimenides paradox.[3] To see this, consider the sentence

All sentences asserted by Cretans are false,

when asserted by Epimenides, a Cretan. Presumably this sentence is equivalent to

This sentence is false and
all other sentences asserted by me and by other Cretans are false.

Yet, since the specifics of the second conjunct of this sentence are not essential to the paradox, the second conjunct can be replaced by any contingent sentence, s. Thus we obtain

(E) This sentence is false & s.

E, however, cannot be true (for if it were, its first conjunct must be true and hence E must not be true). Yet, if E is false it follows that s must

---

3 This relation is made explicit in Laurence Goldstein, 'Epimenides and Curry,' *Analysis* **46** (1986), 117-21.

be false (since at least one conjunct must be false, and its first conjunct cannot be false). So since *E* is false, ~s. This is the Epimenides paradox. What is striking about Curry's paradox and the Epimenides paradox is that in both cases a completely arbitrary, contingent sentence (s and ~s respectively) apparently follows from purely a priori considerations.[4] As Church pointed out with respect to the original Epimenides sentence ('All sentences asserted by Cretans are false'), it is disturbing to think that *from logic alone* it is possible to conclude not just that this sentence must be false, but also that some other (true) sentence must have been asserted by some Cretan.[5] After all, whether or not some additional sentence has been asserted by some Cretan is a completely empirical matter, something normally thought to be discoverable only through experience. (Why, one might ask, isn't it possible for the original Epimenides sentence to be the only sentence ever asserted by a Cretan?) What both paradoxes apparently show is that by purely a priori reasoning, arbitrary empirical claims follow. The question we are therefore faced with is this: Is there a non-ad hoc way of blocking such pathological, a priori inferences?

---

4 Of course, since s is completely arbitrary in both Curry's paradox and the Epimenides paradox, it also follows (by a series of arguments analogous to the ones just given) that not just s (~s), but every contingent sentence is true. From this it follows in both cases that s and ~s are true and, thus, that the sentence s & ~s is true.

5 See Alonzo Church, 'Review of A. Koyré's *The Liar,' Journal of Symbolic Logic* 12 (1946), 131. For additional discussion, see L.J. Cohen, 'Can the Logic of Indirect Discourse be Formalized?' *Journal of Symbolic Logic* 22 (1957) 225-32; as well as A.N. Prior's two articles, 'Epimenides the Cretan,' *Journal of Symbolic Logic* 23 (1958) 261-6; and 'On a Family of Paradoxes,' *Notre Dame Journal of Formal Logic* 2 (1961) 16-32.

II Two Traditional Solutions

It is generally believed that semantic closure and classical logic together yield the paradoxes.[6] Seeing classical logic as sacrosanct, traditional solutions — such as those of Russell and Tarski — have
therefore regularly shared one characteristic in common: they have all
abandoned semantic closure.

A language is said to be semantically closed whenever the following
two conditions are met:

    (i) the language is sufficiently powerful to be able to refer to its
        own expressions,

and

    (ii) the language contains a (universally applicable) truth predi-
        cate.

Of those approaches which abandon semantic closure, most have
done so by attempting to regiment natural language into a hierarchy,
either of types, or of truth predicates, or of formal languages. Russell,
for example, blocked the paradoxes by introducing his famous theory
of types. Tarski did so by introducing his equally famous hierarchy of
formal languages. Both theories resulted in sentences such as C and E
being rejected as ill-formed.

According to Russell's simple theory of types,[7] the universe of
discourse of any (suitably strong) language should be viewed as a

---

6 There are exceptions. For example, see Anil Gupta, 'Truth and Paradox,' *Journal
    of Philosophical Logic* **11** (1982) 1-60.

7 See Bertrand Russell, 'Mathematical Logic as Based on the Theory of Types,'
    American Journal of Mathematics **30** (1908) 222-62, reprinted in *Logic and Knowledge*,
    Robert C. Marsh, ed. (London: Allen & Unwin 1956), 59-102. Also see Bertrand
    Russell, *The Principles of Mathematics* (Cambridge: Cambridge University Press
    1903), Appendix B.

hierarchy.[8] Within this hierarchy individuals form the lowest type (type 0); sets of individuals form the next lowest type (type 1); sets of sets of individuals form the next lowest type (type 2); and so on. Individual variables are then indexed (using subscripts) to indicate the type of object over which they range, and the language's formation rules are restricted to allow only formulas such as '$\alpha_n \in \beta_m$' (where m = n + 1) to be counted among the (well-formed) sentences of the language. Such restrictions mean that strings such as '$x_n \in x_n$' are ill-formed, thereby blocking Russell's own paradox.

The ramified theory of types goes further than the simple theory. It describes a hierarchy, not only of objects, but of closed and open sentences (propositions and propositional functions respectively) as well. The theory then adds the condition that no proposition or propositional function may contain quantifiers ranging over propositions or propositional functions of any order except those lower than itself. Intuitively, this means that no proposition or propositional function can refer to, or be about, any member of the hierarchy other than those which are defined in a logically prior manner. As a result, sentences such as the liar sentence,

(L) This sentence is false,

become ill-formed, referring as they do to sentences other than those which have been defined at previous levels within the hierarchy. Since, for Russell, sets are to be understood as logical constructs based upon propositional functions, it follows that the simple theory of types can be viewed as a special case of the ramified theory.

---

8 At least this is the standard interpretation of Russell. For a contrary interpretation in which Russell is understood as being committed to orders or types of propositional functions, rather than to a hierarchy of entities, see Gregory Landini, 'Reconciling *PM*'s Ramified Type Theory with the Doctrine of the Unrestricted Variable of the *Principles*,' in A.D. Irvine & G.A. Wedeking, *Russell & Analytic Philosophy* (Toronto: University of Toronto Press forthcoming).

In order to justify both his simple and ramified theories, Russell introduced the principle that 'Whatever involves *all* of a collection must not [itself] be one of the collection.'[9] In other words, no well-defined object may presuppose the existence of a totality of which it is a member. Following Poincaré, Russell called this principle the Vicious Circle Principle (or VCP). Once the VCP is accepted, it follows that the claim (first championed by Peano and later by Ramsey)[10] that there is an important theoretical distinction between the set-theoretic and the semantic paradoxes is mistaken. The reason is that in both cases the VCP provides the same philosophical justification for outlawing self-reference. Thus it is by abandoning semantic closure that Russell is able to eliminate both the semantic and the set-theoretic paradoxes.

Like Russell, Tarski also concludes that no paradox-free language can be semantically closed. Like Russell's type theory, too, the details of Tarski's account are familiar.[11] Given an object language, L_0, Tarski takes it to be a condition of the material adequacy of any definition of truth for L_0 that it have as a consequence all instances of the following schema:

(*T*) Ψ is true iff ϕ,

---

9 Or perhaps equivalently, that no collection can be definable only in terms of itself. See Bertrand Russell, 'Mathematical Logic as Based on the Theory of Types,' in *Logic and Knowledge*, Robert C. Marsh, ed. (London: Allen & Unwin 1956), 63; and A.N. Whitehead & Bertrand Russell, *Principia Mathematica*, Vol. 1 (Cambridge: Cambridge University Press 1910), 37.

10 Frank P. Ramsey, 'The Foundations of Mathematics,' *Proceedings of the London Mathematical Society* **25** (Series 2, 1925), reprinted as ch. 1 of Ramsey's *The Foundations of Mathematics*, R.B. Braithwaite, ed. (London: Routledge & Kegan Paul 1931), 20.

11 See Alfred Tarski, 'The Semantic Conception of Truth,' *Philosophy and Phenomenological Research* **4** (1944) 341-75, and 'The Concept of Truth in Formalized Languages,' in *Logic, Semantics, Metamathematics* (New York: Clarendon Press 1956) 152-278.

in which ϕ is replaced by a sentence of the language for which truth is being defined and Ψ is replaced by a name of the sentence which replaces ϕ. To define a truth predicate for L_0 we first specify in a complete and exact way (within a metalanguage, L_1) the syntactic structure of L_0. Using the notion of satisfaction, we then define truth for L_0 from within the metalanguage. Iterating this process results in a hierarchy of languages, L_0, L_1, L_2, L_3, with the truth predicate for each language, L_n, being defined in its metalanguage, L_{n+1}. For those who wish to explicate the natural language truth predicate using Tarski's hierarchy, the usual conclusion is that the natural language predicate 'is true' remains systematically ambiguous (and hence capable of paradox) until it is regimented within an appropriate hierarchy of natural languages. Thus, as with Russell's type theory, Tarski's language hierarchy eliminates the semantic paradoxes, but only by reinterpreting natural language in such as way as to abandon semantic closure.

Both Russell's type theory and Tarski's language hierarchy have been criticized on both technical and philosophical grounds. The details of these criticisms are so familiar as hardly to require mention. Russell's type theory, for example, required the introduction of two logically unintuitive axioms (the axioms of infinity and of reducibility) in order for it to be of any genuine mathematical use. The former of these two axioms has historically been criticized for being non-logical; the latter for being simply too ad hoc. On a less technical level, Ramsey and others have criticized the VCP on the ground that not all self-reference should be abandoned. As Ramsey suggests in a famous example, picking out a man by means of the phrase 'the tallest man in the room' presupposes a collection of which the man himself is a part and, thus, contravenes the VCP. Despite this, such a phrase appears to be a perfectly legitimate one, thus making doubtful the VCP's claim that no well-defined object may presuppose the existence of a totality of which it is a member. The general conclusion has therefore been that to the extent that Russell's type theory was plausible, it was not very useful; to the extent that it was useful, it was not very plausible.

Tarski's theory has met with similar criticism. It, too, can be faulted for failing to provide both a technically satisfactory and a philosophically acceptable solution. In order to see this, Kripke has suggested that we consider a statement such as the following:

(1) Most (i.e., a majority) of Nixon's assertions about Watergate are false.[12]

Nothing appears intrinsically wrong with such a statement. It is grammatically well-formed and will have to be either true or false depending upon which individual statements about Watergate Nixon has made and their independent truth values. For the sake of argument, let us say that statement (1) has been made by Jones. Now, let us also suppose that (1) is Jones's only assertion involving Watergate. Then, should it turn out that Nixon's assertions about Watergate are evenly balanced between the true and the false, except for his assertion that

(2) Everything Jones says about Watergate is true,

it appears to follow quite easily that (1) and (2) are paradoxical, i.e. that each is true if and only if it is false.[13] More importantly, under such circumstances it becomes impossible to assign these sentences in a consistent way to a Tarski-like hierarchy of languages. In order to do this successfully, (1) must be at a level in the hierarchy one higher than all of Nixon's utterances about Watergate (and hence must be higher than (2)). At the same time, (2) must be at a level in the hierarchy one higher than all of Jones's utterances about Watergate (and hence must be higher than (1)).

---

12 Saul Kripke, 'Outline of a Theory of Truth,' *Journal of Philosophy* 72 (1975), 691f.

13 The paradox is similar to the postcard paradox (viz., that which arises when on one side of a postcard is written 'The sentence which is written on the other side of this postcard is true' while on the other side of the postcard is written 'The sentence which is written on the other side of this postcard is false') and to Buridan's 9th Sophism (viz., that which arises when Socrates says, 'What Plato is saying is false' while at the same time, Plato says, 'What Socrates is saying is true'). See G.E. Hughes, *John Buridan on Self-Reference* (Cambridge: Cambridge University Press 1982), 79-83; 173-83.

What this criticism in effect means is that Tarski's theory is unlikely to be applied in any successful way to large portions of natural language. In analyzing natural language, it thus appears that the best one could hope to do would be to claim, not just that the predicate 'is true' will remain systematically ambiguous until it is regimented within a Tarski-like hierarchy, but that — in addition — those portions of natural language which cannot be so regimented should simply be rejected. Natural language, it appears, is neither semantically open nor formally specifiable. In contrast to such a conclusion, though, it was Tarski's belief that, given the unintuitiveness of such a claim, one should be skeptical about identifying his formal definition of truth with that employed in natural language.[14] But from this it seems to follow that the notion of truth as used in natural language is simply incoherent. Thus, like Russell's type theory, the general conclusion is that to the extent that Tarski's hierarchy theory is plausible, it is not very useful; and to the extent that it is useful, it is not very plausible.

Kripke's conclusion is somewhat more modest. In his words, 'many, probably most, of our ordinary assertions about truth and falsity are liable, if the empirical facts are extremely unfavorable, to exhibit paradoxical features.'[15] However, the lesson to be drawn from this is not that the notion of truth is incoherent, but only that it is 'fruitless to look for an *intrinsic* criterion that will enable us to sieve out — as meaningless, or ill-formed — those sentences which lead to

---

14 For example, see Alfred Tarski, 'The Concept of Truth in Formalized Languages,' in *Logic, Semantics, Metamathematics* (New York: Clarendon Press 1956), 165, and passim.

15 Saul Kripke, 'Outline of a Theory of Truth,' *Journal of Philosophy* 72 (1975), 691. (Emphasis removed.) Gupta makes much this same point when he comments that although we have fairly clear intuitions about both paradoxical and non-paradoxical sentences which contain the truth predicate, 'the division between these two classes of sentences is not a straightforward one. It cannot be said, for example, that the first class consists of all and only those sentences that involve one form of self-reference or another.' See Anil Gupta, 'Truth and Paradox,' *Journal of Philosophical Logic* 11 (1982), 1.

paradox.'[16] It follows that some means other than syntactic criteria will be required for this task. As a result, Kripke develops an idea first introduced by Herzberger,[17] to the effect that it is only by grounding sentences within the real (intuitively, non-linguistic) world that they obtain their truth-values.

III Groundedness

Herzberger's basic idea can be explained as follows: a sentence which asserts of another sentence that it is true[18] will itself be true or false depending upon the truth value of the sentence to which it refers. This sentence, if it in turn asserts the truth of another sentence, will itself be true or false depending upon the truth value of the sentence to which it refers; and so on. Should this process eventually terminate with a sentence which does not involve use of the truth predicate, the original sentence is said to be grounded; otherwise it is said to be ungrounded. Intuitively, the idea is that applying the concept of truth requires that there exist sentences at a base level which do not themselves involve the concept in question.[19] In Sainsbury's helpful phrase,

---

16 Saul Kripke, 'Outline of a Theory of Truth,' 692

17 Hans A. Herzberger, 'Paradoxes of Grounding in Semantics,' *Journal of Philosophy* **67** (1970) 145-67

18 Or that it is false, or of a class of sentences that they are all true, or mostly true, or all false, or mostly false, etc. Details of such generalizations are not difficult to construct. For example, a sentence which asserts that all sentences of a certain class are true will be false but grounded whenever at least one sentence in the class is false and grounded, irrespective of the groundedness (or lack of groundedness) of other members of the class.

19 Formally, this basic idea is exhibited within a hierarchy of interpreted languages in such a way that a sentence is grounded if and only if it obtains a truth-value at the smallest fixed point of the hierarchy, and ungrounded otherwise. A paradoxical sentence turns out to be a sentence which cannot consistently be assigned a truth-value at any fixed point. It follows that although all paradoxical sentences are ungrounded, not all ungrounded sentences need be paradoxical.

this situation 'mirrors a putative metaphysical fact: that *truth depends on something outside itself.*'[20]

As a result, it will typically[21] follow that sentences such as

'Snow is white' is true

and

'Some sentence spoken by Tarski is true' is true

will be grounded. In the case of the former, the sentence will be true if and only if 'Snow is white' is true. This in turn will be the case if and only if snow is white, something which has nothing to do with the concept or application of truth at all. In the case of the latter, the sentence will be true if and only if 'Some sentence spoken by Tarski is true' is true. This in turn will be the case if and only if some sentence spoken by Tarski — such as 'Snow is white' — is true. As before, it now follows that some sentence spoken by Tarski — such as 'Snow is white' — will be true if and only if, e.g., snow is white, something which, in this case, has nothing to do with the concept or application of truth at all.

In contrast, a sentence such as the liar sentence,

(L) This sentence is false,

will be ungrounded. For *L* the process of attempting to find a non-truth-predicating fact will never terminate. There simply is no basic,

---

For example, unlike the paradoxical 'This sentence is false,' the sentence 'This sentence is true' is not paradoxical even though it is ungrounded. In other words, it can be assigned a single truth-value, but only arbitrarily. This basic idea of Herzberger's appears to have been anticipated at least by Ryle. See Gilbert Ryle, 'Heterologicality,' *Analysis* **11** (1951) 61-9, esp 67f.

20 R.M. Sainsbury, *Paradoxes* (Cambridge: Cambridge University Press 1988), 117

21 As Kripke's Watergate example shows, groundedness is not, in general, an intrinsic property of a sentence, but typically depends instead upon the empirical context of the sentence's utterance.

foundational fact upon which the truth or falsity of such a sentence rests.

To see how this resolves the liar paradox, recall the argument which purports to prove *L* paradoxical: if *L* is true, then it is false; if it is false, then it is true; and, given bivalence, it follows that *L* is both true and false. However, given that *L* is not grounded, Kripke can consistently claim that *L* is neither true nor false and, hence, that the paradox is resolved. Thus Kripke's resolution of the semantic paradoxes can be summarized as follows: Classical bivalence requires all sentences to have exactly one of the two truth values, truth and falsity. But the fact that some sentences are ungrounded forces us to reject classical bivalence, concluding instead that some sentences may be neither true nor false. This in turn allows sentences such as *L* to escape being paradoxical. On this view it is by accepting truth value 'gaps,' rather than by rejecting semantic closure, that the paradoxes are eliminated.

Unfortunately, the theory of truth-value gaps falls victim to another paradox, the paradox of the strengthened liar.[22] To see this, consider the sentence, *SL* (which stands for 'Strengthened Liar'):

(*SL*)   *SL* is not true.

Now it appears that if *SL* is true, then it is not true; and if it is not true, then it is true. But whether or not bivalence is abandoned with regard to truth and falsehood, surely *SL* is either true or not true. After all, to assert of *SL* that it is neither true nor not true would (on classical reasoning) be equivalent to asserting of *SL* that it is both not true and true. So, since *SL* must be either true or not true even when bivalence is abandoned, it follows that it is both true and not true.

Another way of reaching this same conclusion is as follows: given Tarski's *T* schema,

---

22 The term is introduced in Bas van Fraasen, 'Presupposition, Implication and Self-Reference,' *Journal of Philosophy* **65** (1968), 147.

(T) Ψ is true iff ϕ,

substitute '*SL*' for Ψ and '*SL* is not true' for ϕ. Then we have

SL is true if and only if *SL* is not true.

Thus, even if a theory of truth-value gaps is invoked and *SL* is claimed to be neither true nor false, it follows that it is also true.[23]

Simply put, the conclusion is that the strengthened liar makes any account of groundedness which allows for gaps in truth values incoherent. In addition, having strengthened *L* to form *SL*, it is now also possible to strengthen both *C* and *E*. Since both Curry's paradox and the traditional Epimenides paradox are so closely related to the liar (and hence to *SL*), *C* and *E* can be strengthened to form *SC* and *SE* respectively:

(SC) *SC* is not true $\lor$ *s*,

(SE) *SE* is not true & *s*.

Blocking our original, unwanted a priori inferences will therefore have to involve something other than the postulating of truth-value gaps. It will require the blocking of *SL*, *SC* and *SE*. What moral is to be drawn from this conclusion?

---

23 Yet another way of reaching much this same conclusion is as follows: consider a sentence, s, which is neither true nor false; then the biconditional
    '*s*' is true iff *s*
    fails since "'s" is true' is false but '*s*' is neither true nor false. Thus either *T* must be rejected, or a theory of truth-value gaps abandoned. (See Susan Haack, *Philosophy of Logics* (Cambridge: Cambridge University Press 1978), 101f.)

IV Dialetheism

The moral which Graham Priest draws from the strengthened liar and other arguments like it is that we should be willing to accept some contradictions as being true. In other words we should reject a theory of truth-value 'gaps' in favor of a theory of truth-value 'gluts.' In yet other words, we should accept the doctrine of dialetheism, the doctrine that there exist true contradictions, true sentences of the form 'α and it is not the case that α.'[24]

It is Priest's view that given that there exist valid, a priori arguments from true premises to contradictory conclusions, dialetheism should be viewed as the most natural resolution of the paradoxes. In other words, once we have accepted the semantic closure of natural language at face value, dialetheism follows from the fact that a coherent semantics can be given which allows some sentences to be both true and false. (Others, of course, will remain only true or false simpliciter.) Traditional attempts at resolving the paradoxes require that we give up semantic closure. In contrast, Priest's approach requires only that we should give up classical logic.

Priest's semantics (for the propositional case) are as follows:[25] Let $M = <W, R, w^*, v>$ be a semantic interpretation with W an index set of possible worlds, w_i, R a binary relation on W, w^* the actual world, and v a valuation of the propositional parameters, i.e. a map from W×P (with P the set of propositional parameters) into $\{\{1\}, \{0\}, \{1, 0\}\}$, the set of truth values. More naturally, we can write $v(w, \alpha) = x$ as $v_w(\alpha) = x$.

---

24 See Graham Priest, *In Contradiction* (Dordrecht: Martinus Nijhoff 1987), 11 and passim. Much of the groundwork for this book was laid by Priest in earlier articles, including 'Logic of Paradox,' *Journal of Philosophical Logic* **8** (1979) 219-41; 'Sense, Entailment and *Modus Ponens*,' *Journal of Philosophical Logic* **9** (1980) 415-35; 'To Be and Not To Be: Dialectical Tense Logic,' *Studia Logica* **41** (1982) 249-68; 'Logical Paradoxes and the Law of Excluded Middle,' *Philosophical Quarterly* **33** (1983) 160-5; 'Logic of Paradox Revisited,' *Journal of Philosophical Logic* **13** (1984) 153-79; and 'Semantic Closure,' *Studia Logica* **43** (1984) 117-29.

25 Graham Priest, *In Contradiction*, 94ff.; 'Logic of Paradox,' 226ff.; 'To Be and Not To Be: Dialectical Tense Logic,' 254ff.

Valuation v can then be extended to form a valuation of all formulas as follows:

¬ $1 \in v_w(\neg\alpha)$ iff $0 \in v_w(\alpha)$
   $0 \in v_w(\neg\alpha)$ iff $1 \in v_w(\alpha)$

∧ $1 \in v_w(\alpha \wedge \beta)$ iff $1 \in v_w(\alpha)$ and $1 \in v_w(\beta)$
   $0 \in v_w(\alpha \wedge \beta)$ iff $0 \in v_w(\alpha)$ or $0 \in v_w(\beta)$

∨ $1 \in v_w(\alpha \vee \beta)$ iff $1 \in v_w(\alpha)$ or $1 \in v_w(\beta)$
   $0 \in v_w(\alpha \vee \beta)$ iff $0 \in v_w(\alpha)$ and $0 \in v_w(\beta)$

→ $1 \in v_w(\alpha \rightarrow \beta)$ iff for all w_i such that $w_i R w$,
   if $1 \in v_{w_i}(\alpha)$ then $1 \in v_{w_i}(\beta)$, and if $0 \in v_{w_i}(\beta)$ then $0 \in v_{w_i}(\alpha)$
   $0 \in v_w(\alpha \rightarrow \beta)$ iff for some w_i such that $w_i R w$,
   $1 \in v_{w_i}(\alpha)$ and $0 \in v_{w_i}(\beta)$.

'$1 \in v_w(\alpha)$' is read as 'α is true under v at w' and '$0 \in v_w(\alpha)$' is read as 'α is false under v at w.' Definitions of semantic consequence and logical truth are then introduced in the standard way:

$\Sigma \models \alpha$ iff for all interpretations, M, it is true of the evaluation, v, that
   if $1 \in v(\beta)$ for all $\beta \in \Sigma$, then $1 \in v(\alpha)$.

$\models \alpha$ iff for all interpretations, M, it is true of the evaluation, v, that
   $1 \in v(\alpha)$.

Given Priest's semantics, some rules of inference, such as disjunctive syllogism, fail. (To see this, let $1, 0 \in v_{w'}(P)$ and let $0 \in v_{w'}(Q)$ and $1 \notin v_{w'}(Q)$; then since $1, 0 \in v_{w'}(P)$, it follows both that $1, 0 \in v_{w'}(\neg P)$ and that $1, 0 \in v_{w'}(P \vee Q)$; but then it follows that both $1 \in v_{w'}(P \vee Q)$ and $1 \in v_{w'}(\neg P)$ even though $0 \in v_{w'}(Q)$ and $1 \notin v_{w'}(Q)$; in other words, $P \vee Q$ and $\neg P$ are true while Q is simply false; in yet other words, disjunctive syllogism fails.) The result is that while Priest's theory is clearly inconsistent (since it contains some contradictions), it can also said to be only paraconsistent (since these contradictions do not entail every sentence of the language).

It is also worth noting that, formally, Priest's truth tables for the extensional connectives are identical to those of both Łukasiewicz and Kleene.[26] (Although for Łukasiewicz the intermediate truth-value, *i*, is to be read 'indeterminate' or 'possible,' rather than 'both true and false,' and is to be assigned to statements of future contingents; for Kleene, the third value, *u*, is to be read 'indeterminable whether true or false,' and is to be assigned to undecidable sentences.) As Parsons has pointed out, they are also formally identical to the set of truth tables most commonly used to explain a theory of truth-value gaps. In Parsons's words, where other people see 'gaps,' Priest sees 'gluts.'[27]

Nevertheless, using his non-classical semantics, Priest is able to deal with the paradoxes in (what by some lights) might be viewed as the most natural of alternatives — by simply accepting them into a coherent (although not a consistent) theory. In his words, his position is 'quite self-consistent, though this is hardly a happy way of expressing the matter! So let us just say that it is self-coherent.'[28]

Criticizing dialetheism is no mean task. After all, finding a contradiction — something that in most other contexts would constitute a satisfactory reductio ad absurdum — cannot be viewed

---

26 See Jan Łukasiewicz, 'On 3-valued Logic' (1920) and 'Many-valued Systems of Propositional Logic' (1930), in S. McCall, *Polish Logic* (Oxford: Oxford University Press 1967), and S.C. Kleene, *Metamathematics* (Amsterdam: North Holland 1952), 332ff.

27 See Terence Parsons, 'True Contradictions,' *Canadian Journal of Philosophy* 20 (1990), 336. Of course, as Parsons points out, the formal similarities between theories of truth-value 'gaps' and theories of truth-value 'gluts' mean that criticisms of one account can typically be translated into criticisms of the other. Both accounts, for example, regularly have expressibility problems: the 'gapper' believes that some sentences are neither true nor false, yet typically has difficulty saying this truly; in contrast, Priest believes that some views (including those of the 'gapper') are not true, yet generally has difficulty saying this truly. See 344ff., especially n. 9 and 10 of Parsons.

28 Graham Priest, *In Contradiction*, 91

as a criticism without begging the question. Proving within Priest's system that it is both the case that $(\exists x)(Tx \land \neg Tx)$ and that $\neg(\exists x)(Tx \land \neg Tx)$, i.e. that dialetheia both exist and fail to exist, or even that $(\exists x)[(Tx \land \neg Tx) \& \neg(Tx \land \neg Tx)]$, i.e. that something might both be and not be a dialetheia, will be of very little consequence. Far from being disturbed, Priest takes such contradictions to count as confirmatory instances of his theory.[29] Charitably, however, he does grant that contradictions such as these should not be 'multiplied beyond necessity.'[30]

In this context, not multiplying contradictions 'beyond necessity' is no empty adage. Should contradictions be allowed to spread unchecked within the theory, it would soon follow (as is the case with classical logic) that belief in a contradiction would commit one to belief in everything, clearly an unpalatable result. Thus, Priest's logic must remain paraconsistent; as he himself points out, what this means is that it must not validate the classical principle of absorption, the principle that

$$\{\alpha \to (\alpha \to \beta)\} \models \alpha \to \beta.$$

The reason is that one can use absorption to construct Curry's paradox.

The argument goes as follows: Given an arbitrary sentence, β, construct the sentence, δ, which has the form $T'\delta' \to \beta$, viz. 'If this sentence is true, then β.' From Tarski's T–scheme, $T'\alpha' \leftrightarrow \alpha$, it follows that $T'\delta' \leftrightarrow (T'\delta' \to \beta)$. Now if absorption holds, $\{T'\delta' \to (T'\delta' \to \beta)\} \models T'\delta' \to \beta$, and so, by the substitutivity of equivalents, $\{T'\delta' \to T'\delta'\} \models T'\delta' \to \beta$. But since $T'\delta' \to T'\delta,'$ we have $T'\delta' \to \beta$. And since $T'\delta' \leftrightarrow (T'\delta' \to \beta)$, from above, we have $T'\delta.'$ And so by modus ponens, β.

Since absorption follows from assertion, i.e. the principle that

---

29 Ibid., 91
30 Ibid., 90

$$\models \{\alpha \wedge (\alpha \to \beta)\} \to \beta,$$

one can use an analogous argument to show that Curry's paradox follows from it too. The argument is as follows: Given an arbitrary sentence, β, construct the sentence, δ, which has the form $T'\delta' \to \beta$, viz. 'If this sentence is true, then β.' From the T-scheme, $T'\alpha' \leftrightarrow \alpha$ it follows that $T'\delta' \leftrightarrow (T'\delta' \to \beta)$. Now if assertion holds, $\{T'\delta' \wedge (T'\delta' \to \beta)\} \to \beta$. Then by substitutivity of equivalents, $(T'\delta' \wedge T'\delta') \to \beta$, and then by $\wedge$-elimination, $T'\delta' \to \beta$. But since $T'\delta' \leftrightarrow (T'\delta' \to \beta)$, from above, we have $T'\delta'$. And so by modus ponens, β.[31]

Priest is therefore forced to disallow both absorption and assertion. He does so simply by pointing out that, given the above semantics, both principles fail. For assertion the counter-model is as follows: Let $M = <W, R, w^*, v>$, with $W = \{w^*, w_1\}$, w^*Rw^*, w_1Rw^*, and w^*Rw_1, $v_{w^*}(p) = v_{w^*}(q) = v_{w_1}(p) = \{1\}$ and $v_{w_1}(q) = \{0\}$. Then it follows that $v_{w^*}(p \to q) = \{0\}$ and $v_{w_1}(p \to q) = \{1\}$, and hence that $v_{w^*}(p \wedge (p \to q)) = \{0\}$ and $v_{w_1}(p \wedge (p \to q)) = \{1\}$. Hence it follows that $v_{w^*}((p \wedge (p \to q)) \to q) = \{0\}$.

For absorption the counter-model is $M = <W, R, w^*, v>$ with $W = \{w^*, w_1\}$, w^*Rw^*, w_1Rw^*, and w^*Rw_1, $v_{w^*}(p) = v_{w_1}(q) = \{0\}$ and $v_{\omega^*}(q) = v_{w_1}(p) = \{1\}$.

However, at this point two objections can be raised. The first is that crucial to the success of these counter-models is the failure of reflexivity for R. Yet this is a very strong assumption indeed. In many respects it is quite counter-intuitive. (Under this condition, for example, detachment will not in general hold.) As a result, some philosophical justification is going to be required,[32] and although Priest attempts to provide one, it is less than convincing. According to Priest,

---

31 Similar arguments can be given that are analogous to the Epimenides. For discussion about how Curry's paradox relates to naive set theory, see Robert K. Meyer, Richard Routley, and J. Michael Dunn, 'Curry's Paradox,' *Analysis* **39** (1979), 124-8.

32 In fact, Priest himself criticizes other purported solutions to the paradoxes for lacking just such motivation.

the totality of possible worlds is best viewed as the totality of possible worlds accessible from the actual world, and this doesn't guarantee reflexivity in any case except that of the actual world itself. The reason given by Priest is that on his view it is plausible to identify possibility with that set of situations which is 'conceivable, in some sense, by people living in the [actual world].'[33] Yet this, in turn, is surely a controversial assumption. Why should possibility be identified with conceivability? Why should we assume that possibility is relative to the actual world, or to actual conceivability? Most importantly, why shouldn't (most) worlds be possible relative to themselves? If denying this claim requires accepting one metaphysical account of possibility over another, then the issue is no longer a purely logical one. In other words, regardless of one's answer to the above questions, these are just the kind of considerations that one might plausibly be inclined to believe should *not* enter into a debate on the nature of truth, or on the success or failure of one program or another at solving the paradoxes. Simply put, one's theory of possibility might plausibly be argued to be independent of one's theory of truth. Why should one be forced to identify possibility with real-world conceivability simply in order to avoid Curry's paradox?

The second objection to be raised against Priest's non-reflexivity requirement is even more decisive. This is the objection that, strictly speaking, the failure of reflexivity appears to have nothing to do with dialetheism. In the above counter-models, for example, no sentence takes the values of both truth and falsehood. Thus exactly the same ad hoc move of dropping reflexivity can be made by the advocate of the classical connectives. The lesson appears to be that the acceptance or rejection of reflexivity (and hence the acceptance or rejection of both absorption and assertion) is independent of dialetheism. As a result, one is left wondering just why the acceptance of dialetheism is in any way necessary for this type of (ad hoc) resolution to Curry's paradox.

---

33 Graham Priest, *In Contradiction*, 108

V Sentences, Statements and Empirical Content

At this point it may appear that we have reached an impasse. Neither traditional accounts (such as those of Russell and Tarski) which abandon semantic closure, nor more recent accounts (such as those of Kripke and Priest) which abandon some aspect of classical logic, have proved satisfactory for blocking our original, unwanted a priori inferences. However, underlying the discussion up to this point has been the assumption that eliminating the paradoxes requires a formal solution, that it requires either the regimentation of natural language into, say, a hierarchy of formal languages, or the formalization of a non-classical semantics. Abandoning this assumption will allow us to view the semantic paradoxes, not as formal or structural errors of language or logic, but as informal errors of a priori belief, errors which can only be addressed by linking language and belief more firmly to the empirical world.

The basic strategy is as follows: Priest and Kripke both accept the assumption that sentences like *SL, SC* and *SE* all express meaningful statements. Yet it was exactly this assumption which, in effect, Tarski and Russell questioned. Both Russell's type theory and Tarski's language hierarchy resulted in treating tokens such as *SL, SC* and *SE* as ill-formed and hence meaningless. Once meaningless, such tokens would not simply lack truth-values, they would literally fail to make any assertion at all. Such sentence tokens would be nothing more than uninterpreted syntax, spilled ink on a page. On this strategy, *SL, SC* and *SE* would turn out to be no more paradoxical than would be any other (non-linguistic) physical artifact.

However, given Kripke's Watergate example, we were forced to conclude that it is 'fruitless to look for an *intrinsic* criterion that will enable us to sieve out — as meaningless, or ill-formed — those sentences which lead to paradox.'[34] Another way of putting this is that, given the fact that virtually any sentence involving a truth predicate

---

34 Saul Kripke, 'Outline of a Theory of Truth,' 692

might turn out to be paradoxical in some imaginable state of affairs or possible world,[35] it turns out that formal criteria alone will inevitably prove insufficient for resolving the paradoxes. In contrast, what will prove sufficient is an insistence that meaning itself be taken to be a function of a sentence's material (or empirical) content. By grounding meaningful sentences in the actual world in a case by case way, paradoxical sentences become literally meaningless.

In order to motivate this proposal, compare the following two fables. The first involves Russell's famous 'quasi-paradox,' the paradox of the barber. The second involves *SL*, the strengthened liar:

> *Fable 1*: In a remote village, far away on the other side of a great ocean, there is a barber who shaves all and only those villagers who do not shave themselves. As the villagers regularly explain to visitors, if the barber shaves himself then he does not (since he shaves only those who do not shave themselves); and if he does not then he does (since he shaves all those who do not shave themselves). Thus the villagers have accepted as part of their folklore the belief that the barber both does and does not shave himself.

> *Fable 2*: In the language of a remote village, far away on the other side of a great ocean, there is a sentence, *SL*, which is true if and only if it is not. As the villagers regularly explain to visitors, if the sentence is true, then it is not (since it then truly asserts that it is not); and if the sentence is not true then it is (since what it asserts is that it is not true). Thus the villagers have accepted as part of their folklore the belief that the sentence both is and is not true.

Described in this way, both fables are based upon their own assumption. In the case of the first fable, the assumption is that there is a barber

---

35 Recall, not just Kripke's Watergate example, but Buridan's 9th Sophism and the postcard paradox mentioned in n. 13 above.

who shaves all and only those villagers who do not shave themselves. In the case of the second, the assumption is that there is a sentence which is true if and only if it is not. Seen in this way, the analogy between the barber paradox and the liar paradox is striking.

How do we solve the barber paradox? We do so in a very straight-forward way. We solve it simply by denying its underlying assumption: by concluding that no such barber exists. Without the barber there is no paradox.[36] But if this is so, why can't we say the same with respect to the strengthened liar? Why is this solution not available for solving the semantic paradoxes as well?

The answer appears to be that *SL*, unlike the mythical barber, is real. As evidence, one need merely see it written on a page or hear it asserted, either by oneself or by someone else. But is the situation really as clear-cut as this? Those who answer in the affirmative will believe it sufficient merely to remind us of what *SL* says. As we saw earlier, because of what *SL* says, invoking a truth-value gap only makes the sentence true. Surely the same will happen here. Saying that the sentence is not a statement, or (equivalently in this context) that it asserts nothing, or (equivalently) that it fails to express a proposition, or (equivalently) that it is without meaning, or (equivalently) that it is without truth conditions, apparently commits one to the additional claim that the sentence says nothing true, and hence that it is not true. Yet this is exactly what the sentence says and so, apparently, it says it truly.

---

36 This general strategy not only leads to the resolution of the barber paradox. It is also the same strategy, stripped of all its formal technicality, which lies at the heart of most modern solutions to the set-theoretical paradoxes. Just as in the case of the barber paradox, the conclusion we draw from Russell's paradox is that the Russell set (which both is and is not a member of itself) does not exist. For example, see George Boolos, 'The Iterative Conception of Set,' *Journal of Philosophy* **68** (1971), 215-32, reprinted in Paul Benacerraf & Hilary Putnam, *Philosophy of Mathematics*, 2nd ed. (Cambridge: Cambridge University Press 1983), 486-502. Also compare Jon Barwise & John Etchemendy, *The Liar* (New York & Oxford: Oxford University Press 1987).

But it is at just this point that the skeptic should not be drawn in. After all, if we mean to assert, not just that the sentence is without truth-value, but that the ink on the page or the sounds in the air genuinely fail to assert anything, then we will not be taken in by the strengthened liar. How could *SL* say of itself that it is not true when in fact it says nothing at all?

One might be tempted to say that because the report,

(R) *SL* is not true

is true, the sentence

(SL) *SL* is not true

must be true as well. But this is simply a temptation to which one should not acquiesce. Of course, one might be tempted to think that *SL* is true if one had reason to believe that *SL* was *R*. But what evidence do we have that this is so? None of any consequence:[37] only formal (syntactic) similarity together with the (mistaken) assumption that such similarity is always sufficient for capturing (rather than simply modelling) successful linguistic convention.[38]

---

37 Peter Apostoli has pointed out to me that, strictly speaking, a conclusion this strong is not essential. Even if one accepts the meaningfulness of *SL* as a metatheoretic report, *R*, that an object language sentence, *SL*, fails to be assigned the value True, what the contradictions show is that this fact cannot be expressed in the object language of the model, at least not by the sentence *SL* itself. Indeed, as Apostoli points out, one merely has to inspect the weak-Kleene truth function for negation to see that the composite predicate 'not true' as it occurs in the object language is not co-extensive with the same predicate as it occurs in the metalanguage. Hence, contrary to our assumption, we have failed to achieve semantic closure: there are truths that this language cannot report. Whether this argument should be understood as assuming the meaningfulness of *SL* in actual fact, or merely for the purpose of reductio is, I think, a moot point.

38 In this respect, the proposal being offered here mirrors that of Buridan. By assigning truth values to concrete sentence tokens, Buridan was able to assign

To return to our analogy, simply believing that Russell's barber exists does not force his existence. Beliefs about *SL* (or *SC* or *SE*) are not any different. It does not follow that just because many people believe that *SL* (or *SC* or *SE*) asserts a statement — i.e. that linguistic convention leads us to accept a priori that *SL* asserts a statement — that it does. Just as with Russell's imaginary barber, believing *SL* to be a meaningful statement is not in any way a factor in making it so.

On Kripke's account, ungrounded sentences remain meaningful. On this account they do not.[39] Sentences are not true or false intrinsically. Instead, they obtain their truth conditions only relative to an interpretation or, to make the point in a slightly different way, to a given empirical context. In other words, whether or not a syntactically well-formed sentence token successfully expresses a statement will in every case be a contingent matter. Success in this respect will be dependent in part upon the structure of the sentence and upon conventions relating it to the world; in part it will be dependent upon the nature of that (extra-linguistic) world itself.[40]

---

different truth values consistently to distinct tokens of the same type. However, unlike Buridan's account, this proposal does not assign the value 'false' to the sentence token *SL*. For a lively discussion of whether Buridan is successful in avoiding the semantic paradoxes, see Allen Hazen, '*Contra Buridanum,*' *Canadian Journal of Philosophy* 17 (1987) 875-80, and Ian Hinckfuss, '*Pro Buridano; Contra Hazenum,*' *Canadian Journal of Philosophy* 21 (1991) 389-98.

39 For this reason, this solution has similarities with other 'non-statement' or 'non-propositional' accounts, such as those of Bar-Hillel, Goldstein, Kneale, Prior, and Sobel. It is also motivated by D.C. Stove's 'case by case' view concerning formal inference in general. See Y. Bar-Hillel, 'New Light on the Liar,' *Analysis* 18 (1957) 1-6; Laurence Goldstein, 'Epimenides and Curry,' *Analysis* 46 (1986) 117-21; W.C. Kneale, 'Russell's Paradox and Some Others,' *British Journal for the Philosophy of Science* 22 (1971) 321-38; A.N. Prior, 'Epimenides the Cretan,' *Journal of Symbolic Logic* 23 (1958) 261-6; Jordan Howard Sobel, 'Lies, Lies, and More Lies: A Plea for Propositions,' *Philosophical Studies* 67 (1992) 51-69; and D.C. Stove, *The Rationality of Induction* (Oxford: Clarendon 1986), ch. 9.

40 Of course, this sketch will have to be modified slightly for statements which make reference to language itself.

Thus, language is constrained from two directions: social convention and the world. Since nature itself contains no contradictions, it is appropriate to conclude that contradictory sentences are the result of inappropriate social (i.e. linguistic) conventions; they are the result of inappropriate assumptions concerning the ability of sentences which are either ungrounded or in some other way devoid of material content still to express meaningful assertions. Such assumptions are based upon a priori presuppositions which diverge from nature; upon a priori reasoning gone wrong. In the case of *SL* for example, it is the presupposition that *SL* is a sentence which is true if and only if it is not or, more fundamentally, that *SL* is a truth-bearer at all. Yet if this is correct, then blocking the semantic paradoxes will turn out to be equivalent to abandoning certain inappropriate, a priori assumptions, assumptions which account for the divergence of language from the world and which can only be tested in a case by case way.

To put this point in other words, paradoxes such as the strengthened liar presuppose a theory of language in which sentences such as *SL*, *SC* and *SE* express meaningful assertions simply as a result of certain structural or conventional characteristics they share with other sentences. The contradictions show that this presupposition is wrong. Further, we can show why this is so in terms of a theory of grounding: the purported truth conditions for sentences such as *SL*, *SC* and *SE* fail to reduce, under schema *T* and logical decomposition, to non-truth predicating facts. Hence, whether we recognize it or not, such sentence tokens fail to have truth conditions at all.

The question with which we originally began asked whether there was a way to block the type of pathological, a priori inferences found in Curry's paradox and in the Epimenides paradox without abandoning either semantic closure or classical logic. It turns out that our original question has now been replaced by another: What evidence do we have that specific patterns of ink on the page or the sounds in the air actually do express a meaningful statement? In the case of *SL*, *SC* and *SE*, we have some evidence (grammatical structure and the like) to be sure, but most of this evidence comes from a priori assumptions concerning linguistic conventions, rather than from recognizable material (or empirical) content. At the same time, we do have strong evidence against the claim that such physical tokens express meaningful statements. After all, *SL*, *SC* and *SE* are all ungrounded. If meaningful, they are also paradoxical. Shouldn't this be enough to justify the claim that they are just (non-linguistic) things in the world and nothing more? If so, abandonment of our a priori assumptions to the contrary will amount to an abandonment of the paradoxes themselves.

CANADIAN JOURNAL OF PHILOSOPHY
Supplementary Volume 18

An Essay on Material Necessity[1]

BARRY SMITH

I Hume — Reinach — Searle

At the one extreme stands Hume, who — at least according to common conceptions — rules out entirely the possibility of material or non-logical necessity, and who therefore rules out also the possibility that we might enjoy that sort of certain knowledge that earlier philosophers had assumed as a matter of course to be correlated therewith.[2] At the other extreme stands Adolf Reinach, the hero of our present story, who defends the existence of a wide class of material necessities falling within the domain of what can be a priori known. More precisely, Reinach holds that there are certain categories of entity whose factual instantiation brings with it as a matter of necessity the instantiation of certain other correlated categories. The instantiation of the category *color* necessitates in this fashion the instantiation of the category *visual extension*. Such categories are to be

---

1 My thanks are due to Johannes Brandl, Patricia Donohue, and Philip Hanson for helpful comments on an earlier version of this paper.

2 For a more adequate discussion of Hume's views on this matter see Reinach 1911a.

understood, from Reinach's point of view, after the fashion of Plato's intelligible forms. Thus they constitute an autonomous, natural order that is not capable of being invented or constructed through acts of man; they are such that actual things and events may serve to instantiate them more or less completely or perfectly; and they are such that we enjoy in relation to them (and therefore also in relation to their instances) a special sort of non-inductive knowledge. More consistently than Plato, however, Reinach acknowledges the existence of systems of relations through which the given categories are tied together into larger wholes. Such categories are then intrinsically intelligible precisely as nodes in this system of relations of the given sort, in the sense that anyone who has experience (including imaginative experience) of relevant instances of these categories is implicitly aware also of a corresponding family of relations. It is such intrinsic intelligibility of the basic structures and interrelations of shape and motion, color and sound, for example, which makes it possible for us to learn language and to acquire that sort of a posteriori knowledge on which empirical science is based.

Midway between these two extremes stands Searle. Like Hume, Searle is unwilling to accept special, uninventable categories whose instances would stand in necessary relations to each other. Like Reinach, however, Searle believes that there are categories of entity whose factual instantiation brings with it as a matter of necessity the factual instantiation of other correlated categories. The corresponding categories are for him not eternal and uninventable, however, but human creations; and the necessities in question are purely logical consequences of the 'constitutive rules' by which the given categories are brought into being. As for Vico and Hobbes, so also for Searle; it is only in relation to what a human being has made that he or she is able to enjoy certain knowledge.

The essay which follows has two principal goals. On the one hand I shall summarize Reinach's thinking in connection with the issues of apriorism and material necessity. On the other hand I shall seek to demonstrate that Searle does not, after all, occupy a stable and acceptable half-way house between Hume and Reinach. Searle, too, if he is to be able to do justice to the establishment and to the workings of constitutive rules must, on pain of circularity, embrace something like the Reinachian Platonism outlined above.

There is a commonsensical assumption to the effect that, other things being equal, we can infer from: 'John promised to do such-and-such' to: 'John is obligated to do such-and-such.' Humeans (most philosophers, today) hold that the inference in question is invalid, that an 'ought' can under no circumstances be derived from an 'is.' Reinach holds that our commonsensical recognition of the validity of the given inference flows from our possession of synthetic a priori knowledge of a certain relation of necessitation between the categories in question. Searle, for his part, would have it that we have *made* the institution of promising and that as a result certain inferences are valid because they reflect the manmade rules of that institution.

It will turn out that speech act phenomena manifest in a particularly clear form the necessitation-structures which will be at the heart of our theory of the a priori. Thus I shall start with a brief excursus on the somewhat obscure history of philosophers' deliberations on such phenomena. This history has, I believe, some independent interest of its own, and will provide in addition some useful background for those interested in pursuing further the underpinnings of the Reinachian theory here defended.

II On the Theory of Speech Acts

In the fourth chapter of his *De interpretatione*, Aristotle draws a distinction between two sorts of sentences. On the one hand, he says, there are 'statement-making sentences.' On the other hand there are sentences, such as for example requests, 'in which there is no truth or falsity' (17 a 1-5). The latter, Aristotle affirms, can be dismissed from logic, since consideration of them 'belongs rather to the study of rhetoric or poetry.' Aristotle's attitude here, which remained authoritative throughout the Middle Ages, had fateful consequences. For his remarks ensured that the treatment of non-statement-making sentences came to be banished not merely from logic, but from the realm of science in general.

His remarks seem to have been explicitly challenged only towards the end of the eighteenth century in the work on 'social acts' of Thomas Reid.[3] Reid's ideas in this connection remained without substantial influence, however, and it was not until the early years of the present century that the project of a theory of linguistic action began to take more definitive shape. More precisely, it is in a monograph on the foundations of the civil law, published in 1913 by our hero Reinach, that we find the first truly systematic theory of the phenomena of promising, questioning, requesting, commanding, accusing, enacting, etc., phenomena which Reinach, like Reid before him, collects together under the heading 'social acts.'[4]

Certainly there were philosophers other than Reid and Reinach who had considered the nature of promisings and other social acts. Such philosophers sought, however — in silent tribute to the assumption of Aristotle that only statement-making sentences belong properly to the realm of logic — to reassign such phenomena to the realm of statements or declarations. Thus Bolzano, for example, considers the act of questioning as a statement, to the effect that the questioner 'desires to receive instruction about the object in question.'[5] The act of promising, similarly, is seen by Hume, Lipps and others as the expression of an act of will or as the declaration of an intention to act in the interests of the party in whose favor the declaration is made. There is an obvious inadequacy of all accounts of promising along these lines, however, namely that they throw no light at all on the problem of how

---

3 Cf. Schulthess 1983, 304; Mulligan 1987, 33f.; Schuhmann and Smith 1990.

4 Reinach's theory was in part inspired by the work on logic and ontology of his teacher Edmund Husserl. It incorporated also criticisms of Husserl's thinking derived from the Brentanian philosopher of language Anton Marty and from Reinach's friend and fellow student in Munich Johannes Daubert. On the pre-First World War Munich tradition of speech act theory see Smith 1990 and Schuhmann and Smith 1985. An important role in the development of Reinach's thinking was played also by his background as a student of law: see Schuhmann and Smith 1987, 10-13.

5 *Wissenschaftslehre* (1837), vol. I, § 22

an utterance of the given sort can give rise to claim and obligation. The bare intention to do something has, after all, no quasi-legal consequences of this sort, and it is difficult to see why things should be different in reflection of the fact that such an intention is brought to expression in language.

Certainly *promising* and *communicating one's intention to do something* do have much in common. Thus both belong to the category of what Reinach calls *spontaneous* acts, i.e., acts which involve a subject's bringing something about within his own psychic sphere — as contrasted with passive or receptive experiences of, say, feeling a pain or hearing an explosion.[6] Both are, moreover, acts which involve as a matter of necessity a linguistic utterance or some other *overt performance* of a non-natural (in the sense of conventional or rule-governed) sort. This does not hold of other spontaneous acts such as judging or deciding, nor even of the acts of cursing or forgiving,[7] but it does hold of apologizing, commanding, accusing, entreating, etc. Spontaneous acts can accordingly be divided into two classes, which we might call *internal* and *external*, respectively, according to whether the act's being brought to overt expression is a separable or inseparable moment of the relevant complex whole.[8]

Spontaneous acts are in every case *intentional*, which is to say that there is a (not necessarily existent) object or objects towards which they are directed. Spontaneous acts may in addition however be directed (in a different sense, now) to a subject or subjects, and most typically to a fellow human being. Amongst such subject-directed acts we may distinguish further between those which are *self-directable* and those which are *non-self-directable* (the latter Reinach also calls *other-*

---

6 See Reinach 1913, 706, English trans. 18. The issue whether the distinction between spontaneous and passive acts is an exhaustive one is not important for our present purposes.

7 We leave aside here those acts of forgiving which are prompted by a request for forgiveness.

8 Reinach 1913, 707f., English trans. 20; Mulligan 1987; Schuhmann 1988. On the terminology of 'inseparable moments' see Smith, ed. 1982.

directed or '*fremdpersonal*'). The former are such that the subject toward whom they are directed may be identical with the subject of the act (as in cases of self-pity, self-hatred, etc.). The latter, in contrast, demand as that toward which they are directed a subject other than the one who acts.

Non-self-directable acts may be either internal (for example feelings of envy or resentment), or external (for example acts of baptism or benediction). Certain acts having the property of being both external and non-self-directable are in addition such that the relevant utterance must of necessity not only be directed toward but also *addressed to* and thereby *registered* or *grasped by* the subject in question. A command must as a matter of necessity be received and understood by the one to whom it is addressed (something which does not apply, for example, to an act of baptizing, forgiving or cursing). A command, that is to say,

> is an action of the subject to which is essential not only its spontaneity and its intentionality, but also its being directed towards other subjects and its standing in need of being grasped by those subjects. What has been said of commands holds also for requesting, admonishing, questioning, informing, answering, and many other types of act. They are all social acts which are, in their execution, cast by him who executes them toward another subject that they may affix themselves in his mind [*einem anderen zugeworfen, um sich in seine Seele einzuhaken*]. (Reinach 1913, 707; cf. English trans. 19f.)

What is important about an action of this kind is that it

> is not divided into the self-sufficient execution of an act and an accidental statement [*zufällige Konstatierung*]; rather it constitutes an inner unity of deliberate execution and deliberate utterance. The experience is here impossible in the absence of the utterance. And the utterance for its part is not something that is added thereto as an incidental extra; rather it stands in the service of the social act and is necessary in order that this should fulfil its announcing function [*kundgebende Funktion*]. Certainly there exist also incidental statements relating to social acts: "I have just issued the command." But such statements then relate to the whole social act, *with* its external aspect. (Ibid., 708; cf. English trans. 20)

Social acts, then, for Reinach (exactly as for Reid), involve

> activities of mind which do not merely find in words their accidental, supplemental expression, but which execute themselves in the very act of speaking

itself and of which it is characteristic that they announce themselves to another by means of this or some similar external appearance. (Ibid., 728; cf. English trans. 36)

The closeness to Austin and later speech act theorists here is unmistakable. A promise cannot be the merely incidental expression or intimation of an act of will or of an intention, because the act which underlies a promise is such that it is simply (and as a matter of necessity) not able to exist outside the compass of a whole of just this sort. And similarly there is no independent and self-contained mental experience which is somehow brought to expression, incidentally, in the issuing of a command. Hence, a fortiori, a social act of this sort cannot be a mere report or declaration of such an experience.

To say that there are experiences of such a nature that they exist only if they or their contents are simultaneously brought to expression might seem controversial — the very existence of mutual dependence here implies that it is possible to separate experience and expression only abstractly (that it is in a certain sense illegitimate to speak of two distinct factors here at all). In some cases, however, the existence of an underlying experience is clear. Consider, trivially, the very experience of *bringing to expression* itself. Acts of warning, apologizing, promising, commanding, and so on, are likewise, Reinach holds, necessarily such that they cannot exist except in and through the very act by which they are brought to expression.

Actions of promising and commanding possess, then, as Reinach would have it, not merely an external dimension of utterance and execution, but also an internal dimension, through which they are tied into the domain of mental acts. The given phenomena are further such that they presuppose or are founded on appropriate mental states, for example of belief, and also on states of other kinds, for example the relational state of authority. In this way phenomena of the given sort are multi-categorial: their constituent relations of necessitation span regions of (mental, linguistic, legal and behavioral, factual and normative) reality and combine together into new structures elements derived from each.

We are far from having dealt with every aspect of Reinach's theory here. Thus we could have considered his treatment of conditional acts, of sham and defective and incomplete acts, of acts performed jointly and severally, of social acts performed *in the name of* some other party, of the ways in which such acts can be overridden and undermined, and so on.[9] One aspect of Reinach's work to which we shall return is the way in which his account of social acts is complemented by a theory of legal formations and of the ways in which the universal categories of promise, obligation, etc. are related to the contingent and pragmatically motivated higher-order social acts of the positive law. Reinach's most important contribution, however, at least for our present purposes, is to have drawn attention to the central role of necessitation relations in the sphere of social action and to have grasped the fact that our synthetic a priori knowledge is in large part precisely knowledge of structures held together by relations of the given sort. Necessitation relations had, it is true, been recognized earlier, above all by Husserl and other followers of Brentano in the sphere of psychology. It was Reinach, however, and his fellow Munich phenomenologists, who demonstrated the pervasiveness of the corresponding structures and who showed also how an absolutely general theory of a priori knowledge can be built up on this basis.

III The Ontology of Necessitation Relations

It is an intriguing question whether Reinach's work exerted a direct or indirect influence on the development of speech act theory in Oxford in the nineteen forties and fifties.[10] More important for us here, however, is the nature and content of Reinach's theory itself. The Anglo-Saxon treatment of speech act phenomena arose, familiarly, at a time when philosophy was conceived as a rather informal matter of

---

9 Cf. Mulligan 1987, 78ff., Smith 1990.

10 This question is not at this stage able to be decided. We do know, however, that Austin's early interest in German (and Austrian) philosophy was not confined to his work of translating Frege. Moreover, it is known that a copy of Reinach's *Gesammelte Schriften* was possessed by Austin's colleague Gilbert Ryle. This survives, with annotations, in the library of Linacre College in Oxford.

'conceptual geography.' Reinach, in contrast, treats of speech acts and related phenomena ontologically. That is, he sees promises, claims, obligations, etc., as entities of certain special sorts, embrangled together in systematic ways with entities of certain other special sorts (for example with people, and with acts and states). Social acts are part of the very stock of the world, and not for example mere reflections of our conventional ways of speaking about other, more humdrum entities. This ontological treatment of necessitation *in re* will generate, as we shall see, a corresponding ontological theory of the a priori.

The world *contains* promisings, claims, commands, requests, marryings, and relations of authority, just as it contains instances of biological and logical species such as *lion* and *tiger* or *judging* and *inferring*. The species which people the world can be divided further into two sorts. On the one hand are *independent species*, whose instances do not require instantiations of other species in order to exist.[11] *Lion* might be taken as an example of an independent species in this sense. On the other hand are *dependent species* such as *smile* or *dent*, whose instances do not exist in and of themselves but only in association with instances of complementary species of other determinate sorts. Wherever instances of dependent species exist, there exist also relations of ontological necessitation. The inference from promise to obligation reflects an ontological necessitation of this sort, as also (in Descartes's eyes at least) does the inference from *cogito* to *sum*. Furthermore, where such positive necessitation holds, there obtain also certain correlated constraints or exclusions in a negative direction. Thus for example since color depends for its existence upon extension, it follows that it is excluded as a matter of necessity that two distinct colors should occupy the same area or volume of space. The family of necessitation-relations extends, in this way, to fill out the entire sphere of what, traditionally, had been seen as the domain of a priori knowledge.

---

11 See Smith, ed. 1982 for more details of the theory of dependence and independence as this applies to species.

There is a rigid, autonomous order to the association or connection of dependent and independent entities. As Husserl puts it:

> It is not a peculiarity of certain sorts of parts that they should only be parts in general, while it would remain quite indifferent what conglomerates with them, and into what sorts of contexts they are fitted. Rather there obtain firmly determined relations of necessity ... determinate laws, which vary with the species of dependent contents and accordingly prescribe one sort of completion to one of them, another sort of completion to another. (1900-01, 244f.; cf. English trans. 454)

Judging is an example of a dependent species in Husserl's sense: a judging exists only as the judging of some specific subject (as a smile smiles only in a human face). *Promising*, too, is an example of a dependent species. Here, however, we see that the dependence is multifold: a promise requires that there be at least also the instantiations of the species *claim, obligation, utterance* and *registering act*, reticulated together with language-using subjects in a single whole. As Austin himself recognized, every speech act is dependent on its surrounding circumstances, as it is dependent also on being heard (on uptake, or *'Vernehmung'* in Reinach's terminology).[12] Much more than Austin, however, Reinach was able to do systematic justice to the entire family of such necessitation relations within the framework of a single theory.

Such necessitation relations may be either one-sided or mutual. As an example of the latter, consider the relation of reciprocal dependence between the claim and obligation brought into being automatically with the execution of an act of promising. Or consider the relation between what Reinach calls the internal and external moments of the promising act. Both internal intending act and external utterance-phenomenon are, as we have seen, not able to exist outside the compass of a whole of just this sort. Intending act and utterance-phenomena are accordingly only superficially similar to intending

---

12 See Austin 1962, 22, 52; and compare Reinach 1911, 213, English trans. 373, n. 11; 1913, 707, 796, 801, English trans. 19, 94, 102.

acts or utterance-phenomena of the sort that are able to exist outside the framework of a promise.

The given features of the promise are marked also by a special a priori quality: they seem to be something of which we know not merely through experiment or observation or induction but rather immediately and (in principle) on even cursory acquaintance with phenomena of the relevant sort. They can be grasped without further ado, in the way that we grasp, for example, that red is darker than yellow, that blue is not a shape, that nothing can be simultaneously red and green all over, and so on. The categories in question (promise, color, shape, etc.) seem in some way to be prior to any given factual realization. The corresponding necessary laws can be grasped as necessary even in the absence of factual instantiations.

As the six Platonic solids constrain factually existing processes of crystal-formation, so the categories distinguished by Reinach as basic to the sphere of social acts constrain factually existing institutions. They provide, as it were, a restricted range of natural and in a certain sense inevitable alternatives within the framework of which institutions must then be formed.[13] Through deliberately contrived institutional arrangements, thus through acts of lawgivers and others, such uninventable categories may become modified, in particular cultures and times, above all in the sense that the range of their particular realizations may become narrowed in specific ways. Thus for example it may very well be that in some given society a contract acquires validity only when it bears a certain official stamp. As Reinach saw, however, each such modification must be in keeping with the intrinsically intelligible category which serves as its starting point: hence the given conventional modifications are themselves constrained by certain necessary and intelligible laws. Thus there could be no culture or society in which the validity of contracts is in general made condi-

---

13 This universality manifests itself also in the fact that we naturally tend to understand alien social orders in terms of the same restricted class of basic notions (claim, obligation, etc.), just as we tend naturally to see slightly irregular triangles and squares in terms of the standard concepts of *triangle, square,* etc.

tional on the parties' undergoing painful surgery, or on the finding of a proof for some hitherto unproved conjecture in mathematics. The absurdity of such modifications is grasped immediately by anyone with even a cursory familiarity with entities of the sorts involved. It is an a priori absurdity.

Interestingly, we have to deal here with entities existing in different ways in time. Obligations, claims, and, for example, marital ties are (relational and non-relational) *states* of the corresponding objects. Their dependence consists in the fact that they cannot *endure* unless relevant bearers exist.[14] The spontaneous acts discussed above, on the other hand, are instantaneous *events*: their dependence consists in the fact that they cannot *occur* unless their bearers exist. Now, however, we see that dependence relations can obtain not merely between states or events and their bearers, but also forwards and backwards in time, between the states and events themselves, and even between states and events of different bearers. Thus if, as a matter of fact, certain actions are performed by a suitably authorized speaker under such and such conditions, then as a matter of necessity there begin to exist certain claims and obligations involving this speaker (or his principal) and certain other persons. These claims and obligations then exist for a certain time thereafter, and it may be that an end to their existence can be brought about by further social acts (for example by acts of waiving a claim), whose corresponding effects will then be no less necessary and automatic (and grasped a priori as such).

It is — to repeat once more Reinach's point — in reflection of our prior knowledge of the necessary relations which here obtain that we

---

14 Claim and obligation are in this sense comparable to the individual accidents of the tradition. They differ from standard Aristotelian examples, however, in that they can have a multiplicity of bearers; moreover, they are able to be passed on from one bearer to another (claims and obligations can be inherited; they may migrate from one substance to another). Here, therefore, we have to do not with an individual necessary dependence of one entity upon another, but rather with what might be called a *generic* dependence, whereby it is required only that the dependent entity exist in association with some entity or other from a certain restricted class. (See, again, Smith, ed. 1982.)

are able to derive the 'ought' of obligation (such and such a person ought to do such and such) from the 'is' which is expressed in a certain factual statement (to the effect that an utterance-phenomenon of a certain sort has occurred at a certain time and under such and such conditions).

IV The Logical Conception of Material Necessity

There is a deep-rooted temptation, now, to suppose that such a priori necessities are one and all a matter of the logical relations which hold among the corresponding concepts. An account along these lines does indeed enjoy considerable purchase in relation to necessary laws in the purely formal spheres of for example mathematics. Such an account has however failed repeatedly when the attempt has been made to extend it to the necessary laws obtaining in such material spheres as those of colors or tones or social acts.[15] To say of the truths of mathematics that they are 'formal' is to say that they are topic-neutral, that they are not specific to any given qualitative or material sphere.[16] Such truths can at least in principle be applied unrestrictedly to all qualitative or material regions (as one can count, for example, everything from ring nebulae to canzonettas). When once the transition is made to laws whose content involves a restriction to what is qualitatively or materially determined, however, the logical account can no longer be successfully applied.

This follows from the ineliminable presence of materially specific concepts (or corresponding terms) in the formulations of these laws themselves. On the logical account, propositions or sentences seemingly expressing material necessities are seen as being characterized by the fact that they can in every case be exposed as mere analytic truths which are entirely empty of content. Such exposure is effected

---

15 The argument which follows is developed at greater length in my 1986, 15-18.

16 See my 1981 for further consideration of the meaning of the terms 'formal' and 'material' in the present context.

via a process of stripping out defined terms, replacing each such term with a *definiens* consisting of more primitive expressions. 'All bachelors are unmarried' is revealed as analytic in this way, by being converted to 'All unmarried men are unmarried,' a substitution instance of the logical truth: 'All *A*s which are *B* are *B*.'[17]

If, however, we wish to hold on to the view that all the necessary propositions of the theory of (say) social acts are analytic in this sense, then we shall have to insist that all such propositions can be formulated in terms of at most one single primitive non-logical concept. For suppose that even two such concepts were needed, say α and β, neither (by hypothesis) definable in terms of the other. Consider now the propositions expressing relations between α and β, even such trivial relations as the relation of non-identity. These cannot (again by hypothesis) be analytic. For propositions expressing non-identity of concepts (green is not yellow, color is not sound) are clearly not substitution-instances of logical truths as they stand. But there are (again by hypothesis) no defined non-logical terms which could be eliminated in such a way as to reveal the corresponding statements as logically true. But nor (again by hypothesis) can they be merely factual. On the logical reading of necessity, however, no further alternative is available, which implies that the original assumption that there are two (or more) such concepts must be rejected.

When, however, we consider the wealth of independent concepts involved in the theory of social acts — concepts of language, of mental acts of intending, willing, registering, of mental states of sincerity and good faith, of obligation, claim, authority, concepts of action and performance, etc. — then it is clearly impossible that the entire family of such concepts might be capable of being reduced, by a process of definition, to at most one single non-logical primitive. The corre-

---

17 This is no mere incidental mark of analyticity, but a statement of what it is for a proposition to be analytic. There are, to be sure, competing accounts as to what 'analytic' might mean, drawn for example from Wittgensteinian 'logical grammar.' None of these accounts has, however, succeeded in establishing itself as a clear and natural alternative to the Fregean account adopted here.

sponding laws, therefore, or the bulk of them at least, are matters of non-logical necessity, and our corresponding knowledge of such laws is synthetic and a priori.

V Institutional Concepts and Constitutive Rules

If we cannot understand the necessary laws which obtain in the sphere of social acts in purely logical terms, then how are we to understand them? Reinach, as we have seen, adopts a Platonistic answer to this question, an answer according to which there obtain necessary and intelligible relations between categories of certain sorts (for example promises, claims, and obligations) as these are realized in the world. It is in reflection of our knowledge of such relations that the derivation of 'ought' from 'is' in the case of the promise is grasped as valid a priori.

Between this Platonic extreme and the Humean position which would deny the given derivation tout court, we have the conventionalism of Searle. For Searle, too, there are necessities obtaining in the sphere of social acts. For him, however, these necessities follow from the special character of those forms of behavior which involve what he calls 'constitutive rules,' rules whose adoption at a certain time by a certain culture or society brings into being the corresponding categories or forms of behavior.

There are, Searle tells us, two different kinds of rules or conventions:

> Some rules regulate antecedently existing forms of behavior. For example, the rules of polite table behavior regulate eating, but eating exists independently of these rules. Some rules, on the other hand, do not merely regulate an antecedently existing activity called playing chess; they, as it were, create the possibility of or define that activity. The activity of playing chess is constituted by action in accordance with these rules. Chess has no existence apart from these rules. (1969a, 131)

The same can be said also, from Searle's point of view, of the institution of promising:

> The institutions of marriage, money, and promising are like the institutions of baseball and chess in that they are systems of such constitutive rules or conventions. (Ibid.)

Searle is appealing here to an opposition between 'institutional' and 'brute' facts, the former being distinguished in this way: that they presuppose deliberate constitutive arrangements of the given sort. Many forms of obligations, commitments, rights, and responsibilities are, Searle holds, a matter of institutional facts in this sense. As for Reinach, so also for Searle, the oughtness of obligation follows as a matter of necessity from the isness which is the making of a promise. For Searle, however, this is a definitional matter, for the making of a promise is for him by definition a case of acting according to certain conventional rules and in these rules the notion of obligation is involved in the relevant sense.

There are on this view no special universal and uninventable categories which our everyday acts of promising might reflect and by which the very institution of promising might somehow be constrained and made intelligible. The illusion that there are such categories arises only as a result of the fact that, because certain parts of reality have themselves been shaped by rules of the constitutive sort, we are able to utilize corresponding concepts and to apply them to corresponding pieces of behavior.

There are clearly, however, as Searle himself must recognize, certain constraints on the constitutive rules that human beings can adopt. Thus, for example, we cannot have a rule which enjoins walking through walls, or travelling back in time, or making 2 + 2 equal 5. Institutions are in this sense constrained by brute facts and also by the requirement of logical consistency of the underlying rules. It seems that for Searle, however, they cannot be constrained by anything other than this; for what could this something else be? All conceivable constitutive rules which are factually realizable and logically coherent must from his perspective be at least *ex ante* of exactly equal status, however absurd or unnatural they might seem.

Reinach, in contrast, has a means of doing justice not merely to the necessary laws and necessary constraints governing the field of institutional facts, but also to our capacity to grasp immediately the absurdity of institutional arrangements which violate such constraints (as we can grasp immediately the a priori absurdity of eating a phoneme or weighing a number). He holds, as we have seen, that there is a family of uninventable and intrinsically intelligible categories which serve as the necessary basis for rule-formation in the institutional sphere. Thus there could not, according to Reinach, arise institutions which did not reflect the basic categories of, for example, utterance-phenomena, claims, obligations, and their interrelations.

For Reinach promise and obligation are elements in a complex natural hierarchy of universally instantiable categories. It is in reflection of this autonomous hierarchy of categories that the relevant concepts and the rules we follow in speaking and acting have in large part arisen. These categories and their instantiations may involve, e.g., linguistic elements, but they are not contributed by language or convention. On the contrary, *the very practices involved in formulating and adopting conventional rules presuppose universal categories of the given sorts*, not least those universal categories which concern rules and conventions themselves and all that goes together therewith. Clearly, on pain of circularity, we cannot hold with Searle that such universal categories could themselves have been invented via rules and conventions.

Note that Reinach accepts that certain institutional conveniences may in the course of history come to be attached to universal categories of the given sorts as these are realized in particular societies. Thus he is willing to concede to Searle that even a world which manifests the given uninventable universal categories in the realm of social acts might still have room for *purely conventional* arrangements built up on these, reflecting constitutive rules of the sort Searle favors.[18]

Cases of concepts which are 'purely conventional' in this sense might be: *endowment mortgage, lien bond, football team-manager*, and so on. These (we may reasonably suppose) correspond to no special universal categories, but are rather imposed upon the world via

---

18 Cf. Reinach 1913, 801f.; English trans. 104, where the parallels between Reinach's notion of enactment and Searle's notion of constitutive rule are especially clear. See also Paulson 1987 and Burkhardt 1986.

Barry Smith

constitutive rules in the way that Searle describes. The criterion of pure conventionality here, a criterion which Reinach, too, could readily accept, is the possibility of our introducing the concepts in question via non-circular definitions expressible in terms of concepts which are truly and unproblematically more basic. For Reinach, however, we must by these means eventually arrive at *basic institutional concepts,* which is to say: institutional concepts not capable of being further defined on the institutional level. *Ownership,* presumably, is a concept of this sort; others might be: *rule, obligation, benefit, exchange, utterance, uptake, understanding, agreement, preference, sincerity,* and so on. Similar basic institutional concepts are required also, e.g., in the realm of games — concepts such as *winning, losing, playing, breaking a rule,* and so on. And clearly such basic institutional concepts, or the corresponding natural categories, must be involved also where constitutive rules are formulated and adopted in the realm of the positive law, concepts such as *command, decision, authority, consent, acknowledgement, jurisdiction,* and so on.[19]

Consider, now, the truths holding of such basic institutional concepts. The question for Searle is: are such truths *purely conventional* in the sense defined above? Clearly not: for the very formulation and adoption of constitutive rules *presupposes* concepts of the given sort. Are they, then, merely analytic? This alternative, too, can be ruled out, by the argument given above on the inapplicability of the analytic conception to relationships of material necessity. Can we, then, suppose that all such concepts can be defined in non-circular ways in terms of non-institutional concepts? Not at all, for then all institutional concepts would turn out to be thus definable, an outcome which Searle quite rightly rules out.[20] The only alternative which remains, therefore, is for Searle to accept that the given truths express irreducible material necessities of the Reinachian sort, that is, that they

---

19 Note that nothing in what follows turns on the question as to whether we have provided even partially adequate lists of basic institutional concepts here: the lists provided in the text are intended to serve as illustrative examples only.

20 1969, 56

318

express necessary relations between certain uninventable sui generis categories. (That Searle has not faced the necessity of drawing this conclusion follows from the fact that he has always already *presupposed* a rule-positing society, without ever asking how this society and its rule-positing practices came about — not, clearly, by prior rules.)

Not only Reinach, then, but also Searle must accept the notion of basic institutional concept. Moreover, both must accept also the irreducible institutional categories to which such concepts must correspond. Where they might still disagree is in relation to the question as to where the line is to be drawn between what we have called purely conventional concepts (concepts which can reasonably be held to have been introduced by definition) and basic institutional concepts (concepts reflecting irreducible categories for which non-circular definitions cannot be supplied). Promising, in particular, is taken by Searle to be a purely conventional concept, where Reinach insists that it is basic.[21] Such borderline disputes need not detain us long, however, so long as it is accepted that we are in possession of clear cases on either side of the disputed border. For then it will at least have been established that there is an order of categories that is at least to some degree prior to any imposed order which we might seek to contrive, e.g., by definitional fiat. Recall, in this connection, the reconstructive endeavors of Whitehead and Russell in *Principia Mathematica*. Number, in their framework is defined (though not before *100 of volume II) in terms of certain other, not intuitively more basic concepts, including *propositional function* and *type*. That such a definition can be constructed (albeit, notoriously, at a certain price in terms of other dis-

---

21 Searle has indeed offered a definition of 'promising' in terms of other, more basic concepts (see his 1969, 57ff.), though it has to be said, e.g., in relation to clause 7 of this definition, that it is not at all clear that the mere fact that someone intends that his utterance shall place him under an obligation to do such and such is sufficient to bring it about that his utterance will indeed have this effect. In regard to clause 9, similarly, we must ask whether the semantical rules of a language really can be such that a given sentence is correctly and sincerely uttered if and only if this sentence brings it about that the speaker is brought under an obligation.

puted assumptions in the system) does not, from the Reinachian perspective, imply that numbers *are* what they are reputed to be in the context of that system. Rather, it shows that we have a certain limited free play in constructing definitional systems adequate for example to our deductive purposes in mathematics.

VI A Theory of the A Priori

Let us summarize the results of our deliberations as far as the phenomenon of a priori knowledge is concerned. Our thesis is as follows: that a priori knowledge relates first and foremost to the relations (above all relations of necessitation) which obtain between intelligible categories of for example color, sound or shape. Man, it is suggested, is born with an innate capacity to discriminate between instances of categories of the given sorts — for this is not itself something that could have been learned — and hand in hand with this innate capacity goes the ability to grasp the associated relations of necessitation. One incidental advantage of the view in question is that it yields a systematic accounting of all the various types of a priori laws (laws relating to one-sided and mutual necessitation, laws of exclusion and compatibility, and so on), where more familiar treatments of the a priori are constrained to conceive the latter as amounting to little more than a collection of ad hoc examples. Our view amounts, as already suggested, to an ontological (realist, reliabilist) theory of the a priori: we enjoy synthetic a priori knowledge of, say, the basic relations between colors, because there are corresponding intrinsically intelligible relational structures in the world. This view, once the common possession of all philosophers — who rightly saw the existence of such structures as providing the necessary and sufficient conditions for the existence of their discipline — is diametrically opposed not only to standard Humean conceptions (which simply deny the existence of necessity in re), but also to the Kantian view, which sees the a priori as a result of the imposition of structure by experiencing subjects. Kant was, to be sure, correct in recognizing the central importance of synthetic a priori knowledge not only to philosophy but also to science and to our everyday experience. He was wrong, however, not only in his estimation of the scope of such knowledge — which he saw as being restricted, effectively, to not much more than arithmetic, geometry (Euclidean) and mechanics (Newtonian) — but also, and disastrously, in his account of where such knowledge comes from.

References

Austin, J.L. 1962 *How to do Things with Words*. Oxford: Oxford University Press.

Burkhardt, A. 1986 *Soziale Akte, Sprechakte und Textillokutionen. A. Reinachs Rechtsphilosophie und die moderne Linguistik*. Tübingen: Niemeyer.

Burkhardt, A. 1987 'Verpflichtung und Verbindlichkeit. Ethische Aspekte in der Rechtsphilosophie Adolf Reinachs,' in Mulligan, ed., 155-74.

Burkhardt, A., ed. 1990 *Speech Acts, Meanings and Intentions*. Berlin/New York: de Gruyter.

Husserl, E. 1900-1 *Logische Untersuchungen*, as reprinted in Husserliana vol. XVIII (E. Holenstein, ed.) and XIX/1, XIX/2 (U. Panzer, ed.). The Hague: Nijhoff 1975/1984.

Mulligan, K. 1987 'Promisings and Other Social Acts: Their Constituents and Structure,' in Mulligan, ed., 29-90.

Mulligan, K., ed. 1987 *Speech Act and Sachverhalt. Reinach and the Foundations of Realist Phenomenology*. The Hague: Nijhoff.

Paulson, S.L. 1987 'Demystifying Reinach's Legal Theory,' in Mulligan, ed., 133-54.

Reinach, A. 1911 'Zur Theorie des negativen Urteils,' in A. Pfänder, ed., *Münchener Philosophische Abhandlungen*, Leipzig: Barth, 196-254, reprinted in Reinach 1989, 95-140; English trans. as 'On the Theory of the Negative Judgment,' in Smith, ed., 1982, 315-77.

Reinach, A. 1911a 'Kants Auffassung des Humeschen Problems,' *Zeitschrift für Philosophie und philosophische Kritik*, 141, 176-209, reprinted in Reinach 1989, 67-94; English trans. by J.N. Mohanty as 'Kant's Interpretation of Hume's Problem,' in *Southwestern Journal of Philosophy* 7 (1976) 161-88.

Reinach, A. 1913 'Die apriorischen Grundlagen des bürgerlichen Rechts,' *Jahrbuch für Philosophie und phänomenologische Forschung*, I/2, 685-847, reprinted in Reinach 1989, 141-278; English trans. as 'The Apriori Foundations of the Civil Law,' by J.F. Crosby, *Aletheia* **3** (1983), 1-142.

Reinach, A. 1989 *Sämtliche Werke. Kritische Ausgabe mit Kommentar*, 2 vols., K. Schuhmann and B. Smith, eds. Munich/Hamden/Vienna: Philosophia.

Schuhmann, K. 1988 'Die Entwicklung der Sprechakttheorie in der Münchener Phänomenologie,' *Phänomenologische Forschungen* **21** 133-66.

Schuhmann, K. and Smith, B. 1985 'Questions: An Essay in Daubertian Phenomenology,' in *Philosophy and Phenomenological Research* **39** 763-93.

Schuhmann, K. and Smith, B. 1987 'Adolf Reinach (1883-1917),' in Mulligan, ed., 1-27.

Schuhmann, K. and Smith, B. 1990 'Elements of Speech Act Theory in the Work of Thomas Reid,' *History of Philosophy Quarterly* **7** 47-66.

Schulthess, D. 1983 *Philosophie et sens commun chez Thomas Reid (1710-1796)*. Berne.

Searle, J.R. 1969 *Speech Acts. An Essay in the Philosophy of Language*. Cambridge: Cambridge University Press.

Searle, J.R. 1969a 'How to Derive "Ought" from "Is",' in W.D. Hudson, ed., *The Is/Ought Question*. London: Macmillan, 120-34.

Smith, B. (ed.) 1982 *Parts and Moments. Studies in Logic and Formal Ontology*. Munich: Philosophia.

Smith, B. 1981 'Logic, Form and Matter,' *Proceedings of the Aristotelian Society, Supplementary Volume* **55** 47-63.

Smith, B. 1986 'Austrian Economics and Austrian Philosophy,' in W. Grassl and B. Smith, eds., *Austrian Economics. Historical and Philosophical Background*. London and Sydney: Croom Helm, 1-36.

Smith, B. 1990 'Towards a History of Speech Act Theory,' in Burkhardt, ed., 29-61.

Smith, B. 1990a 'Aristotle, Menger, Mises: A Categorial Ontology for Economics,' *History of Political Economy*, supplement to **22**, 263-88.

Index

Ackerman, Felicia, 93, 109
Allison, Henry, 183, 187, 228, 233, 237, 241, 242, 248
Alquié, F., 182
Ameriks, Karl, 187
Apostoli, Peter, 273, 296
Appiah, Anthony, 109
Aquinas, T., 10
Aristotle, 7, 8, 9, 10, 13, 56, 267, 270, 303, 304
Armstrong, D.M., 32, 153, 268
Aspect, A., 264
Audi, Robert, 150
Austin, J.L., 307, 308, 310
Ayer, A.J., 4, 64, 116, 117, 118, 119, 120, 129, 142, 143, 145, 269

Bar-Hillel, Y., 297
Barnes, J., 7, 8, 10
Barwise, Jon, 295
Beck, L.W., 225, 237
Bell, 255, 256, 260, 263, 264, 265, 266, 270
Benacerraf, P., 255, 267
Bennett, Jonathan, 228, 237
Berkeley, G., 266
Bigelow, J., 15, 16, 19, 31, 32, 36, 37, 38, 39, 40, 41, 42, 44
Bird, Graham, 183
Bohm, D., 258
Bohr, Niels, 256, 257
Bolzano, B., 304

BonJour, L., 5, 14, 16, 20, 24, 25, 27, 29, 30, 33, 40, 48
Boolos, George, 295
Born, Max, 256
Brandl, Johannes, 301
Brentano, F., 308
Brittan, Gordon, 213
Brook, Andrew, 30
Brown, Bryson, 273
Brown, James R., 16, 19, 36, 50, 51
Buchdahl, Gerd, 195, 204
Buridan, J., 294, 296, 297
Burkhardt, A., 317
Butchvarov, Panayot, 65, 68, 69, 115, 150

Carnap, Rudolf, 16, 25, 136, 137, 138, 139, 181, 214, 225
Cartwright, Richard, 168, 170, 171, 172
Casullo, Albert, 4, 24, 26, 36, 46, 114
Chisholm, Roderick, 8, 9, 11, 12, 202
Church, Alonzo, 276
Cioffa, A., 16
Cohen, L.J., 276
Curley, Edwin, 182, 184, 185, 190, 191, 211
Curry, Haskell B., 273, 274, 275, 276, 286, 290, 291, 292, 298

Daubert, Johannes, 304

Davidson, Donald, 102, 103, 104, 105, 110, 111
De Pierris, Graciela, 2, 28, 29, 48
Dennett, D., 250, 251
Descartes, R., 2, 101, 179, 181, 182, 183, 184, 185, 186, 187, 188, 189, 191, 192, 193, 194, 195, 196, 198, 200, 202, 203, 204, 205, 206, 210, 211, 309
de Vleeschauwer, H.J., 242
Donohue, Patricia, 301
Dretske, Fred, 268
Dryer, D.P., 225, 233, 236, 239, 241, 242, 245, 248
Dummett, Michael, 89
Dunn, J. Michael, 291

Einstein, A., 257, 258, 264
Etchemendy, John, 295

Field, H., 255
Firth, R., 13
Foley, Richard, 103
Frege, 64, 138, 308
Friedman, Michael, 206, 235, 236, 237, 250
Fumerton, Richard, 103

Galileo, 157, 270, 271, 272
Gibson, J.J., 31
Gödel, K., 267
Goldman, A., 33, 53
Goldstein, Laurence, 275, 297
Grandy, Richard, 105
Grice, H.P., 73
Gueroult, Martial, 183, 184, 187, 203, 211
Gupta, Anil, 277, 282
Guyer, Paul, 219, 237

Haack, Susan, 89, 286

Hacking, Ian, 190
Hanson, Philip, 150, 272, 273, 301
Harman, Gilbert, 38, 83, 85
Harper, William, 231, 233
Hazen, Allen, 297
Heisenberg, W., 256, 257
Hempel, Carl, 116, 117, 118, 119, 120, 121, 122, 123, 124, 125, 126, 127, 128, 129, 130, 131, 132, 133, 134, 135, 136, 137, 145
Henrich, Dieter, 30, 211
Herzberger, Hans A., 283
Hilbert, 257, 258
Hinckfuss, Ian, 297
Hobbes, T., 302
Hughes, G.E., 281
Hugly, Philip, 150
Hume, D., 23, 28, 195, 196, 216, 221, 266, 301, 302, 304
Humphrey, Ted B., 236, 242
Hunter, Bruce, 150, 272
Husserl, Edmund, 304, 308, 310

Irvine, Andrew, 36, 46, 47, 51
Irwin, T., 8

Jammer, M., 256
Jubien, Michael, 150

Kant, I., 2, 16, 22, 23, 24, 28, 29, 30, 34, 37, 48, 58, 59, 60, 61, 146, 147, 148, 160, 182, 186, 187, 188, 189, 195, 199, 206, 207, 209, 210, 215, 216, 217, 218, 219, 220, 220, 221, 222, 223, 224, 225, 226, 227, 228, 229, 230, 231, 232, 233, 234, 235, 236, 237, 238, 239, 240, 241, 242, 243, 244, 245, 246, 247, 248, 249, 251, 252
Kaplan, David, 168, 170, 171, 178
Kazmi, Ali, 43, 44, 46

Kemp Smith, Norman, 215, 228
Kenny, Anthony, 182, 191, 205
Kim, Jaegwon, 107, 108
Kitcher, Patricia, 218, 225, 226, 228, 230, 231, 232, 234, 249
Kitcher, Philip, 11, 12, 18, 31, 32, 33, 34, 35, 36, 37, 38, 39, 40, 41, 47, 114, 164
Kleene, S.C., 289, 296
Kneale, W.C., 297
Kornblith, Hilary, 253
Kripke, Saul, 49, 115, 116, 174, 223, 251, 281, 282, 283, 284, 285, 293, 294, 297

Landini, Gregory, 278
Leibniz, G., 2, 3, 4, 5, 6, 7, 12, 13, 22, 23, 24, 25, 27, 28, 41, 43, 57, 185, 214
Levin, Michael, 94, 95, 96, 98, 99, 104
Lewis, David, 32, 173, 174, 175, 176
Lipps, T., 304
Locke, 57, 266
Lukasiewicz, Jan, 289

Maddy, Penelope, 150
Mares, Ed, 273
Marty, Anton, 304
McGinn, C., 50
Mendola, Joseph, 150
Mersenne, M., 203
Meyer, Robert K., 291
Mill, J.S., 266
Miller, Richard, 250
Morton, Adam, 89, 97
Mulligan, K., 304, 305, 308

Orenstein, Alex, 75

Pap, Arthur, 16, 24, 99, 139

Parsons, Charles, 130, 237
Parsons, Terence, 289
Patton, Tom, 273
Paulson, S.L., 317
Peano, G., 137, 138, 140, 141, 279
Plato, 56, 272, 302
Podolsky, B., 258, 264
Poincaré, 279
Pollock, J., 18, 19, 27, 35
Posy, Carl, 109
Priest, Graham, 287, 288, 289, 290, 291, 292, 293
Prior, A.N., 102, 276, 297
Putnam, Hilary, 21, 30, 49, 89, 91, 100, 114, 129, 225, 226, 255, 267
Pythagoras, 31, 41

Quine, W.V., 21, 27, 45, 49, 56, 58, 70, 71, 72, 73, 74, 75, 76, 77, 79, 80, 81, 82, 83, 84, 85, 86, 87, 89, 90, 91, 94, 95, 96, 97, 98, 99, 104, 105, 129, 134, 153, 162, 163, 165, 168, 221, 228
Quinton, Anthony, 67, 68, 115, 146, 147

Ramsey, Frank P., 279, 280
Reid, Thomas, 304, 306
Reinach, Adolf, 23, 301, 302, 303, 304, 305, 306, 307, 308, 309, 310, 311, 312, 315, 316, 317, 318, 319
Richard, Mark, 168
Robinson, Dick, 273
Rosen, N., 258, 264
Routley, Richard, 291
Russell, Bertrand, 16, 17, 20, 138, 277, 278, 279, 280, 282, 293, 294, 297, 319
Ryle, Gilbert, 284, 308

Sainsbury, R.M., 283

Index

Savitt, Steven, 273
Schrödinger, Erwin, 256
Schuhmann, K., 304, 305
Schulthess, D., 304
Salmon, Wesley, 62, 250
Searle, J.R., 302, 303, 315, 316, 317, 318, 319
Sellars, Wilfrid, 8, 10, 25, 27, 181
Smith, Barry, 19, 23, 27, 36, 49, 304, 308, 309, 312
Sobel, Jordan Howard, 297
Sosa, Ernest, 15, 109, 202
Spinoza, 214
Steiner, Mark, 126, 129, 130, 139, 140, 141
Strawson, P.F., 73, 233, 237
Stroud, Barry, 210
Stumpf, E., 9

Swinburne, R.G., 147, 148, 149

Tait, W.A., 4
Tarski, Alfred, 277, 279, 280, 281, 282, 284, 285, 290, 293
Tennant, Neil, 91
Thompson, M., 237
Tooley, Michael, 51, 268

Van Cleve, James, 5, 45, 46
Van Fraasen, B., 20, 285
Vico, G., 302

Waxman, Wayne, 239
Whitehead, A.N., 16, 279, 319
Williams, Bernard, 205
Wilson, Margaret, 182, 191
Wittgenstein, L., 21, 181, 214